Multiculturalism
and Intergroup
Relations

Multiculturalism and Intergroup Relations

Psychological Implications for Democracy in Global Context

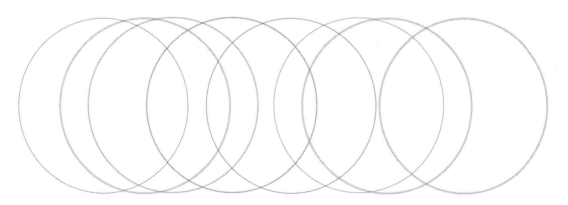

Fathali M. Moghaddam

American Psychological Association • *Washington, DC*

Published by
American Psychological Association
750 First Street, NE
Washington, DC 20002
www.apa.org

To order
APA Order Department
P.O. Box 92984
Washington, DC 20090-2984
Tel: (800) 374-2721; Direct: (202) 336-5510
Fax: (202) 336-5502; TDD/TTY: (202) 336-6123
Online: www.apa.org/books/
E-mail: order@apa.org

In the U.K., Europe, Africa, and the Middle East, copies may be ordered from
American Psychological Association
3 Henrietta Street
Covent Garden, London
WC2E 8LU England

Typeset in Goudy by Stephen McDougal, Mechanicsville, MD

Printer: Maple-Vail Book Manufacturing Group, Binghamton, NY
Cover Designer: Naylor Design, Washington, DC
Technical/Production Editor: Devon Bourexis

The opinions and statements published are the responsibility of the authors, and such opinions and statements do not necessarily represent the policies of the American Psychological Association.

Library of Congress Cataloging-in-Publication Data

Moghaddam, Fathali M.
  Multiculturalism and intergroup relations : psychological implications for democracy in global context / Fathali M. Moghaddam.
    p. cm.
  Includes bibliographical references and index.
  ISBN-13: 978-1-4338-0307-9
  ISBN-10: 1-4338-0307-0
  1. Multiculturalism. 2. Intergroup relations. 3. Globalization. I. Title.

  HM1271.M63 2008
  305.8001—dc22   2007025838

British Library Cataloguing-in-Publication Data
A CIP record is available from the British Library.

Printed in the United States of America
First Edition

To Donald M. Taylor

Razor mind, roaring wit, wild heart
Harnessed to level a fair start

CONTENTS

FOREWORD

It is inspiring to see a social psychologist address some of the major issues of our time—notably, globalization, democratization, and strategies for managing ethnic and cultural diversity—in a way that demonstrates that psychological theories and research have a great deal to say about how society should deal with core concerns. In addition, it is gratifying to see how much of value Fathali Moghaddam is able to draw from psychology that is relevant to such broad issues. This is in part a tribute to the breadth of literature he brings to bear on these questions. The scope of the material brought together in this volume is truly striking, as is the way the author is able to weave it together in a coherent and compelling fashion.

The beginnings of the modern social psychology of group dynamics lie in the aftermath of World War II. After the world was engulfed in this terrible conflict, it was easy for people to see the importance of understanding the social forces that motivate and shape intergroup conflict as well as the attitudes that encourage it. This led to psychological research on prejudice, leadership–followership, and the dynamics of behavior in groups and societies. All of this research was based on the premise that the roots of social dynamics lie in the effect of social forces. In recent decades the field of psychology has shifted toward cognitive- and neuroscience-based models of human behavior. Social psychology has shifted with it, moving toward intrapsychic models reflected in social cognition– and social neuroscience–based perspectives on the person. Therefore, the study of intergroup dynamics has been increasingly neglected.

This volume is a powerful statement of the centrality of the study of the social aspects of groups to understanding the key questions that preoccupy our society today. If we hope to understand the social changes occurring throughout the world, we must look to the psychology of intergroup dynamics. We must, as Moghaddam tells us, understand how it is that people are connected to groups and how these connections are reinforced or stressed by the forces of globalization and democratization that are sweeping through various societies. We must also understand how it is that structures can be placed around and above people with loyalties to diverse ethnic, religious, and cultural values. These are truly the core issues of our times and, as this book makes clear, they are issues of social dynamics. Hence, many of the core issues and insights of research on group dynamics are of striking relevance today.

In Part I, Moghaddam sets the stage for his efforts by painting a broad picture of social evolution across the globe. To do so, he draws on a wide range of examples from current events. This part of the book is compelling, as the forces of democratization and globalization are outlined and considered from the point of view of people within different societies, all undergoing different forms of change. The key tension highlighted is linked to the psychological finding that people find it easier and more comfortable to identify with small groups of people with whom they have personal contact or at least share cultural, ethnic, or religious ties; because of this, the changes associated with globalization are disorienting and stressful. Moghaddam paints a striking picture of the tension between a broad globalism (i.e., a society in which subgroup differences are minimized) and the efforts of ethnic, religious, and cultural groups to create smaller, more differentiated entities by separation from others—a core conflict in the evolution of our world today, a conflict of fractured globalism, and one presented in stark profile in this volume.

One especially appealing feature of Moghaddam's overview is his effort to bring our understanding of economic and political systems into a common psychological framework. *Globalization* is a term sometimes used to refer to the spread of free markets. There have also been discussions of the global spread of democracy. This review recognizes that both of these forces need to be considered from the perspective of how they influence the individuals who are subjected to them. If democracy, for example, encourages loyalty to large societies that have values inconsistent with the values held by people within particular subcultures, then the move toward democracy imposes psychological costs. People need to be able both to feel loyalty toward a group so large that they may never have seen its leaders and to have the capacity to tolerate views and lifestyles inconsistent with their own. Moghaddam argues that democracies are most likely to flourish when they minimize these psychological burdens. He makes a compelling case for the virtues of thinking through issues of globalization, democratization, and diversity with an eye to our understanding of the nature of human nature.

The key effort to draw on social psychological theories and research is found in Part II of this volume. In Part II Moghaddam builds his efforts to examine contemporary issues around a set of core psychological ideas—rationality, materialism, identity, and justice—each having its own theories and research history. Moghaddam then provides a clear and concise discussion of the origins and history of each of these areas, ending by pointing out their relevance to current concerns about globalization, democracy, and the relationship of these two ideas.

In each section Moghaddam's integration of classic and modern approaches is remarkable. In addition to framing his discussion through classic authors—Freud, Marx, Tajfel—Moghaddam, in each chapter, clearly explains recent contributions. For example, the chapter on irrationality begins by presenting the work of Freud and Adorno but ends with a presentation of recent writing on terror management. Similarly, his presentation on social justice is framed by classic writing on relative deprivation but also presents more recent work on distributive and procedural justice. This book provides an easy and complete introduction to both the theories and the research findings of the core areas. In each case, Moghaddam ends the chapter with a direct discussion of the relevance of the material discussed to issues of globalization and democratization.

Finally, Moghaddam returns in Part III to the issue of diversity. He paints a contrast between two alternative approaches to dealing with diversity: assimilation and multiculturalism. The choice between them is crucial to the evolution of globalism because they lead to dramatically different social policies. Using a variety of examples ranging from American and Canadian experiences to recent European Union struggles over diversity, Moghaddam clearly lays out the issues involved. As before, he stresses the centrality of social psychological research to making social policy decisions about how to manage questions of ethnic, religious, and cultural diversity.

Overall, this book is striking for the range of issues the author explores and the literatures he brings to bear on those issues. As it was following World War II, the world is in a time of change and turmoil. There are large transformations afoot and big issues at stake. Moghaddam brings a big picture perspective to these issues, and his core argument is crucial—we need to try to understand what is possible through the perspective of what we know about people. Although human psychology alone does not shape the evolution of society or social institutions, what people want, or what they find stressful and difficult to deal with, shapes social change. In grappling with the large forces of globalization, democratization, and diversity, we need to begin by considering what we know about human psychology. It is to that task that this compelling book turns.

Tom Tyler, PhD
University Professor
Department of Psychology
New York University

PREFACE

I wrote this book to explore both the challenges and opportunities presented by globalization and increased intergroup contact. The potential rewards of a peaceful, open, and diverse global village are spectacular and historic but so are the potential consequences of a failure to manage diversity and intergroup conflict. To borrow a Dickensian phrase, one can say this is the best of times, this is the worst of times.

Globalization and increased contact between different groups, particularly those with little previous history of living together, presents humankind with glorious opportunities but also confronts people with terrifying perils. At the dawn of the 21st century, with the tragedy of 9/11 and the "war on terror" in the background, Denmark became the eye of a storm thundering through much of Western Europe as Muslim protesters showed their anger against the publication of cartoons that depicted the Prophet Mohammed. Meanwhile, wars raged in Iraq and Afghanistan, and the Israeli–Palestinian conflict and dozens of other conventional violent conflicts continued to simmer, and periodically come to a boil, in Africa, Latin America, Asia, and Eastern Europe. The evolving global village is characterized not only by diversity but also by major violent conflicts, fragmentation, separatism, radicalization, and terrorism.

On the domestic front, many Western and non-Western societies are confronted with the growing challenge of how to best manage cultural, ethnic, religious, linguistic, and other types of diversity. This challenge is heightened by enormous population movements to Western Europe and North America, resulting in an influx of tens of millions of first-generation immigrants from non-Western societies, such as Latinos in the United States, South Asians in the United Kingdom, North Africans in France, and Turks in Germany. A number of other countries, such as Japan and Russia, that do not have a tradition of accepting immigrants now have birth rates well below replacement level and face the danger of experiencing significant population decline over the next few decades unless they import labor—and then deal with the challenges and opportunities associated with increased diversity.

How can we best manage cultural diversity and avoid intergroup conflict in the fast-changing world of the 21st century? In exploring this question, I draw from four main sources. First, I examine psychological theories and experimental research on intergroup relations. I give the highest priority to critically exploring theories because I deeply believe in the Lewinian dictum that "the most practical thing is a good theory." Second, I draw on the wider social science literature on multiculturalism and critically assess the psychological foundations of policies for managing cultural diversity. Third, I incorporate the theme of democracy and culture, drawing on literature in political science and political psychology. It is of particular importance to explore the implications of intergroup theories, research, and policies for democracy, because globalization is leading to increased intergroup contact— often between groups with no previous history of extensive contact. The implications of these trends must receive attention from supporters of democracy. Fourth, I explore a source that is of vital importance to me—my personal experience of living and researching in various democracies and dictatorships around the world.

A particular focus of this book is the implications of psychological research and theory for (a) democracy and (b) policies for managing diversity. These implications are profound, given that the characteristics of the *psychological citizens* (i.e., the psychological features of individuals sustaining a given sociopolitical order) in any society limit the political systems and public policies that can be successfully implemented.

This book is primarily intended for readers interested in diversity, intergroup relations, and democracy in national and international contexts. Students in a number of courses will find this book particularly useful, including those studying social psychology, cultural and cross-cultural psychology, multiculturalism, international relations, ethnicity, group behavior, intergroup relations, conflict resolution, peace and justice studies, American studies, and gender or women's studies.

ACKNOWLEDGMENTS

This book has benefited from feedback provided by two groups of very thoughtful students: first, students in my course "Multiculturalism, Democracy and Intergroup Relations" at Georgetown University in Washington, DC; second, students in several series of lectures I delivered at Lund University, Sweden, in 2005, 2006, and 2007 (in highly innovative international programs directed by Alf Bang and Christina Erneling). In teaching courses based on preliminary drafts of this book, I learned some valuable lessons from my students in terms of both style and content, and I have endeavored to reflect these lessons in the published book. I also owe thanks to the peer reviewers, who provided critical feedback on the manuscript.

With regard to personal history, this book reflects my deep debt to Henri Tajfel, Mick Billig, John Turner, and Howard Giles in England; Serge Moscovici in France; Willem Doise in Switzerland; Don Taylor and Wally Lambert in Canada; and Muzafer Sherif in the United States, who all pioneered groundbreaking lines of research in intergroup relations and inspired me to explore research and policy concerning diversity and group relationships. In dedicating the volume to Don Taylor, I am paying tribute to his more than 4 decades of inspiring and inspired research toward improving our understanding of intergroup relations and his achievement of greater justice for minorities.

Rom Harré and Bill Bryson at various times attempted to straighten out my thinking with bottled advice at Pommeroy's, and I hope I drank the correct measures.

I am indebted to the staff of the American Psychological Association, particularly Maureen Adams, Emily Leonard, and Devon Bourexis, for the superb support and guidance they provided throughout the development and publication of this book.

I

DIVERSITY IN INTERNATIONAL AND NATIONAL CONTEXTS

INTRODUCTION:
DIVERSITY IN INTERNATIONAL
AND NATIONAL CONTEXTS

We humans have been hurled into the 21st century on a tidal wave of globalization and change, the vast scope of which is difficult for us to recognize. The Romanian American historian Eugen J. Weber (1925–2007) pointed out that it took roughly the entire 19th century for "La Marseillaise" to become the national anthem of France because when it was first introduced, so few people in France spoke French (E. J. Weber, 1991). Until fairly recently, France consisted of a multilingual society, characterized by major regional differences. Rapid changes in communication and transportation systems, along with urbanization and industrialization, have given rise to what we now recognize as the fairly uniform French-speaking nation of France. Yet, having achieved a national character, France is now melting economically and in some ways culturally into the European Union, as well as the larger global village. Symbolic of this change, "foreign" fast food outlets are now scattered all around Paris.

As a university student in England during the 1970s, I used to travel regularly to France, where important academic meetings were conducted primarily in French. In the 21st century, English has become the language of international science and commerce, and more and more important academic meetings in France are now conducted primarily in English. The European academic journals, such as the *European Journal of Social Psychology*, are published in English, and papers at major European conferences are delivered in English. Whereas in the early 19th century those who wanted to get ahead in France had to learn French in addition to any other local language they spoke, in the 21st century those who want to get ahead in France have to learn English as well as the "local" language, French. This includes the millions of Muslim North African immigrants now settled in France.

However, at the same time that France is becoming part of the European Union and the global village, there are strong nationalist sentiments to keep France "French" and to limit or end immigration into France, particularly from Algeria and France's other former non-Western colonies. The French, like people in many other European Union member states, are finding it much easier to identify with "their own country" than with the entire European continent, to see themselves as French rather than as European. Similarly, the natives of England, Germany, Italy, and other European countries still tend to see themselves first and foremost as English, German, Italian, and so on, rather than as European. On a broader level, despite globalization and the emergence of a global village, most people around the world identify with the local, as a member of a village, a neighborhood, a city, a religion, and so on, rather than the entire world.

The resistance to identifying with the largest category, humankind, is reflected in a question that people often ask when they are confronted by group-based prejudice and discrimination: "Why can't we just treat one another as human beings rather than seeing each other as Black or White, male or female, Muslim or Jew, Catholic or Protestant, liberal or conservative, prolife or prochoice?" Perhaps one day we shall be able to ignore smaller categories and just treat one another as human beings, but this is not what currently takes place in most parts of the world. Group membership has an important impact on how we think and act toward ourselves, toward *ingroup* members (those who share our group membership) and toward *outgroup* members (those who belong to a group to which we do not belong).

The major themes that dominate our lives in the process of intergroup interactions are introduced in the two chapters that compose Part I of this book. Such interactions are taking place in the context of what seems to be assimilation and the melting away of intergroup differences, such as the different nationalities of Europe becoming "European." However, there is also strong evidence to suggest the emergence of a second trend, one involving differentiation and the highlighting and exaggeration of intergroup differences, such as the reemergence of Scottish nationalism and other nationalist and break-away movements. Just as globalization speeds ahead and group-based differences seem to be disappearing, there is also an ethnic revival and the reemergence of ethnic pride and "being different." A wealth of theories with psychological foundations address these themes in intergroup relations and are introduced in four groups: rationality, material resources, identity, and perceived justice.

Perhaps the most basic question concerns the extent to which we assume that individuals are malleable and can be changed: Is it possible for people to not see themselves and others as group members but simply as human beings? For example, is it possible for "Sam" to be seen as a person and not as a man or woman who is either Black or White, young or old, Muslim or Jewish, and so on? The discussion in chapter 2 explores this question by considering how social categorization takes place within a biological and cognitive framework. Social categorization is a natural process in the sense that it is highly functional and seems to be universal.

However, although social categorization is pervasive, the boundaries and contents of social categories are socially constructed. How we divide up the social world is malleable and dependent in large part on political factors, particularly the political interests of majority groups. Consider, for example, the case of Sandra Lang, a brown-skinned natural child of two White Afrikaaners living in South Africa during the apartheid era (Stone, 2007). Sandra's dark skin coloring apparently resulted from a preapartheid time when interracial sex was common, rather than from her mother having slept with a Black man. Despite having White parents, the South African government classified Sandra as "Colored," and she was expelled from the White-only school she had been attending. Eventually, the girl became an outcast from her own White family, with tragic consequences for all the family members.

Consider the arbitrariness of categorizing people into "White," "Colored," and "Black" groups on the basis of the color spectrum that in nature is continuous (in South Africa during apartheid, people were placed into racial groups by an official Race Classification Board). Why were three groups used? In the United States prior to desegregation in the South, only two groups were used: White and Colored. But one can envisage many more categories (Pale White, Dark White, Dark Brown, Light Black, etc.) based on equally arbitrary and malleable criteria designed to meet particular political ends (typically, to maintain the power monopoly of a certain group, such as Afrikaaners of European descent in apartheid-era South Africa). Interactions between groups using different criteria for categorization need to be seen against the backcloth of rapidly moving globalization.

The vast scope and speed of globalization is creating new challenges in intergroup relations and the management of diversity. In 1907, movies could be seen in a very small number of places in a few major Western cities. A century later, the movie *Pirates of the Caribbean: At World's End* was released on Memorial Day weekend 2007 in more than 10,000 theaters in 104 countries (Waxman, 2007). Against this juggernaut of globalization, basic psychological needs such as those related to identity and perceived justice will continue to influence how we think and act as group members, interacting with ingroup and outgroup members. The simultaneous release of movies such as *Pirates of the Caribbean* in over 100 countries is seen by some as a sign of progress, helping world unity and peace, but by others as further evidence of attacks on indigenous cultures and traditional moral and religious systems as well as a justification for conflict and even terrorism against the West and the United States in particular. It is clear that managing intergroup relations and diversity in the 21st century will be a challenge, perhaps the greatest challenge, facing humankind.

1

MULTICULTURALISM, DEMOCRACY, AND INTERGROUP RELATIONS: INTERNATIONAL AND NATIONAL CONTEXTS

It was April 1979, and I had returned from studies in England to my native country of Iran to experience the exhilarating spring of revolution. The downfall of the last Shah's corrupt dictatorship had given way to great hope but also to revolutionary turmoil and the threat of Iran breaking apart because of growing ethnic separatist movements, including those by Kurdish, Azari, and Baluchi separatists. Within another year, Saddam Hussein's Iraqi army had invaded Iran and there followed a grueling war that tied the two oil-rich dictatorships together in a macabre dance until finally, after 8 long years of bloody fighting, they both collapsed in utter exhaustion, adding to instability and the threat of fragmentation in the entire Near and Middle East region. Almost a quarter of a century later, after several more regional wars and two U.S.-led invasions of Iraq (in 1992 and 2003), Saddam Hussein's reign of terror finally came to an end, but now the threat looms of Iraq fragmenting into separate Kurdish, Shi'a, and Sunni regions. This tendency toward fragmentation in the Near East is within the context of the nearby

"Stans" (i.e., Kazakhstan, Kyrgyzstan, Tajikistan, Turkmenistan, Uzbekistan), the Ukraine, and other territories, breaking away from the clutch of Russia after the collapse of the Soviet empire in 1989.

Separatism and fragmentation, such as in the case of the former Soviet states, strengthens diversity and bolsters multicultural and multilingual tendencies. By achieving greater political independence, smaller states can enjoy fuller independence in economic decision making and can implement policies to maintain local linguistic and cultural traditions. For example, by gaining political independence, Ukraine and other members of the former Soviet empire have been able to strengthen their distinct cultural and linguistic traditions, similar to what the Kurds are striving to do in northern Iraq. However, the strengthening of separatism and independence carries the risk of fragmentation and discord.

INTEGRATION IN THE WESTERN WORLD

Looking from the vantage point of Western societies at the continuing threat of societal fragmentation in the Near East, the former Soviet Union, and other regions of the world, we are prone to see our experiences as rather different. On the surface, at least, Western societies seem to be moving in a different direction, toward greater integration, unification, and assimilation. The North American Free Trade Agreement of 1994 (see http://www.dfait-maeci.gc.ca/nafta-alena/agree-en.asp) has further integrated the United States, Canada, and Mexico, and there are serious ongoing efforts to integrate greater parts of the American continent. The European Union has united Western Europe; the expansion of the European Union to almost 25 states (with further expansion planned) means that it includes most of Eastern Europe.

This integration of Western societies is taking place within the context of *globalization* (i.e., increasingly deeper forms of interconnectedness between economies, organizations, and people across national boundaries and the realization of the global village). For example, the *New Partnership for Africa's Development* represents an effort to strengthen economic, political, and cultural cooperation across Africa (see Murithi, 2005; for critical perspectives on integration itself, see Rosamond, 2000).

In many important ways, our 21st-century world seems to be shrinking as assimilation speeds ahead at the global level. Internationalization of trade, vastly improved communication and transportation systems, and large-scale movements of people around the world are leading to the realization of the global village (different visions of the global village are available, see Huntington, 1996; Ohmae, 1990; Sen, 2006). Employees of international corporations, tourists, diplomats, and other people can move from New York to Bombay to Prague to London to Beijing and to scores of other internationalized cities around the world and enjoy basically the same lifestyle at each new destination.

The goods and services that the international community enjoys, including clothing, electronics, cars, household appliances, films, food, information and services via the telephone and computers, and so on, are as likely to be provided by people in China and India as they are by people in the European Union and North America. Through the use of electronic communications and computer screening, patients in U.S. hospitals are now being provided services by medical specialists thousands of miles away in other countries, and the same trend of outsourcing is expanding in most professional service areas, including insurance, accounting, architecture, publishing, and of course, computing (Merchant, 2003).

This increasing globalization and movement of people, services, and goods around the world is associated with the globalization of values. Research shows, for example, that at least among young people, basic attitudes toward human rights are, in important ways, now similar across scores of different countries (Spini & Doise, 2005). An important aspect of this globalization of values is related to democracy.

Rhetoric about democracy seems to be influencing the political, economic, and social aspirations of people in different countries in a number of key ways. First, there is a *top-down* process, led by powerful politicians, particularly in the United States and the United Kingdom, espousing the goal of exporting democracy around the world. Irrespective of the extent to which we accept as genuine the new stance of "democracy belongs to all the world" among some Western political leaders, we must accept that simply by expressing support for global democracy, Western leaders have raised expectations among hundreds of millions of ordinary people, particularly those still living under the crushing force of dictatorships. Just as various kinds of democracies are emerging in the former dictatorships of Eastern Europe (Roberts, 2006), forms of democracies could emerge in the present dictatorships of Asia and Africa.

However, the successful implementation of a political system, be it democratic or otherwise, depends in large part on the characteristics of the available psychological citizens—the cognitive, developmental, social, and other key psychological characteristics of the citizens of a society. The psychological citizen has two sets of characteristics: those particular to one or a few societies (i.e., *emics*) and the smaller number of characteristics common to all or most societies (i.e., *etics*). When political systems are "parachuted" into a society without regard for the characteristics of the psychological citizens, there is likely to be a mismatch between the formal political system and the actual citizens occupying society, as in the disastrous case of Iraq after the 2003 American-led invasion. The implication is that in planning macrolevel policies, we must pay close attention to social and psychological processes, particularly those that influence intergroup peace and conflict.

Second, associated with rhetoric about democracy, is a *bottom-up* process, arising from consumerism and the right to enjoy free choice in the marketplace. Mass communications have spread the image of a better life to the farthest corners of the earth, so that even people in remote Asian and African villages have been influenced by media representations of Western middle-class affluence. True, choice in the economic marketplace does not guarantee political choices, but nevertheless, the trend of rising expectations places new demands on political leaders, both elected and unelected. Consequently, there is increasing commonality around the world in support of citizens having greater choice in either the consumer market, the political arena, or both.

A SECOND LOOK AT TRENDS IN THE WESTERN WORLD

From a Western perspective, then, globalization seems to be associated with greater integration and uniformity. The global village seems to be becoming a reality. But a closer look at social, political, and economic trends reveals that the experiences of Western societies are in some respects very similar to those of non-Western societies, and a movement opposing globalization persists internationally: a movement involving fragmentation, differentiation, and a highlighting of cultural differences. Some aspects of this apparently contradictory movement are discussed by economists, political scientists, geographers, sociologists, anthropologists, as well as psychologists, under the title of *regionalism* (Breslin, Hughes, Phillips, & Rosamond, 2001; Farrell, Hettne, & Van Langenhove, 2005; Gamble & Payne, 1996; Katz, 2005). However, discussions of regionalism have not fully captured the breadth, power, and passion of the push for independence and differentiation. This push is clearly reflected in numerous separatist movements in different parts of the world in attempts to break apart from existing states and form new states while retaining and reconstructing avowedly unique cultures, religions, languages, and authentic identities (Moghaddam, 2006b). For example, the citizens of the small state of Belarus have voted to break free from their alliance with Montenegro, another small state in post–Soviet Eastern Europe.

In its extreme form, tactics of differentiation, independence, and anti-globalization include varieties of terrorism, such as ecoterrorism political-religious terrorism. Examples of terrorist organizations in recent history are the Black Tigers—a special suicide terrorism group within the Tamil Tigers fighting for independence in Sri Lanka—as well as Al Qaeda and various other groups that are part of the Islamic terrorist movements fighting for a return to "pure Islam" (Moghaddam, 2005a). At the heart of most terrorist movements is a motivation to weaken or destroy central authorities and to, in some way, strengthen differentiation and separation from global trends. Islamic terrorism reflects the deep identity crisis experienced by Islamic communities around the world in reaction to the global reach of secular Western culture (Moghaddam, 2006b).

However, it would be a mistake to assume that North America and the European Union are immune from this trend of fragmentation and drive toward independence. In North America, the Quebec independence movement has, since the 1960s, come very close to breaking Canada apart; in the United States, the Hawaiian independence movement is gaining momentum and likely to achieve greater successes in the future toward the goal of full independence from the U.S. mainland (a Puerto Rican independence movement is also active). On the European continent, the expansion of the European Union has to be considered in the context of a backlash against European integration, as reflected by the rejection of the proposed EU constitution by majorities in France and the Netherlands in 2005, and the flourishing of numerous independence movements such as Scottish nationalists and Basque nationalists. Also, within the European Union there are now large ethnic immigrant groups, such as millions of South Asians in the United Kingdom, North Africans in France, and Turks in Germany, that are retaining their distinct and separate identities rather than assimilating and melting away into the mainstream. The violent riots that shook France in 2005, when thousands of Muslim youth clashed with authorities, are a sharp reminder of this trend.

Just as globalization and unification is challenged by an opposite tendency toward fragmentation and independence, the rhetoric of democracy and the spread of freedom to all corners of the world are challenged by trends suggesting a continuation and even strengthening of dictatorships. Regime changes and elections seem to indicate movement toward democracy and freedom, but these changes can remain surface level and superficial and hide a very different, deeper trend. For example, there have been numerous elections in Iran since the 1978 revolution, just as citizens in Russia have voted many times since the collapse of communism, but neither country has made serious progress toward democracy.

TWO PSYCHOLOGICAL LIMITATIONS: MAXIMUM SPEED OF PSYCHOSOCIAL CHANGE AND LIMITED IDENTIFICATION WITH LARGER INGROUPS

How do we explain these two contrasting international trends—one toward unification, assimilation, and the formation of larger and larger units and the other toward fragmentation, independence, attempts to reconstruct or retain smaller units (with a result of strengthening diversity)? An important part of the explanation lies with two psychological processes that are integral to universal aspects of the psychological citizen.

The first psychological process concerns the maximum speed of change at the micro psychosocial level as compared with the macro level of economic and political transformations. Change at the macro level of politics and economics can, in some conditions, come about very quickly: Revolutions and coups d'etat can bring about regime change and political transformation almost overnight, and economic policy can change just as quickly, such as through government decisions or natural disasters. However, the psychosocial transformations needed for individuals to change their styles of thinking and action to fit in with the new macro system are often much slower (Moghaddam, 2002, chap. 2).

Consider, for example, the events that followed two of the most important revolutions of the late 20th century: the revolution that brought an end to the Soviet dictatorship in 1989 and the 1978–1979 revolution that toppled the dictatorship of the Shah in Iran. In both cases, revolutions led to the collapse of a political system—communism in the Soviet Union and monarchy in Iran. These political changes resulted in great hope for freedom, fairness, and the creation of open societies. However, these relatively speedy macro-level political changes failed to bring about, and were even resisted by, much slower changes at the micro level of thought and action (see Moghaddam & Crystal, 1997).

A consequence is that political freedom proved to be short lived, and dictatorship has returned to both Iran and Russia. The same trend of macrolevel changes being speedier than microlevel changes, in part through the influence of subtle cultural *carriers*—"the means by which styles of social thinking and doing are sustained and passed on from generation to generation" (Moghaddam, 2002, p. 8)—is reflected in the 1917 revolution in Russia (Figes & Kolonitskii, 1999) and the great French Revolution (Schama, 1989).

The second psychological process that helps explain the persistence of trends toward fragmentation is the difficulty of achieving rapid identification shifts from smaller to larger ingroups. This difficulty can best be understood in evolutionary context. The lives of our hunter–gatherer ancestors were spent in small bands (see Panter-Brick, Layton, & Rowley-Conwy, 2001), and the earliest settled communities consisted of relatively small populations. Although bipedalism began among our ancestors over 5 million years ago, it is only in the past few thousand years that settlements, nations, and empires with large populations have emerged. Thus, our evolutionary history has almost exclusively involved identification with small groups. The shift to identification with groups numbering more than a few hundred is very recent when considered on the timescale of animal and human evolution.

FRACTURED GLOBALIZATION

We can propose a general rule that all things being equal, individuals more easily identify with, and form allegiance to, smaller rather than larger groups (research evidence supports this view; see Abrams, 1994; Hornsey & Jetten, 2004, p. 251). Smaller groups allow for greater intimacy and more likelihood of direct contact between members as well as between members and leaders. Larger groups, such as the European Union, often remain as abstract concepts, even though they have important economic advantages, at least for some members.

Globalization is unidirectional, involving a move from smaller to larger units. For example, nation states in Europe are expected to integrate into a larger unit—the European Union. But allegiances to and identification with smaller states, such as France, Great Britain, and Spain, evolved over very long time periods, spanning at least many centuries. Identification with France as an ingroup is central to the identity of most French people, just as identification with Italy is integral to the identity of most Italians. To change such allegiances so that French and Italian citizens now feel themselves part of a much larger unit—a united Europe—would take generations. In contrast, the formal laws and political and economic systems creating the new European Union are coming about relatively faster. Thus, there is a clash between the relatively fast-pace maximum speed of macrolevel political and economic changes and the slower maximum speed of psychosocial change.

Psychological limitations to (a) the speed of change and (b) the shift from identification with smaller to larger groups are contradicted by economic pressures toward globalization. Business corporations are expanding to take advantage of economies of scale and international markets (R. Tilly & Welfens, 2000). These contradictory economic and psychological pressures are summed up in the phrase *global economy*, *local identity* and the concept of *fractured globalization* (i.e., the tendency for sociocultural disintegration to pull in a local direction at the same time that macroeconomic and political systems are set up to accelerate globalization).

Fractured globalization reflects the fact that idealistic rhetoric pointing to one humankind and the unity of all people is in the shorter term, at least, more in line with economic trends than it is with psychological processes. In the early decades of the 20th century, this is perhaps most clearly represented by the relationship between China and the United States. From an economic standpoint, the two giants of the 21st century are strongly linked and interdependent, but this economic unity is not translating into shifts in psychological identification. The United States continues an arms embargo against communist China and has used its influence to ensure that the European Union also continues the same policy. There, at least, does not seem to be a shift in the "us versus them" attitude of Americans. Indeed, since the collapse of the Soviet empire, in the United States there has been a shift to seeing communist China as the major rival and threat to American interests.

Despite psychological processes that inhibit identification with larger and larger units, globalization is surging ahead, driven by technological and economic forces. A result is that local languages and cultures are under threat, and some have disappeared. The same technological and economic forces are influencing biological diversity, and it is necessary to consider together the lockstep decline of biological and cultural diversity.

TWO PARALLEL DEBATES: CULTURAL AND BIOLOGICAL DIVERSITY

Two parallel debates are underway concerning diversity and globalization (Moghaddam, 2006a). A first debate involves biologists, ecologists, veterinarians, and other scientists who are exploring plant and animal diversity and highlighting the rapid decline and extinction of numerous nonhuman life forms. It is estimated that species extinction is taking place at about one every 20 minutes (Gorke, 2003). The natural world we are passing on to future generations clearly will be far less diverse than the one we inherited. Unfortunately, the lack of effective global and regional, and in some cases national and local, policies for preserving ecological balance as well as the rapid rise of hundreds of millions of new consumers in developing societies (N. Myers & Kent, 2004), particularly China and India, indicate greater future pressures on the natural environment. Consequently, it is unlikely there will be a halt to the decline in diversity among animals and plants in the foreseeable future.

Parallel to the debate concerning diversity in plants and animals is a debate about a decline in diversity in human cultures and languages that involves psychologists, political scientists, anthropologists, sociologists, and linguistics, among others. Decline in cultural and linguistic diversity is associated with colonial and imperial expansion that has occurred since the 16th century and, more recently, globalization trends. For example, new estimates of the number of Native Indians in North and South America in 1491 (the year before Columbus landed in America) total 100 million; by 1800 they were down to one tenth of their original population (Mann, 2005).

Language death has been just as sharp. About 15,000 living languages are estimated to have existed in the world in 1491. Now, only about 6,000 languages are left, and most of these are in danger of extinction (Crystal, 2000). Even the languages of powerful nations such as France and Germany are under pressure: The European Union does not yet have an official language, but English is the commonly used language in European political meetings and communications, as it has become the official language of science and business internationally. Almost half a billion people speak English as their first language, and nearly 1 billion more speak English as their second language. (Mandarin Chinese remains the most widely used first language; see Saville-Troike, 2006, p. 9, Table 2.1.)

Conditions that give rise to *catastrophic evolution*, a swift, sharp, and often fatal decline in the numbers of a particular life form, are now common to diversity trends in both cultural and biological spheres (Moghaddam, 2006a). In most cases, catastrophic evolution has resulted from human activities associated with cultural change. Just as colonial and later imperial expansion led to Westernization and the decline or extinction of numerous indigenous cultures and languages in Africa, Asia, Australia, and the Americas, the introduction of new plants and animals to the colonies led to the decline or extinction of numerous local species. For example, the arrival of European settlers in Australia, New Zealand, and nearby islands led to the annihilation of a number of indigenous human groups, such as the Tasmanians (Tasmania was discovered by Europeans in 1642, and by 1876 the entire Tasmanian population had been wiped out—see Ryan, 1981; there have recently been claims that some Tasmanians did survive and that these survivors should enjoy land rights), as well as the disappearance of numerous local animals and plants (Baskin, 2002).

But why should this matter? One argument is that it does not matter because evolutionary changes necessarily involve the death of some species and the rise of other species. This process has always existed and ensures the survival of those species that are best adapted to new environmental conditions. However, an alternative argument, common to discussions of both biological and cultural diversity, is that greater diversity has benefits and advantages, and by reducing diversity we are damaging our own chances of long-term survival. As ecological conditions change—because of global warming, for example—we may find that some of the characteristics of the animals and plants as well as human cultures that are now facing extinction, or are already extinct, could have increased our chances for survival. By reducing diversity, the argument goes, we are shrinking the pool of resources we have to meet new challenges in an unpredictable environment.

These arguments are directly relevant to ongoing debates about the best policies for managing culturally diverse societies. On the one hand, there are policies supportive of *assimilation*, involving the melting away of differences between different groups toward a society in which intergroup similarity is maximized and differences minimized. On the other hand, there are policies supportive of *multiculturalism*, involving the strengthening and highlighting of intergroup differences. Assimilation leads to decreased diversity; multiculturalism leads to the maintenance of, or even increases in, diversity.

The two contrasting trends discussed earlier, globalization and unification versus fragmentation and differentiation, are respectively in line with policies for assimilation and those for multiculturalism. Which policy should we favor? A first set of arguments in response to this question concern the possible advantages of diversity for meeting future ecological challenges. Changing ecological conditions could create unforeseen demands and challenges, which could be met far better through a wider range of biological and/or cultural resources—resources that are continually dwindling.

A second set of arguments also rest on the assumption of certain psychological limitations, such as limitations to shifting identification from smaller to larger groups that influence the viability of assimilation and multiculturalism. Assimilation is associated with globalization and movement toward larger and larger units, such as the European Union. In theory, this movement could ultimately result in one global village and a world government. However, this assimilationist movement is challenged by the psychological tendency of people to resist identifying with larger and larger groups.

Finally, a third set of arguments are based on justice issues, particularly *rights* (i.e., what is demanded of others) and *duties* (i.e., what is owed to others). For example, do minority groups have the right to receive support for the preservation of their distinct cultures and languages? In addition, do majorities have a duty to support the preservation of minority cultures and languages? Or, do minority groups have a duty to abandon their heritage cultures and languages, to adopt the cultures and languages of the majority groups, and in this way, contribute to the realization of a global village? Further, do majorities have a duty to support minority assimilation? Such questions must be considered in the broader context of *intergroup relations*, characterized by competition, conflict, power inequalities, leadership struggles, changes in membership, and so on.

Intergroup relations is perhaps the most challenging domain of human behavior, particularly because of the continued danger of destructive intergroup conflict and war at local, regional, and global levels. I believe that the best tools available to us for meeting this challenge are the major theories of intergroup relations.

PLAN AND ORIENTATION OF THIS BOOK

Globalization and the large-scale movement of people, goods, services, and other cultural products around the world have had two consequences that have helped to shape this book. First, whereas questions about diversity and multiculturalism have traditionally been raised in the local and national contexts, it is now necessary to also raise such questions at the international level. Intergroup contact and the challenge of managing diversity are now global, not just local, issues. Indeed, in some respects national boundaries have become irrelevant in many parts of the world because the vast flow of people, goods, services, and other cultural phenomena has created global cultural continuities across national borders. Thus, the discussions in this book are set in local and national as well as regional and international contexts.

A second impact of globalization that has influenced the orientation of this book is that traditional cross-cultural comparisons have become less appropriate, and in some situations, redundant. Globalization means that culture is no longer synonymous with fixed geographical space and national boundaries (if it ever was). Over the past few decades, there has been a tremendous growth in continuities in culture across physical space and across national boundaries. For example, the Internet and Weblogs have brought into being new communities that share important cultural characteristics but that are physically located in different nation states. Consequently, I treat the traditional idea of cultural differences being associated with geographical location critically and cautiously throughout this book.

The book chapters are organized in three main sections. The two chapters composing Part I establish the context and scope of the discussion. After introducing the main research themes and questions here, in chapter 1, I discuss the foundational topic of group formation in chapter 2. For intergroup relations to take place, groups must first come into existence. I examine the psychological, biological, and cultural factors that shape categorization and group formations.

The four chapters in Part II of this volume critically review the major psychological theories of intergroup relations, organized around four themes: rationality (chap. 3), material resources (chap. 4), identity (chap. 5), and perceived justice (chap. 6). These themes implicitly or explicitly underlie theories not only in psychology (Gaertner & Brown, 2002; Worchel & Austin, 1986) but also in international relations (Sterling-Folker, 2006; C. Weber, 2005). The major theories reviewed differ in a number of important ways, but in each case the implications of the theories for democracy are examined.

RANGE OF THEORIES

Since the mid 20th century, a variety of psychological theories have been developed specifically to explain intergroup relations (Brewer & Miller, 1996; Gaertner & Brown, 2002; Hogg & Abrams, 2001; D. M. Taylor & Moghaddam, 1994; Worchel & Austin, 1986). In addition, the writings of Sigmund Freud (1856–1939) yielded a rich psychological account of intergroup relations. Also, Vilfredo Pareto (1884–1923) and Karl Marx (1818–1883) provided dynamic intergroup theories that have psychological underpinnings and should receive more attention from psychologists. Although my focus is the psychology of intergroup relations, I do not shy away from crossing disciplinary borders when psychological ideas are found in other fields of study. Indeed, I believe that setting aside disciplinary boundaries leads to important practical and research benefits.

The organization of the discussion of major intergroup theories revolves around four main themes (i.e., rationality, material resources, identity, and perceived justice) and allows for a more integrated and critical assessment. The following sections provide a more detailed discussion of each theme.

Rationality

The discussion on the theme of rationality is particularly influenced by the writings of Freud, with some attention also given to Pareto's (1935) and Marx's (1852/1979; Marx & Engels, 1848/1967) research on the authoritarian personality as well as more recent developments such as terror management theory and system justification theory.

The main questions addressed in relation to the theme of rationality are as follows:

1. Are humans rational creatures? By this is meant, do humans know what they do and why? Do they understand the real motivations behind intergroup conflict and war, for example? Of course, this is very different from asking whether humans can rationalize and present rational arguments. For instance, after initiating a war against another country, invaders can and often do rationalize their actions by arguing that they waged war to expand freedom or democracy (or the word of God or some other apparently positive motive).
2. What are the implications of displacement of aggression, experiences of terror, and other outcomes of unconscious motives, fears, and so on?
3. What is the role of leadership in intergroup relations?
4. What are the psychological characteristics that are more likely to support dictatorial leadership?
5. What are the implications of irrationalist theories for democracy?

Material Resources

The theories discussed in this section all give central place to the role of material factors in intergroup relations. The major materialist theories include realistic conflict theory and resource mobilization theory, with some attention also given to the psychological underpinnings of Marxist theory. Also examined are evolutionary psychology, sociobiology, social dominance theory, and various other adaptations of classic evolutionary theory. Some thematic questions in this section are as follows:

1. Does conflict arise from competition for material resources?
2. Do material conditions and material interests determine the consciousness of group members?
3. Are group-based inequalities inevitable?
4. Does competition among human groups reflect a deeper competition among gene pools?

5. What are the implications of materialist theories for democracy?

Identity

What kind of person am I? To what kind of group do I belong? Questions about identity have become even more central to our lives in this era of identity politics. Appropriately, theories of intergroup relations that give primacy to identity have gained prominence. The major theory discussed in association with the theme of identity is social identity theory, but attention is also given to self-categorization theory, optimal distinctiveness theory, and the collective identity model. Some thematic questions in this section are as follows:

1. Is the desire for a positive and distinct identity universal?
2. Does categorization necessarily lead to intergroup bias?
3. Is there a universal motivation to achieve a balance between belonging to groups and remaining an independent individual?
4. What is the relationship between individual identity and collective identity?
5. What are the implications of identity theories for democracy?

Perceived Justice

"We are not being treated fairly!" "Our rights are being violated!" Such complaints are often heard during the processes of intergroup conflict when people feel a sense of injustice and unfair treatment. The final theme of perceived justice is discussed primarily with a focus on equity theory and relative deprivation theory, with some reference to more recent research on the psychology of human rights and duties (Finkel & Moghaddam, 2005). The thematic questions in this section are as follows:

1. Why are people inclined to see the world as just, even when objective criteria suggest a high level of injustice?
2. What is the role of ideology in perceptions of injustice?
3. What is the role of social comparison processes in feelings of deprivation?
4. What is the relationship between perceived rights and duties among minority and majority groups?
5. What are the implications of justice theories for democracy?

DEMOCRACY, DIVERSITY, AND INTERGROUP RELATIONS

The major theories of intergroup relations have direct implications for democracy as well as for policies for managing diversity. These implications are particularly important in the domains of justice and the characteristics needed for psychological citizens in democracy.

Intergroup Relations, Rights, and Duties

Central to intergroup relations are what each group perceives to be ingroup and outgroup rights and duties. Rights exist where vulnerabilities exist, where something can be taken away by others. If there was no possibility of a group (e.g., journalists) losing free speech, it would not make sense to support a "right" to free speech (e.g., in the face of government restrictions). A right to clean air is only now being discussed because of the recognition that this right is being threatened by environmental pollution, the activities of powerful industrial interests, and so on. In situations of change, rights are given priority by minority groups, vulnerable because they have less power than the majority to uphold and extend their rights (Moghaddam, 2004).

In contrast, duties are associated with majorities in two important ways. First, duties imply power. To put it in a Kantian way: *oughts* imply *cans*. Because the majority group enjoys greater power, the majority has the greater ability to define *oughts*, both for itself and for others. A second, more subtle way in which duties are associated with majorities is that majorities are served by the status quo; consequently, majorities are apt to give priority to the duty of the members of both majority and minority groups to uphold the status quo.

When minority–majority relations are stable and there is little possibility of change, minorities are more likely to buy into the narrative used by the majority group and (implicitly or explicitly) neglect their own collective rights. However, in times of changing intergroup relations, minority groups give priority to rights and attempt to bring about changes more favorable to themselves.

Globalization and transformations in trade, communication, and transportation have created conditions for, and expectations of, greater change. Thus, associated with globalization are shifts in the priorities given by majority and minority groups to rights and duties (discussed further in chap. 6). Rights and duties are central to all political systems, and a shift from dictatorship toward democracy involves major changes in the rights and duties of both minority and majority groups.

Contextualized Democracy and Globalization

Despite regionalism and tendencies toward fragmentation, the drive toward further globalization and assimilation remains strong. Globalization raises the possibility of the global spread of democracy, particularly after the collapse of the Soviet empire (Sharansky & Dermer, 2004). Just as free-market capitalism has been exported in some shape or form to different parts of the world, including communist China, perhaps democracy can be exported to become global? The popularity of a phrase such as *exporting democracy*, particularly among a number of powerful Western politicians (e.g., President George W. Bush of the United States, former Prime Minister Tony Blair of the United Kingdom) in the early 21st century, raises questions about the relationship between democracy and culture as well as about the core or essentials of democracy.

With respect to democracy and culture, I argue that if democracy is to be successfully introduced to societies with very different cultures, there must develop *contextualized democracy* (i.e., the use of local cultural symbols and meaning systems as a way of strengthening democratic trends and bringing into place a democratic state; Moghaddam, 2006b, p. 129). There must be considerable flexibility in how democracy takes shape in different societies. The possibility arises that democracy can come to look different in some important ways across societies. Careful study of developing societies in which democracy has taken root, such as the insightful examination of Chile, Costa Rica, Kerala (India), and Mauritius by Sandbrook, Edelman, Heller, and Teichman (2006), demonstrates this to be the case.

At the same time, however, there must surely be some common core, some essential elements that are at the heart of democracy, that are indispensable and without which a system would not be recognized as democratic. What is this common core?

Sifting through various alternatives to identity to serve as a common core for democracy, we can quickly dispense with some possibilities. For example, it would be a mistake to assume that mass participation and large-scale social movements necessarily result in, or are a precondition for, democracy. The relationship between social movements and democracy is complex; social movements can be both pro- and antidemocracy (see readings in Ibarra, 2003). However, other possibilities seem more essential for a common core. For example, following Sen's (1999) argument for the central place of choice in national development, we can also interpret choice as having a central place in democracy: for example, having the choice to vote out a leader, to express an opinion in public, or to withdraw support from or add one's support for a cause.

Another core feature of democracy is the rule of law, in the sense that everyone must be dealt with according to the law. It may be that the law gives, in some respects, different rights and duties to different groups. For example, rights and duties ascribed to the young may in some respects differ from those ascribed to adults. However, the key essential is that everyone be treated as required by the law.

Even when we identify certain core features of democracy, such as the availability of choice and the rule of law, it is clear that there is a great deal of variation in the particular ways in which democracy can be brought to fruition. For example, democracy can be *direct* (as in some of the small Greek city states of 2,500 years ago, where democracy, rule by the *demos*, originated), in which citizens could personally participate in debates and decision making, or *indirect*, in which (usually because of the huge size of populations in modern societies) citizens elect representatives who undertake debates and decision making on their behalf. The electoral systems of democracies vary, examples being *plurality rule* (i.e., candidate with the most votes wins), *proportionality* (i.e., representation of a political party in the country's assemblies is proportional to the votes they receive), and *majoritarian* (i.e., candidates must win a majority to be elected). There is also variation in democracies in the relationship between the ruling party in elected assemblies (e.g., the Senate, Parliament) and the head of the legislative branch of government. For example, in the United States, the president can be from a party other than the party in the majority in Congress; in the United Kingdom, the prime minister is the head of the party with the majority in Parliament.

Three other ways in which democracies vary have received far less attention than is warranted. First, in some societies voting is considered a right, and the government is obligated to create conditions for individuals to practice this right, whereas in other societies voting is considered a duty, and the onus is on the individual to fulfill this duty. For example, in the United States, citizens have a right to vote (voting is referred to as a right in the 15th, 19th, and 24th amendments to the U.S. Constitution), a right that only a numerical minority actually exercises in most elections; in Australia, citizens have a duty to vote and are punished if they fail to do so.

A second variation across democracies that deserves far more attention concerns economic inequalities: Does democracy require certain limits to economic inequalities in society? On the one hand, it could be argued that as long as citizens enjoy equal rights in the courts and in the political sphere, the amount of money they have is irrelevant: In elections the vote of a poor person has the same influence as the vote of a rich person. For example, in U.S. national elections the vote cast by Bill Gates, reportedly the richest person in the world, is given the same value as the vote cast by a penniless person. On the other hand, when wealth disparities within a society become too great, members of the poor group become relatively so disadvantaged that they lose the ability to freely exercise choice. I use the term *planned democracy* to denote societies, such as those of Scandinavia, in which greater effort is made to control economic disparities between the richer and the poorer sectors. In contrast, *free-market democracy* denotes other societies, such as the United States, in which less effort is made to control economic disparities between the richer and the poorer sectors. Of course, dictatorships can also be planned or free-market.

The various alternatives can be conceived as lying at some point in a space delimited by two vectors (see Figure 1.1). The first vector has as its polar opposites democracy and dictatorship (acknowledging that examples

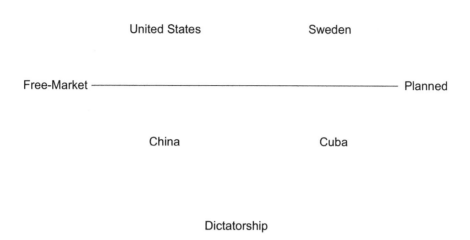

Figure 1.1. Diagrammatical representation of alternative approaches to describing planned and free-market democracies and dictatorships.

of pure democracy or dictatorship are not found among contemporary nation states). The extreme poles of the second vector are free market and planned (again, examples of these in their pure forms do not exist). The resultant four possibilities are free-market democracy, free-market dictatorship, planned democracy, and planned dictatorship.

A third important type of variation across democratic societies that deserves far more attention concerns the management of *cultural diversity*. By *culture* I particularly mean the normative system and values that people use as guides to their behavior, and by *cultural diversity* I mean variations in normative systems and values that exist within a society. Democracies have adopted different policies for managing cultural diversity (see the highly insightful discussion of Walzer, 1997). We can conceptualize these policies as lying on a continuum—at one extreme, complete assimilation through which all cultural differences are melted away and there is cultural and linguistic homogeneity; at the other extreme, complete multiculturalism through which cultural differences are maintained, strengthened, and celebrated and there is a high level of cultural and linguistic diversity.

A common challenge confronting all four types of societies is the question of how best to manage cultural diversity, and a common experience in all four societies has been the overwhelming influence of globalization leading to de facto assimilation as the dominant trend, with some slight variations. These variations arise, for example, from government interventions in Canada, Australia, and some other (mainly historically immigrant-receiving) societies, to support cultural and linguistic diversity (although Australia is rethinking its support for diversity in reaction to terrorist and radicalization threats).

Another source of such variation is religiously inspired governments, such as in Iran, intervening to strengthen traditional religious practices and values in the face of globalization. Thus, it is ironic that the challenge of maintaining diversity has been taken up by governments in democracies (e.g., Canada, particularly the provincial government of Quebec) and dictatorships (e.g., Iran) that share a feeling of being under siege from globalization forces.

Democracy, in particular, is challenged by globalization and its implications for minority rights and diversity. The enormous movement of people from Asia, Africa, South America, and Eastern Europe to North American and Western European democracies has highlighted a number of key questions regarding democracy, diversity, and intergroup relations:

1. Does diversity hurt democracy? Are the requirements and constraints of a diverse society incompatible with those of democracy?
2. Irrespective of our answer to the previous question, are we obligated by fairness principles to support diversity and minority rights?
3. What is the relationship between diversity and social capital?

CONCLUDING COMMENTS

Globalization has been associated with spectacular progress in science, technology, and trade, including advancements in communication and transportation systems, medicine, and agriculture. We can now electronically communicate with other humans across the other side of the earth, land people on the moon and use international collaboration to help run space stations, and carry out medical treatments that just a few years ago were assumed to exist only in the realm of science fiction.

However, these miraculous scientific and technological advances are in sharp contrast to our continual struggles to overcome intergroup discrimination, conflict, and multinational wars. We continue to fight, kill, and destroy—so much so that our aggression threatens to annihilate us. It is not clear whether we will survive our own "advanced" weapons.

As the world is brought closer to the realization of a global village, we must apply ourselves more diligently and sincerely to improving intergroup relations and conflict resolution. Our policies for managing conflict must improve because the stakes are now far too high, and the cost of major intergroup conflict is far too great for any group to shoulder. Toward contributing to this effort, this book brings to bear intergroup research and theory on the problem of managing conflict and developing effective policies for managing diversity in national and international contexts. An underlying bias in this work is that democracy and the open society is a desirable goal but that there is considerable cultural variation in the ways in which this goal can be realized. Thus, contextualized democracy (Moghaddam, 2006b, chap.10), which uses local symbols and traditions to develop democracy, is viewed as the most effective and desirable strategy.

2

CONSTRUCTING GROUPS: BIOLOGY, CULTURE, AND CATEGORIZATION

Each one of you shall help to make things slip
By telling two stories on the outward trip.

—Chaucer (trans. 1977, p. 24)

In the epigraph above, the host invites the pilgrims to recount tales to one another on their way to Canterbury in Geoffrey Chaucer's 14th-century narrative *The Canterbury Tales*. The individual pilgrims join together to form a group for functional reasons, and as they progress on their pilgrimage, social ties and emotional connections are forged between the group members. In various situations in our everyday lives, we join groups for functional reasons, particularly to carry out tasks at school and at work. After the pilgrimage is over, Chaucer's pilgrims disband and go their separate ways, as is the case with most groups that are formed with a specific goal in mind (e.g., reaching a particular destination, completing a class project, or attending to a task at work). However, some other groups are much longer lasting and develop identities that are influential across many generations (Moghaddam, 2002). For example, the historian Geoffrey Elton (1994) closed his lucid profile of the English in this way:

> We have now brought the English through a thousand and more years of history, and despite all the often drastic changes in circumstances and behaviour the main features of the scene have proved surprisingly con-

tinuous. Formed into one people out of diverse war-bands and farmers, they quite early acquired what can fairly be called a sense of nationhood. (p. 213)

The "sense of nationhood" that Elton (1994) referred to is still very much alive among the English, but it is now being pulled and pushed in new directions by global and regional forces. The English are now part of an enlarged European Union, and they are being encouraged to develop a European identity as well as to embrace the global economy. This move toward a greater Europe within a global village reflects a top-down trend toward establishing larger and larger groups. I say "top-down," as previously discussed in chapter 1, instead of "bottom-up" because the main impetus for change is coming from elite economic and political forces rather than from the desires of ordinary people expressed in their everyday lives.

Of course, advocates of free-market economics argue that European unification and an open global economy will benefit ordinary people. From the perspective of a liberal market economy, it would be best if there were no barriers to trade and the world population served as one enormous market. This would require us to perceive all people as members of one gigantic group of consumers.

In practice, far from being one single market, economic markets remain fragmented and full of barriers, just as in the political and social arenas in which modern human societies are characterized by numerous divisions and groupings. Such group distinctions are a universal feature of human societies rather than being unique to modern life. There is no doubt that part of the reason is functional: Just as Chaucer's (trans. 1977) pilgrims found it more effective to travel in a group, humans, at least since their hunting and gathering days, have found it more effective to organize themselves into groups. At a cognitive level, also, we find it useful and necessary to categorize the world around us (Ahn, Goldstone, Love, Markman, & Wolff, 2005), placing into groups both social and nonsocial phenomena.

The moral philosopher John Rawls (1971) formulated an influential thought experiment in which people of approximately equal ability agree on how to organize society without knowing the group membership of themselves or others. What principles of social relations and justice would people agree on if they did not know to which racial, sex, class, religious, age, or other groups they and others belonged? Could it be presumed that such a veil of ignorance would lead people to agree on fairer social arrangements? Even more basic questions lurk behind this thought experiment: Given the human tendency to think, act, and organize life using groups, how malleable is human thought and action with respect to groups? What are the constraints on getting people to think without using groupings? The research evidence suggests that both biological and ideological constraints influence our thoughts and actions in this arena.

CONSTRAINTS ON CATEGORIZATION

At the foundation of intergroup relations is the basic process of categorizing the world and identifying individuals as belonging to different groups. By changing how the social world is categorized, we could alter group memberships and intergroup relations. In this section, I identify and assess certain constraints on how we can change categorization.

Biological Constraints

> They came to their journey's end late in the evening. Close to the railway was an immense white edifice, like an ugly hospital, on which was painted "NATIONAL HOTEL." There was a wooden gallery or verandah in front, in which it was rather startling, when the train stopped, to behold a great many boots and shoes, and the smoke of a great many cigars, but no other evidence of human habitation. By slow degrees, however, some heads and shoulders appeared, and connecting themselves to the boots and shoes, led to the discovery that certain gentlemen boarders, who had a fancy for putting their heels where the gentlemen boarders in other countries usually put their heads, were enjoying themselves after their own manner in the cool of the evening. (Dickens, 1843–1844/1994, p. 320)

The above description is from the viewpoint of two newcomers to 19th-century America in Charles Dickens's novel *Martin Chuzzlewit*. The New World is unfamiliar to the newcomers, and as they are transported by train to another settlement, it takes them time to make sense of their surroundings. In any situation, an infinite amount of information is available to us in the environment. We make sense of and structure this mass of information through a number of mechanisms, some of which rely on our inbuilt biological characteristics.

The idea that we arrive in this world predisposed to organize our experiences in particular ways is in line with Kant's (1787/1996) argument that all human experience is shaped by 12 schemas. Thus, for example, space, time, and causation are a priori categories of experience; inbuilt schemas predispose us to synthesize the streams of information reaching us so that we experience relationships in space, the passing of time, and cause–effect associations in particular ways. For example, although we have to be taught how to use clocks to tell time, we do not have to be taught that time passes; the experience of passing time is common to all humans, irrespective of whether they use clocks or other instruments to measure the passage of time (readings in Helfrich, 2003, explore some of the continuities in the psychological experience of time).

Perceptual Constraints

The Kantian tradition is reflected in psychology by the research of the Gestalt school (see Ellis, 1959). Gestalt researchers designed demonstrations to show that our perceptual system predisposes us to structure incoming information and impose patterns on that information. Such patterns arise out of laws of perceptual organization, important examples being similarity and proximity. When looking at phenomena in the world, we tend to group things together when we see them as similar (e.g., when watching a football game, we group the players according to the team colors they wear), and when we see them as physically close to one another (e.g., we perceive different groups of children playing in a park on the basis of how each child is physically located in relation to other children—those physically closer to one another are seen as a group).

Despite increasing awareness of the importance of ecological factors in perception, the tradition continues in psychological research of emphasizing predispositions to structure information (Gibson, 1979). This includes a predisposition to first attend to shape in forming categories (Landau, 1998), which appears in children as young as 2 years old, as well as an ability to discriminate on the basis of conceptual primitives of geometry (Dehaene, Izard, Pica, & Spelke, 2006). In a study of villagers in a remote area of the Amazon, where there is no formal schooling and no maps or tools that incorporate geometric concepts, Dehaene et al. showed that an understanding of the basics of Euclidean geometry seem to be universal and part of our inborn, human inheritance.

The processing of *light*, the part of the electromagnetic spectrum detected by humans, provides an excellent example of how our biological characteristics predispose us to perceive the world in particular ways. Our receptors respond only to wavelengths from 400 to 700 nanometers, and this is labeled *visible light*—constituting only a small part of the electromagnetic spectrum (e.g., it does not include Gamma rays, X-rays, or infrared rays). This visible light is processed by specialized visual receptors: Cones are adapted for detail, color, and daylight; rods are coded for dim light and night vision. Visible light is categorized by us into a color spectrum, with some cultural variation in how we partition and label categories (Lindsey & Brown, 2002).

Rethinking the Cognitive Miser

As suggested by the partitioning of visible light into a color spectrum, categorization is a foundational mechanism used by humans to rapidly process the infinite amount of information reaching us (Rosch & Lloyd, 1978). However, this "cognitive miser" view only tells part of the story and is oversimplified. The boundaries of categories tend to be fuzzy rather than rigid and sharp (as suggested by the research of Rosch, 1978). For example, some birds (e.g., eagles, pigeons) are clearly more birdlike than others (e.g., penguins, ostriches), and belonging to the bird category is not all or none. Also, there are differences in the extent to which our cognitive representations of categories are concrete rather than abstract (E. R. Smith & Zárate, 1990). For example, Katherine thinks of a hammer as a concrete example of a hammer rather than as an abstract concept.

Inherent in the cognitive miser view is a danger of depicting humans as inactive, as being pushed along passively to partition the world in particular ways. Clearly, although we can be passive at times, we are often active in our interpretations of the world. Each of us enters a social context with our particular ways of viewing the world, or *constructs*, as George Kelly (1955) put it. Such constructs guide us to impose meaning on the world and construct and reconstruct our experiences in different ways.

In addition, the view that our categorization of the world arises out of our need to cope with infinite amounts of information can be turned on its head: Perhaps, at least in some contexts, we impose categories not because of too much but too little information (Oakes & Turner, 1990). In situations in which we have too little information to work with, imposing a category allows us to make assumptions easily about a category member. Although such assumptions are often to some degree inaccurate, they help us interact with the world in situations in which we have too little information.

Thus, there is a predisposition for humans to categorize both social and nonsocial phenomena, and children learn the (often biased) categorization systems of their cultures through the socialization process. For example, children learn color classifications appropriate for their particular culture (Lindsey & Brown, 2002).

Continuities Across Nonsocial and Social Categorization

In line with the idea that there is a general predisposition to categorize both nonsocial and social phenomena, research suggests there are a number of continuities in the cognitive effects of categorization across nonsocial and social domains. The most influential conceptual account of this continuity was developed by Henri Tajfel during the *new look* cognitive revival (i.e., the movement that overtook behaviorism) of the 1950s, starting with his pioneering research on the categorization of nonsocial stimuli (Tajfel, 1959; Tajfel & Wilkes, 1963). Building on earlier research on the categorization of nonsocial stimuli (Campbell, 1956), Tajfel (1959; Tajfel & Wilkes, 1963) argued that categorization results in two important cognitive consequences: first, in the accentuation of between-group differences and, second, in the minimization of within-group differences. Thus, phenomena categorized as belonging to two different groups, Group A and Group B, will be seen as more different than they are, and those phenomena within Groups A and B will be seen as more similar than they actually are.

In a seminal study (Tajfel & Wilkes, 1963), participants were presented with eight lines that differed in length from one another by a constant ratio. In Condition 1, the four shorter lines were labeled A and the four longer lines were labeled B. In Condition 2, the eight lines were randomly assigned to Categories A and B. In Condition 3, the eight lines were presented without labels. In assessing the lengths of lines in the three different conditions, participants demonstrated between-group accentuation: In Condition 1, but not in Conditions 2 and 3, they accentuated differences between lengths of Line 4, the longest line in the short category, and Line 5, the shortest line in the long category. However, in this study there was little evidence of minimization of within-group differences following categorization, although evidence for this effect had been earlier found by Campbell (1956) using nonsense syllables (i.e., a nonsocial stimuli) and more recently by Rothbart, Davis-Stitt, and Hill (1997) using job candidates varying in similarity (i.e., a social stimuli).

Of course, there are important differences between the categorization of nonsocial and social stimuli (see D. J. Schneider, 2004, pp. 75–83). For example, social categories are more complex, they are value laden and associated with emotions, and people tend to belong to multiple categories. "Ahmed" belongs to the categories *male*, *young*, *Muslim*, *soccer player*, and *ambitious*. This is rather different from a glass bottle, belonging to the general category *bottle*. Experimental evidence on cross-cutting group membership suggests that the highlighting of multiple group membership (e.g., that although "Joe" and Ahmed belong to two different religious groups, they are both professional engineers, fathers, and Manchester United supporters) is worth considering as a possible strategy for reducing intergroup prejudice in human groups (Brewer, 2000). We are obviously not concerned with such challenges when considering the categorization, cross-cutting or otherwise, of nonsocial phenomena.

Despite some differences between the categorization of nonsocial and social phenomena, there are foundational similarities. First, categorization is a basic, universal cognitive strategy that develops early in humans (Eimas & Quinn, 1994). Second, categorization tends to be associated with between-group differentiation and within-group minimization of differences (Billig, 1976; McGarty, 1999; D. J. Schneider, 2004). Third, cultural factors influence the criteria selected for categorization, although the categories of sex, race, and age seem to be salient in most cultures, at least in the 21st-century context.

THE CONSTRUCTION OF DIVERSITY

In the Twelfth Month there was a royal outing to Oharano. Like everyone else, the ladies of Rokujō set out in their carriages to watch. . . . The princes and high officials were beautifully fitted out. Their guards and grooms, very good looking and of generally matching heights, were in the finest of livery. All the ministers and councillors and indeed the whole court had turned out for the occasion, the highest ranking dressed uniformly in yellow-green robes and lavender singlets. . . . The princes and high courtiers in charge of the falcons were in fine hunting dress. The falconers from the guards were even more interesting, all in printed robes of the most fanciful design. Everything was very grand and very novel, and the carriages of the spectators fought for places. Some among the spindly carriages of the lesser ladies emerged from the struggle with broken wheels. The better carriages had gathered at the approaches to the floating bridge. (Shikibu, trans. 2000, pp. 467–468)

The above passage from Murasaki Shikibu's 11th-century masterpiece *The Tale of Genji*, perhaps the earliest great novel in world literature, describes the categorization of the elite in 11th-century Japanese society. Although the specific criteria used in this categorization scheme (e.g., the yellow-green and printed robes) are different from those used to categorize elites in Western societies during the same historical period, the general idea of a hierarchy among the elite is similar to all societies with centralized government, not just those with a king or an emperor. Consider, for example, how one might describe an outing by the U.S. President to the U.S. Senate on the occasion of a State of the Union Address, an annual report the President is obligated to make to Congress on the health of the nation. Such a description would include categories of members of the Senate, the House of Representatives, the Supreme Court, the military, and leading citizens as well as categories among the elite families (e.g., the First Lady and her entourage).

Flexibility in Categorization

Now consider social categorization in a very different cultural context, one in which there is no central authority. One such society is the traditional Tiwi, residents of Bathurst and Melville Islands off the coast of North Australia (Hart, Pilling, & Goodale, 2001). Among the Tiwi,

There was no tribal government, there were no tribal officials, and no occasions that required the whole tribe to assemble together as a collective entity. For daily and yearly living, the important group was the band or horde, of which there were nine. (Hart et al., 2001, p. 13)

Each band consisted of about 100 to 300 people and roamed a territory of about 200 or 300 square miles, but it was the territory that was stable and not the people who occupied it.

Changes in band membership arose in large part because of the traditional Tiwi custom that all females of all ages and conditions must be married. The Tiwi believed that a woman becomes pregnant because a spirit has entered her body (thus ignoring the role of the man in pregnancy). The unpredictability of the spirits required females to always have husbands from birth until death so that their children would have fathers. Females were typically given as wives to men who could reciprocate and return some material benefit to the man offering the wife (this man was often, but not always, the father of the bride). In many cases, females were offered as wives to men in other bands, and so there was considerable movement across bands and fluctuation in band membership.

The identification of Tiwi individuals with bands of several hundred people reflects a general trend among traditional societies. As I proposed in chapter 1, identification with smaller groups is more easily achieved, in the sense that it requires less investment in formal socialization institutions. The ethologist Eibl-Eibesfeldt (1989) pointed out that through most of human history people have lived in relatively small groups: "Even today, in hunter–gatherer societies, a people speaking one language number only several hundred (usually about 500) members" (p. 100), and local groups among hunter–gatherers are often even smaller: "Local group size of the !Kung is an average of 25 persons . . . in the !Ko 35–45 . . . and in the G/wi 22–60. . . . Each local group is composed of 6 to 15 families" (pp. 614–615).

In addition to categorizing the social world in terms of the nine bands and on the basis of gender, the Tiwi system of categorization emphasized age, particularly for men. In traditional Tiwi society, a man's influence increased with age. Men below the age of 30 were typically without a wife because they had not accumulated the connections and resources needed to be offered a wife by the old men who controlled resources. A man would typically acquire his first wife when he had reached his 30s, and she would be about 15 years older than he. Successful men would continue to acquire more wives as they grew older, and the ages of their new wives would typically be much younger.

Although the social and political arrangements of the traditional Tiwi are unusual, their use of age and sex as bases for categorization is part of a near universal trend. Next, we turn to the question of flexibility and continuity. Given that humans are predisposed to categorize the social world, what are the criteria used for categorization in different societies? This discussion paves the way for an assessment of continuity in the categorization systems in different cultures.

Variations in the Criteria for Categorization

> The Long-ears came from the east first, the Short-ears from the west later. The first were industrious and in charge of monuments and the great works. The Short-ears patiently toiled for two hundred years with the monuments in honor of the Long-ears; then they conspired and made revolt. They pushed the Long-ears down into their own burning pyre and ruled the island alone thereafter. (Heyerdahl, 1989, p. 239)

According to the ancient oral traditions of Easter Islanders, the key grouping on Easter Island used to be Long-Ears and Short-Ears. The Long-Ears were the dominant group, but the Short-Ears staged a revolution and became the rulers. This is one of numerous examples of categorization on the basis of what in other contexts would be interpreted as a trivial criterion; after all, on an objective basis, why should ear length be of any importance? For instance, Maquet (1961) highlighted the use of height for categorization in Ruanda. The Tutsi were the traditionally dominant group, and they exaggerated the height difference between themselves and the Hutu, who were the power minority and (objectively) slightly shorter.

In many cases the criteria used for categorization are only recognized by those who are familiar with local cultural traditions. For example, in Shi'a Islam, the mullahs wear white or black turbans. Those with black turbans are *sayyeds* and enjoy a lofty status, because the color of their turban signifies that they are descendants of the prophet. The categorization of mullahs on the basis of turban color, or titles denoting status in a hierarchy of power and influence, starting from *talabeh* (i.e., student–seeker) and culminating in *ayatollah-ozma* (i.e., grand ayatollah), requires appropriate cultural knowledge.

Majority groups tend to use their superior power and resources to construct requirements for inclusion in the elite group that serve as barriers to exclude minority group members. For example, consider the symbolic value of ceremonial spears among the Tiwi. From the perspective of locals, the possessor of ceremonial spears was necessarily one of the elite who could afford to invest in painted spears that were seldom ever used (Hart et al., 2001, p. 54). As Veblen (1899/1953) articulated over a century ago, dominant groups continually search for and invest in activities and objects that have no function other than to help distance them from the members of other groups. The more "useless" the object of investment and the higher its cost, the less likely that members of less affluent groups could afford to adopt it. For example, Veblen (1899/1953, chap. 14) argued that the classics continue to enjoy a particularly exalted position in higher education exactly because they serve as evidence of wasted time and effort and, consequently, of the additional resources needed to afford them.

Differentiation between groups using criteria that have little or no practical use, other than to distinguish between groups, is similar to the runaway selection identified by Fisher (1930/1999) and other biologists since the early 20th century. Consider, for example, the classic example of the peacock's very long and elaborate feathers, which make the peacock an easier target for predators and serve no "practical" functions. Why should the peacock have evolved such feathers? An explanation from the perspective of runaway selection is that peahen began to use the size of peacock feathers as an indicator of fitness: Peacocks that could survive the burden of carrying useless longer feathers must be fitter. Each generation of peahen selected peacocks with longer and more elaborate feathers until we reached the contemporary pea-cocks with their spectacular, but impractical, display. The animal world provides numerous other examples of markers that serve the same runaway-selection function as tail feathers in the case of the peacock.

Carriers and Categorization

Just as there seem to be few limits in the characteristics that could be used as markers in runaway selection, there are few limits in the criteria that could be used by people to categorize and to differentiate between human groups. Often differentiation is achieved using symbols and other carriers. For example, a carrier such as the cross is used to store meaning (see Geertz, 1958) and to categorize people in terms of religious affiliation. At a functional level, the cross is just two pieces of wood joined together, but at a symbolic level it serves as a powerful basis for Christian identity and differentiation.

In a similar fashion, the veil used to cover the heads of women in countries such as Saudi Arabia and Iran is just a piece of cloth, but the highest meaning is ascribed to the Islamic veil, so much so that any women appearing in public in these Islamic societies without the veil would face the harshest punishments. This is a "piece of cloth" that many have died for—reminding us of fights over other pieces of cloth, such as the Confederate Flag and "Old Glory" in the United States (see Moghaddam, 2002, particularly pp. 8–10).

The vital importance of carriers as a basis for categorization and the development of group identity is recognized by groups and reflected in attacks on carriers during intergroup conflict. For example, there have been increased hostilities between Shi'a and Sunni populations in Iraq, after an attack that destroyed the dome of the Golden Mosque in Samarra, Iraq. The shrine has special meaning for Shi'a Muslims, because it is the burial place of Ali al-Hadi and Hassan al-Askari, 2 of the 12 imams revered by Shi'a (as Shiism is practiced by the majority of the population in the region), as well as the place where, according to Shi'a tradition, the "Hidden Imam" Muhammad al-Mahdi made his last appearance. The attack on the Golden Mosque resulted in the Shi'a-dominated Iraqi government declaring 3 days of national mourning, and violent clashes between Shi'a and Sunni Muslims have dramatically escalated, resulting in well over a thousand killings within a week.

Although categorization using religious carriers is often associated with traditions that span many centuries, fashion carriers can change far more quickly (Walters & Cunningham, 2005). In the 1960s, afro hair styles sported by some young African American men served to differentiate between them and mainstream society. In the new millennium, hip-hop fashion serves the same differentiation purpose. Of course, the carriers for hip-hop, from hairstyles to music, are in some ways different from the carriers used by the 1960s Black Power generation. What remains the same is the media depiction of the latest Black fashions as dangerous and even criminal (Jackson, 2006).

In conclusion, as the example of fashion demonstrates, there is considerable flexibility with respect to the criteria that can be used for categorization and differentiation. However, there are also fundamental constraints on the criteria that actually become salient in any given cultural context, the most important constraint being ideology, discussed in the following sections.

IDEOLOGICAL CONSTRAINTS ON CATEGORIZATION

So far in this chapter, I have argued that (a) humans are predisposed to categorize the social world, (b) social categorization tends to have certain cognitive consequences (such as between-group differentiation), and (c) there seems to be both consistency and variation across cultures with respect to the criteria used for categorization. In this section I explore further the consistency raised in the third point. In this case, my focus is not on biological constraints; rather, I highlight ideological constraints on the criteria used for categorization.

There is no doubt that biological and ideological constraints are in many situations interacting to bring about particular outcomes. This is particularly the case with respect to sex, age, ethnicity and race, which traditional Western research suggests are the "primary categories" (see D. J. Schneider, 2004, p. 96), in the sense that they serve as important bases for categorization across cultures. To what extent is it possible to alter the roles of even these primary categories? This question is best addressed in the context of a broader discussion about the role of ideology in setting constraints on the criteria given prominence as a basis for social categorization. In the context of Western capitalism, two trends in ideological constraints are (a) the focus on the individual rather than the group and (b) the focus on sex, age, ethnicity, and the minimization of social class as criteria for social categorization.

The Self-Contained Individual

Our greatest moments are personal, self-motivated, not to be touched. The things which are sacred or precious to us are the things we withdraw from promiscuous sharing. But now we are taught to throw everything within us into public light and common pawing. To seek joy in meeting halls. We haven't even got a word for the quality I mean—for the self-sufficiency of man's spirit. . . . I think the only cardinal evil is that of placing your prime concern within other men. I have always demanded a certain quality in the people I liked . . . a self-sufficient ego. Nothing else matters. (Rand, 1943/1971, p. 609)

This is one of many passages in which the architect Howard Roark, the hero in Ayn Rand's novel *The Fountainhead*, exhorts the nobility and superiority of the self-contained, independent individual. Before I lived in the United States, I was mystified by the continued role played by Rand's novels in American culture. They are far from being great novels, yet they continue to serve as a source of intellectual inspiration for particular groups of well-read Americans. After I lived in the United States for some years, I realized that Howard Roark reflects a celebration of the self-contained individual—who believes a self-sufficient ego is all that matters—in modern America. I say "modern America" because at least in the early centuries the American experience was not characterized by individualism (e.g., Shain, 1994). It was the dual influence of industrialization and Western expansion that gave rise to modern American self-contained individualism by the 19th century.

Industrialization and capitalism developed roots in Western Europe earlier than in America, and the rise of the new middle class brought with it an emphasis on personal responsibility and individual merit. However, it was the addition of the Western frontier experience, explored in F. J. Turner's (1920) seminal studies, that gave a unique character to individualism in America (for a review of the narrower empirical evidence for uniqueness in American individualism, see Oyserman, Coon, & Kemmelmeier, 2002). The frontier strengthened the myth of a level playing field and the idea that everyone has an equal chance of becoming a success. After all, the frontier is natural and "unbiased," a tough "neutral" environment that underlines the belief that everyone "is created equal" and has "equal rights." Long after the West was settled and the moving frontier in effect came to an end, the myth of the Western frontier continues to be celebrated, and its influence is expanded through Hollywood movies.

The self-contained individualism celebrated in the United States has bolstered the idea that group membership is unimportant and what really matters is personal characteristics. The American focus has remained firmly fixed on the individual rather than on the group as the prime unit of social mobility. This is not to claim that there has been general agreement about an ideal world created through individual mobility:

> Since the decline of the aristocratic ideals associated with Federalism, most Americans have spoken the language of opportunity, self-improvement, and mobility. But they do not mean the same thing. Franklin and Jefferson were hopeful that, in the new American republic, men might achieve a new ideal of human development and a new kind of social order. Others . . . were more concerned with the perpetuation in the new world of traditional religion and social patterns. . . . Yet, more often than not, the young Americans of the nineteenth century . . . went on to mark

out their own conception of the self-made man as an aggressive, go-getting, and rapidly moving entrepreneur. (Cawelti, 1965, pp. 35–36)

The common feature, then, of the American value system is the celebration of the individual as the important unit for social mobility, rather than the wider societal goals of social mobility.

Ideology and Class: Perceived Differences and Used Differences

The term *class* has been used to denote different strata in society (Joyce, 1995), and the term *social class* has been used to denote stratification based on status and cultural characteristics, such as those associated with the lifestyle of working-class people (Zandy, 2001). Marx (1867/1976) discussed, but did not precisely define, *class* in terms of the position of individuals in the production process. In the era of capitalism, the old-landed aristocracy was swept away by capitalists who owned the means of production and used their capital monopoly to purchase labor for the lowest possible price in the economic marketplace. Marx influenced a conflict tradition that remains robust but has new strands in the contemporary era (Giddens & Held, 1982; hooks, 2000; Joyce, 1995), according to which capitalists and workers have competing interests and the interests of workers will only be met through explicit class consciousness and class warfare.

Class is a social construction, and as such it is dependent on subjective perceptions (Argyle, 1994). There is enormous plasticity and variation with respect to the shape, role, and importance a social construction can take on (see the discussion of social constructionism in Moghaddam, 2005a, chap. 20). Irrespective of one's political position, one can agree that class has not become an important enough basis for categorization to lead to class warfare in capitalist societies. Why is class not a primary category, such as sex, age, and race (see D. J. Schneider, 2004, p. 96), for grouping the social world? Why have we not given as much importance to class as we have to gender or race? A classic Marxist explanation rests on the concept of false consciousness: The ideology dominant in capitalist societies influences people to misperceive their own class membership as well as the true interests of the different classes. For example, workers fail to recognize that the interests of their class—the working class—directly contradicts the interests of the capitalist class. Instead of focusing on class differences, workers have become distracted, particularly by differences in race and sex.

There is no doubt that the dominant ideology does have an important influence on how social class is perceived, and in the next section I focus on this issue in the context of the United States. For now, however, I turn to the psychological factors that make it easier for people to categorize the social world on the basis of sex, age, and race than on the basis of class. Sex, age, and race are tangible; in most cases, we can clearly recognize physical differences between women and men, young and old, Black and White. Just as children seem to be predisposed to give priority to shape when forming categories (Landau, 1998), in the social domain, tangible physical characteristics are more accessible for use as a basis for categorization: In categorization, seen differences are used differences.

A number of factors make social class less likely to be used as a basis for categorization. First, the markers of social class are often variable and might (for longer or shorter time periods) be adopted by outgroup members. For example, consider situations in which members of the lower classes emulate the dress and behavioral style of members of the upper classes (e.g., a working-class couple dressing up to walk around an exclusive part of town), and members of the upper classes emulate the dress and behavioral style of members of the working classes (e.g., rich kids dressing as hip-hop "gangsters"). Second, and most important, the self-help ideology dominant in capitalist societies socializes individuals to give priority to individual social mobility rather than collective action, a tendency demonstrated in experimental studies (e.g., Lalonde & Silverman, 1994; Wright & Taylor, 1998; Wright, Taylor, & Moghaddam, 1990). Even when they are mistreated as members of a disadvantaged group, individuals are guided by the self-help ideology to try to take individual rather than collective action to improve their lot.

Of course, it could be argued that it is not socialization but human nature that leads people to give priority to individual rather than collective action. People are selfish by nature, the argument goes, and first and foremost interested in the improvement of their own personal lots. Socialization can do little to change this "natural" tendency. However, as pointed out by a leading biologist, there are human natures (multiple) rather than human nature (single): "Human nature is not the same from society to society or from individual to individual, nor is it a permanent attribute of *Homo Sapiens*" (Ehrlich, 2000, p. 12). Moreover, even if we assume that individuals are selfish by nature, a selfish survival strategy is most effective when it involves cooperation in groups (Moghaddam, 2005a, chap. 19). Collaboration in social groups is a skill that very probably evolved early in the evolution of our ancestors as a primitive social relation (Moghaddam, 2002, p. 40) and well before we developed complex forms of collaboration characteristic of contemporary human societies. Chimpanzees have been shown to be skilled in recruiting other chimpanzees when they needed help as well as to know which other chimpanzee would be the most effective collaborators on the basis of earlier experience (Melis, Hare, & Tomasello, 2006).

The Exceptional Case of America

"Here's another thing I always carry. A souvenir of Oxford days. It was taken in Trinity Quad—the man on my left is now the Earl of Doncaster." It was a photograph of half a dozen young men in blazers loafing in an archway through which were visible a host of spires. There was Gatsby, looking a little, not much, younger—with a cricket bat in his hand. (Fitzgerald, 1925, p. 67)

In the quintessentially American novel *The Great Gatsby*, the fantastically rich Gatsby relies on props from England to try to achieve some authenticity as a person who "has made it." *Gatsby* is an American story, involving a protagonist with an unsure past but a rapid rise to extravagant financial success. In the land of the American dream, Gatsby has won his fortune. However, being rich does not guarantee being "high class." It is through particular markers in his speech, such as his repeated use of the phrase *old sport*, and various props, such as Oxford spires and the Earl of Doncaster, that he tries to present himself not only as rich but also as upper class.

Although Gatsby attempts to use speech markers and props from England to try to position himself as upper class, the American society in which he lives is dominated by an ideology that is fundamentally different from the ideology traditionally dominant in England (at least prior to the 1980s Thatcher–Blair revolution). The ideology of the American dream involves the assumption that American society is open and meritocratic, meaning that the rewards and status achieved by individuals depends on their personal merit. Discussions of class in America often invoke *American exceptionalism*, the idea that the American experience with social class is different from class-ridden countries of old Europe (Lipset, 1996). However, we need to determine whether there is a factual basis to American exceptionalism or whether it is merely popular belief.

There is some evidence challenging the idea that Americans are exceptional in terms of their consciousness or perception of class differences (Devine, 1997). It seems that Americans do recognize class differences and the enormously disparate opportunities and benefits available to the rich and the poor. Furthermore, America is not exceptional in terms of social mobility, because a working-class person in America has about the same chance of joining the professional middle class as a working-class person has in major European countries, with social mobility being slightly higher in some countries (e.g., Sweden) compared with in America (Beeghley, 1996; McMurrer & Sawhill, 1998). Moreover, America is by no means exceptional in terms of the economic equality achieved; on the contrary, economic inequalities are greater in the United States than in other industrialized societies (e.g., as reflected in the *Human Development Reports* of the United Nations; see http://hdr.undp.org/). Income disparity in the United States has been growing at a sharp rate. This is a well-documented fact that is sometimes reported in some U.S. news outlets, such as the following report in *The New York Times*:

Between 1972 and 2001 the wage and salary income of Americans at the 90th percentile of income distribution rose . . . about 1 percent per year. . . . But income at the 99th percentile rose 87 percent; income at the

99.9th percentile rose 181 percent; and income at the 99.99th percentile rose 497 percent. (Krugman, 2006, p. 23)

In addition, an article from *The Washington Post* noted the following:

In 1971 the top 5 percent of Americans made about 6.3 times what the bottom 20 percent made. In 2001 . . . that same group made 8.4 times what the bottom 20 percent did. Income inequality in the United States is now not only at a record level and not only the greatest since we began measuring it—it is also on par with that of a Third World country. (Rattner, 2003, p. A23)

Furthermore, there are daily reminders in the United States press that at least 47 million Americans do not have health insurance (e.g., see Cohen, 2007). There are also best-selling books that focus attention on the super rich (R. Frank, 2007) and on how the American education system further skews income disparities by giving hugely preferential treatment to the children of the rich (Golden, 2006), with the result being that about three quarters of students in the most selective American universities come from the top socioeconomic quartile.

There is some evidence that American workers are aware of growing economic inequalities and their own relative decline: "Three new polls released yesterday found deep pessimism among American workers, with most saying that wages were not keeping pace with inflation and that workers were worse off in many ways than a generation ago" (Greenhouse, 2006, p. A17). Clearly, American exceptionalism does not, in practice, mean that at least a large number of Americans fail to recognize economic inequalities, as recognition is indicated in major newspapers and popular books.

However, there are two important ways in which America is exceptional, and I see these differences as relating to immigration and the American dream. First, America is the largest and by far the most important immigrant-receiving country in the world and is seen, not only by people inside the United States but also by billions of others around the world, as the land of opportunity, a place where anyone from anywhere in the world could have a chance at success. Second, the enormous and exceptional class disparities in America have a paradoxical "lottery" effect of motivating immigrants, and many others, not only to perceive the system as legitimate but to join the race to "get ahead." Rather like ticket holders in a giant lottery, most Americans, and particularly immigrants, see the "winner-takes-all society" (R. Frank & Cook, 1995) as giving them a shot at the big time. No matter how small the odds, they still want to invest in a ticket (Wright & Taylor, 1998).

Thus, social categorization on the basis of class continues to be less important in the United States, as well as in most Western societies, in large part because of the perceived permeability of social classes. Individuals are assumed to be able to move from one class to another if they work hard and are talented enough. Moreover, the exceptional inequalities that exist in the United States, with the super rich amassing an increasingly greater share of the national wealth, have the paradoxical lottery effect of motivating immigrants and many others to want to buy into the system in the hope that they will end up holding a winning ticket. Just like the tens of millions of lottery ticket buyers in America who fail to win this week but look forward to buying another ticket for next week's lottery, those who do not make progress up the system look to their children to break through and land a winning ticket.

CONCLUDING COMMENTS

Any serious effort to change intergroup relations and progress toward better policies for managing diversity must begin with a consideration of certain psychological processes associated with categorization. All humans categorize phenomena as a basic strategy for more effective information processing. An implication is that there is a strong tendency for us, initially at least, to perceive other humans in terms of category membership (e.g., as female or male; Black, White, or Latino; young or old) rather than merely as individuals without group affiliations.

This universal tendency to categorize is coupled with, on the one hand, certain cognitive consequences (e.g., within-group minimization and between-group exaggeration of differences) and, on the other hand, tremendous variation in the criteria used for categorization, with importance given to category membership as well as to the kinds of stratification arrived at in society. In the next section, I critically discuss the major theories that attempt to explain intergroup relations and group-based inequalities that have social categorization as a starting point. I also consider the implications of these theories for democracy.

II

PSYCHOLOGICAL THEMES, THEORY, AND RESEARCH

INTRODUCTION: PSYCHOLOGICAL THEMES, THEORY, AND RESEARCH

Democracy has traditionally been defined in terms of legal requirements such as free and open elections, universal suffrage, rule of law, and freedom of expression (although there is considerable variation in how democracies can come about, be sustained, and actually meet the needs of citizens; Murphy, 2007; Shapiro, 2003). A number of scholars have placed particular emphasis on requirements of democracy in terms of social relations. For example, C. Tilly (2003) focused on relations between citizens and government agents and particularly on protected consultations: "Any move toward protected consultation constitutes democratization, any move away from protected consultation constitutes de-democratization" (p. 26). However, this approach still takes as its point of departure the formal requirements of democracy rather than the nature of social relations.

In this analysis, I take as my starting point social and, in particular, intergroup relations and proceed to consider their implications for democracy. Underlying the major theories of intergroup relations are assumptions about the psychological citizen and how citizens interact as group members. Theories and empirical research on intergroup relations attempt to get at how humans actually are rather than just how they should be in the ideal.

47

First, I examine the irrationalist perspective: the idea that intergroup behavior is in large part shaped by unconscious motives, wishes, fears, and so on. Although intergroup conflict arises from unconscious forces that humans typically fail to recognize, humans rationalize conflict by citing material interests or "democratic," "human rights," or some other high-sounding principles. The role of leadership is given the highest importance by irrationalist theories, with the implication that democracies need constant protection against destructive, potentially dictatorial leadership.

Second, I consider the materialist theories, which share the assumption that psychological experiences are shaped by material conditions so that groups that monopolize material resources can dominate social norms, beliefs, values, and ideology more broadly. Intergroup peace and conflict are assumed to depend respectively on shared and competing material interests of different groups. The materialist theories lead us to give particular importance to group-based material inequalities and to also attend to the nature of ideology dominant in society (Jost, 2006). Can true democracy survive in an age of increasing group-based inequalities?

Third, I turn to identity theories of intergroup relations, which focus on what kinds of persons individuals see themselves to be and to what kinds of groups they think they belong. Do their ingroups enjoy positive status in society, or are they seen as distinct? Do the individuals acquire an adequate identity by belonging to their particular ingroups? If not, what options do individuals see open to them for gaining adequate identity? Empirical research and theories in the identity tradition highlight the strong tendency humans have to divide up the social world into "us" and "them" and for showing bias in favor of "us" against "them." The dangers of fragmentation and the disengagement of groups are also highlighted. This is highly relevant to contemporary democracies, in which minority groups often remain outside political discourse and large numbers of minorities are in one way or another disenfranchised.

Finally, I consider theories centered on subjective justice. Do individuals perceive the world to be just and fair? How does this perception of fairness relate to their actual living conditions? Justice research reveals that there is not a simple relationship between how individuals are objectively treated and their subjective sense of justice. An implication is that even in democracies certain "normal" psychological processes can help sustain enormous injustices. A combination of individual tendencies to want to see the world as just and societal ideologies interpreting the world as just can (and often does) result in people putting up with huge injustices.

Thus, the chapters in Part II have two main goals: (a) to critically examine intergroup theories and research around the themes of irrationality, materialism, identity, and justice and (b) to consider some implications of these four perspectives for democracy.

3

RATIONALITY: FROM FREUD TO THE AUTHORITARIAN PERSONALITY

Writing about the bloody European wars of the 19th century in his monumental novel *War and Peace*, Tolstoy (1869/1957) asked,

> If the object of the European wars of the beginning of this century had been the aggrandizement of Russia, that object might have been attained without any of the preceding wars and without the invasion. If the object was the aggrandizement of France, that might have been attained without either Revolution or the Empire. If the object was the propagation of ideas, the printing-press could have accomplished that much more effectually than soldiers. If the object was the progress of civilization, one may very readily suppose that there are other more expedient ways of diffusing civilization than by slaughtering people and destroying their wealth. Why then did things happen thus and not otherwise? (p. 1342)

Extending this line of questioning, we could ask why in the 20th century "progress" had to be achieved through two devastating world wars—from 1914 to 1918 and from 1939 to 1945—as well as hundreds of regional and national wars, and why "advancement" in the 21st century has already required dozens of other major wars, including the highly controversial U.S.-

led invasion of Iraq in 2003, with its bloody aftermath, associated terrorism, and tragically high civilian casualties (Moghaddam, 2006b).

Why do human societies continue to engage in highly destructive national, regional, and international wars? Each war is justified as defending freedom, spreading democracy, or liberating people, or even being "a war to end all wars," but wars have not ended, and after the passage of time the justifications for different wars seem to blend into one another.

According to *irrationalist* intergroup theories, human beings are capable of rationalizing their behavior, but this does not mean that they are rational agents. Indeed, humans are for the most part *irrational*, meaning that they are not fully aware of what they do and why they behave as they do (Moghaddam, 2005a, chap. 4). Individuals are influenced by unconscious factors (e.g, hidden motives, wishes, fears) to show loyalty to particular groups, discriminate against outgroups, justify intergroup inequalities and discrimination, engage in intergroup conflict and war, and generally behave in ways that favor some groups (typically ingroups) and show bias against some other groups (typically outgroups). However, in explaining this type of prejudice and aggression, people are not aware of the unconscious factors influencing them and are always ready to rationalize their behavior by referencing culturally acceptable, "politically correct" explanations such as the fight for freedom and democracy.

Similarly, people come to see themselves as members of groups that are in fundamental respects different from other groups, but actually in many cases the intergroup differences are minor. This narcissism of minor differences involves the construction of differences even when objectively there are none. In this, as in a number of other areas concerning collective behavior and conflict, Freud was ahead of his time; more than half a century later, the role of minor differences in intergroup relations was experimentally studied by social identity theorists (see the discussion of the minimal group paradigm in chap. 5, this volume).

The irrationalist perspective encourages us to see explanations for war, such as the exportation of democracy, as often serving a self-justification function—as a rationalizing front displayed by groups that are basically irrational. However, a key factor is that those who rationalize their irrational behavior are convinced by their own arguments. They are not consciously participating in a conspiracy to mislead other people.

On this important point, the irrationalist perspective of Freud is in line with the ideas of Karl Marx (1852/1979; Marx & Engels, 1848/1967): Both Freud and Marx presented theories that give an important role to people being convinced by their own rationalizations. Marx's main focus was on the justifications propagated by the ruling class for the continuation and extension of class inequalities. The ruling class is convinced by its own rationalizations as to why prevailing inequalities, and even greater ones, are fair and just. For example, consider the case of a company (e.g., ENRON) that declares bankruptcy, but the company executives are given "golden parachutes" worth hundreds of millions of dollars at the same time that thousands of regular employees receive almost nothing in compensation and even lose their pensions after many years of work for that company. The executives are convinced by their own arguments, such as, "This really is fair because our brain power created the wealth of the company and our rewards should be in line with our extraordinary contributions."

IRRATIONALITY AS A THEME IN MAJOR THEORIES

The irrationalist theme in explanations of thought and action is primarily influenced by the writings of Sigmund Freud, but variations of this theme are present in a number of materialist and cognitive theories, examples of which I identify in this chapter.

An irrationalist assumption underlies at least some versions of the evolutionary psychology account of intergroup relations, including Dawkins's (1989) selfish gene thesis and E. O. Wilson's (1975) sociobiological paradigm (the abandonment of the term *sociobiology* for evolutionary psychology came about in large part because of political attacks against sociobiology— see Palmer & Palmer, 2002, pp. 15–16—and is itself a suitable topic for intergroup research). The proposition that genes causally influence intergroup behavior, acting like a whispering within to lead people to be biased against genetically dissimilar others and in favor of genetically similar others, implies that people do not consciously recognize the real factors shaping their behavior. Thus, "John" really discriminates against "Ahmed" in favor of "George" because he is genetically more similar to George than he is to Ahmed; John himself fails to see this connection and rationalizes his bias using various false explanations (e.g., "George is more creative than Ahmed").

Whereas the genetic-based theories assume hidden causal factors to be material and internal to individuals, some materialist theories, including those influenced by Marx (e.g., Marx, 1852/1979; Marx & Engels, 1848/1967), place greater focus on hidden causal factors outside individuals. In the Marxist tradition, the assumption of irrationality is associated with the notion that people are influenced by the prevailing ideology to construct a false social reality so that the true picture of intergroup inequalities is kept hidden to both the rulers and the ruled. This ideology maintains the status quo and actually works in favor of those who enjoy the greatest power and resources. Thus, people are influenced by the dominant ideology to justify prevailing inequalities, as suggested, for example, by the system justification theory (Jost & Banaji, 1994), and are not conscious of their own behavior and its societal consequences.

A final example worth noting concerns irrationality in cognitive theories. Although the theme of irrationality is associated with the psychodynamic approach pioneered by Freud—an approach that is qualitative, highly interpretative, and based on case studies—this theme has also been present, implicitly at least, in the cognitive school that has dominated psychology since the 1950s and is quantitative, more data driven, and experimental. For example, consider the classic scenario discussed in cognitive dissonance research (Festinger, 1957): Subjects who only received $1 for participating in a long and very tedious psychology experiment reported it to have been a more interesting and rewarding experience than subjects who received $25. According to cognitive dissonance theory (discussed in more detail in chap. 4), the subjects who received only $1 are not aware that they are justifying their participation by exaggerating how interesting and rewarding the experience really was for them. In a sense, they are fooling themselves without being aware of it. A solid body of subsequent research has shown that people are very ready to confidently construct stories about why they behave in particular ways or say particular things, even when their stories are mistaken (D. Myers, 2003; Nisbett & Ross, 1980). Thus, the theme of irrationality has gained prominence even in cognitive psychology.

From a cognitive perspective, then, one could argue that just as people can fail to recognize the real reasons why they prefer a particular nightgown over another (Nisbett & Wilson, 1977), or why they get up and walk across a room (Gazzaniga, 1992), they can be mistaken about complex group-related issues such as the nature of their group interests and the real reasons they fight against outgroups.

Freud's irrationalist perspective has directly influenced research on the authoritarian personality, displaced aggression, and terror management theory (discussed later in this chapter). Irrationality is also an underlying theme in a number of other theories that will be discussed in following chapters.

Freud's Psychology of Intergroup Relations

Freud remains the most influential thinker in the history of psychology, and his influence is increasing in non-Western societies as globalization proceeds (e.g., see Akhtar, 2006, for a discussion of Freud's ideas in a non-Western context). Unfortunately, both critics and supporters of Freud have traditionally focused on aspects of his psychology that concern reductionist, microlevel processes such as the proposed psychosocial stages of development and the notorious *Oedipus Complex*. Furthermore, Freud's psychology is traditionally depicted as dealing with a subjective inner world rather than an objective material world. In contrast to this traditional reductionist interpretation of Freud's psychology, I argue that Freud's writings have more important and long-lasting implications for macrolevel, societal processes (Moghaddam, 2007). My thesis is that Freud's intergroup theory is actually very close to the harsh realities of the larger material world.

I begin by clarifying an essential distinction between rationality and rationalization. Next, I critically assess Freud's ideas about groups, leadership, and intergroup conflict.

Rationality and Rationalization

Preempting the research of Leon Festinger (1919–1989) and other cognitive researchers of the 1950s and later, Freud gave importance to a distinction between rational action and the rationalization of action. An important implication of Freud's ideas is that we should not accept a rationalization of action as indicative of the rationality of that action. For example, consider the role of defense mechanisms that protect individuals against feelings of anxiety.

Feelings of anxiety arise because of the struggle within individuals between instinctive desires, motives, wishes, urges, and inclinations in general, on the one hand, and the morality of society that is intended to keep such inclinations in check, on the other hand.

> civilization and higher education have a large influence on the development of repression, and we suppose that, under such conditions, the psychical organization undergoes an alteration . . . as a result of which what was formerly felt as agreeable now seems unacceptable and is rejected with all possible psychic force. The repressive activity of civilization brings it about that primary possibilities of enjoyment, which have now, however, been repudiated by the censorship in us, are lost to us. But to the human psyche all renunciation is exceedingly difficult. (Freud, 1905/1960, p. 101)

Renunciation is particularly difficult in two domains where the taboos of "civilized" society clash with the basic human instincts of sex and aggression. Repressed inclinations seep through the defense mechanisms, acting as "the voice within us that rebels against the demands of morality" (Freud, 1905/1960, p. 110), and surface in various forms in thoughts and actions. However, even though the resulting thoughts and actions are irrational, we rationalize them in the narratives of our lives. For example, a father comes home from a frustrating day at work and beats his son, justifying the beating with the explanation that "It's a tough world out there, and I'm teaching him a lesson, thickening his skin. He'll be grateful for this when he grows up."

The father's rationalization of why he beats his son should not distract us from the irrational nature of his behavior, just as a claim by a political leader that "we wage war to make the world a safer and more democratic place" should not necessarily persuade us that this particular act of war is rational.

In discussing the international situation at the start of World War I (1914–1918), Freud (1915/1957) argued that different nations explain why they go to war by citing their interests, but this rationalization hides their real motivation to satisfy "their passions" (p. 288). In other words, economic, political, and other interests are cited in surface explanations, but the underlying causes for war lay deeper in our irrational passions. Just as Tolstoy (1869/1957) pointed out, if the objective is to maximize material profits, then nations could adopt strategies that are far more effective than war (see the quotation cited at the beginning of this chapter).

To understand why the path of conflict continues to be adopted, we must attend to Freud's ideas about group dynamics.

What Is a Group?

Two elements are essential for understanding the nature of the group from a Freudian perspective: identification and leadership. Identification represents the earliest form of an emotional tie between two people: A person identifying with another acts as if she were the target person. For example, a little girl identifying with her mother tries on her mother's shoes and walks on high heels, imagining she is her mother.

Identification can be conscious, but it is often unconscious. In the group context, group members (in large part unconsciously) develop emotional ties with one another through what they see to be a common quality: the introjection of the same leader in their egos. Freud's (1921/1955) formal definition of a group was a number of individuals who have "identified themselves with one another in their ego" (p. 116). However, what about individuals who are members of groups without leaders?

Freud exclusively concerned himself with groups that have leaders. This is because he believed it is only through a leader that a group can attain the superior organization needed to achieve a high level of performance and effectiveness (see D. M. Taylor & Moghaddam, 1994, chap. 2). When they join a group, individuals are susceptible to a lowering of intellectual performance, or regression. Joining a collective can result in the "dumbing down" of individual decision making, so-called mob behavior, and acting and thinking at the level of the lowest common denominator. Later research showed that group opinions tend to become divorced from reality and polarized, particularly because group members seek concurrence (Janis, 1989), repeat each others' explanations (Brauer, Judd, & Gliner, 1995), and develop a common narrative. Effective leadership can help avoid such shortcoming and guide the group to better performance (Janis, 1989).

From a Freudian perspective, it is not surprising that African Americans made gains in the 1960s and 1970s. They were led by Martin Luther King Jr. at that time but have since not found leadership of the same extraordinary, forward-looking quality. Just as leaders such as King and Nelson Mandela (the Black South African who led the successful and largely peaceful struggle against apartheid) can mobilize a group and channel its energies to make progress, leaders can direct group energies toward destructive goals. It is unfortunate that there are numerous examples of such destructive leaders in history. To understand in more depth the role of the group leader, I turn next to the issue of emotional ties in groups.

Libidinal Ties and Displacement of Aggression

A continuous theme in all of Freud's psychology is the negative and positive aspects of the human experience: love and hate being two sides of the same coin. Libido, the energy of instincts that come under the label *love*, is complex and also involves intense feelings that are potentially or actually negative.

Lovers, parents and children, best friends, husband and wife—in all relationships involving intense feelings of love, there is also complexity and ambivalence. Love can switch to hate in some situations. The swooning lovers can become fierce enemies, the best friends can fight mercilessly, and the happily married couple can (and sometimes does) end up in a bitterly fought divorce battle. All libidinal ties involve negative feelings that could become channeled toward destructive ends.

Within a group, the positive aspects of libidinal ties lead to greater cohesion, higher productivity, and better social atmosphere. Bring to mind the positive team spirit that thrives in a winning group.

However, what about negative feelings? What about hostility, jealousy, and other potentially destructive aspects of libidinal ties between the members of the same group? These negative aspects could immobilize a group, rendering it helpless in competition with outgroups. This happens when the group's leadership is ineffective, in contrast to when effective leadership emerges. Thus, a great deal depends on the characteristics of the group leader.

A potent strategy favored by some group leaders is the *displacement of aggression*, involving the channeling of negative sentiments toward targets who are situated outside the group and are not responsible for the negative sentiments but who are too weak to retaliate when attacked. Freud pointed out (D. M. Taylor & Moghaddam, 1994, chap. 4) that such targets are not randomly selected but are identified on the basis of similarity: The less similar an outgroup, the more likely it is to be selected to serve as the target of displaced aggression. Through this insight, Freud preempted modern research demonstrating the powerful role of similarity in intergroup relations (see Osbeck, Moghaddam, & Perreault, 1997, and the discussion in chap. 8, this volume, on the role of similarity in multiculturalism policy).

Freud's model of group and intergroup dynamics can be described as hydraulic, in the sense that the pressure from negative sentiments that builds up in a group has to find an outlet, otherwise the group could experience the equivalent of a destructive explosion. As negative sentiments build up, feelings of frustration lead to aggressive action, and one way in which such energies can be redirected is to target dissimilar outgroups.

The strength of the redirected negative sentiments corresponds to the strength of the positive sentiments binding the group members together. For example, lower religious persecution in Western Europe and some other parts of the world should not be interpreted as a sign of greater religious tolerance; rather, it is a sign of a decline of religiosity. Where there is a rise in religiosity, such as among Christian fundamentalists in the United States, there is a corresponding displacement of negative sentiments onto outgroups—as in the case of increased attacks by Christian fundamentalists on gays, liberals, Muslims, and other "outgroups."

This implied association between frustration and aggression has been experimentally examined by teams of researchers led by John Dollard in the 1930s and 1940s (Dollard, Bood, Miller, Mowrer, & Sears, 1939), Leonard Berkowitz (1969) in the 1960s and 1970s, and Norman Miller since the 1990s (N. Miller, Pederson, Earlywine, & Pollock, 2003). The result of these research programs over 8 decades is a shift from the original conception of frustration always causing aggression to a more nuanced picture. Frustration can, but need not, result in aggression. If a first frustrating event has already taken place, the pent-up frustration could be triggered by a second (and third, fourth, etc.) frustrating event, resulting in a cascade effect in which case aggression becomes more likely.

Also, with respect to the characteristics of the aggressor, more powerful agents can show aggression more openly and directly. However, this does not mean that less powerful agents, even the weakest ones, would not show aggression covertly and indirectly. For example, unskilled workers seem powerless compared with senior management, but when unskilled workers experience frustration with company policies, they can commit acts of sabotage, "goof off" at every opportunity, and generally act to lower efficiency without publicly declaring their opposition.

The Correlates of Displacement. Displacement of aggression is associated with certain dynamics both within and between groups. Within groups, displacement is associated with increased (a) cohesion, (b) conformity, and (c) obedience, as well as the rise of more aggressive leadership.

Within the group, individual members are tied to one another and to the group leader through libidinal ties. The members of the Catholic Church, to cite an example discussed by Freud (1921/1955), are tied to Christ, their "substitute father" (p. 94), and to all other church members whom they are urged to treat with brotherly love. Strong bonds between church members mean that the behavior of individual members is more closely regulated by the rules and norms of the group and a high level of conformity with the church culture and obedience to the church leadership is maintained. Measures such as *excommunication* (i.e., expulsion from the church) are used to control nonconformists.

The crucial role of the leader involves soliciting and maintaining obedience, which must take place if the group is to function effectively. The members of an army must obey the commander-in-chief (to use another example cited by Freud, 1921/1955), who, like the head of a church, plays his role on the "illusion" that all group members are loved equally by the leader. Without obedience, the army, the church, and other groups could not achieve a high level of performance to fight a military or spiritual battle (or a combination of the two).

The identification of an external target as a threat (e.g., to an army or church) channels negative energies toward an enemy outside and binds group members more tightly together inside. In one of his sharpest and seemingly most pessimistic insights, Freud (1930/1961) argued that it is always possible to bind a great many people in love "so long as there are other people left over to receive the manifestations of their aggressiveness" (p. 114). The implication is that there is a perpetual cycle of displacement of aggression as leaders attempt to direct negative sentiments to targets outside the group.

With respect to a perpetual cycle of displacement of aggression, similar to Vilfredo Pareto (1935; discussed in chap. 4, this volume), Freud seemed to be presenting a pessimistic view of intergroup relations. Just as Pareto argued that there is an inevitable and perpetual cycle of counterelite versus elite conflict throughout history, Freud argued that a strong, cohesive group has a dark side: displacement of aggression onto dissimilar targets outside the group. The views of both Freud and Pareto point to the irrational nature of intergroup relations and the political "usefulness" of displaced aggression for leaders. By focusing attention on external threats, leaders can minimize dissent at home (e.g., critics of the government can be labeled *unpatriotic*) and mobilize the populations behind their "nationalist" policies.

The Authoritarian Personality. Who among the group members would be more likely to support leaders in their attempts to displace aggression? Researchers were particularly interested in this question after the horrific events of World War II (1939–1945), when hundreds of thousands of "ordinary" citizens in Germany, Japan, and Italy, among other societies, had obeyed fascist dictators to attack and try to destroy "outgroups." To identify individuals who were more prone to follow orders from fascist dictators, Adorno, Frenkel-Brunswik, Levinson, and Sanford (1950) developed the Potentiality for Fascism Scale, or F-Scale. The F-Scale was described as a measure of authoritarianism, and those who scored high tended to be obedient and subservient toward authorities but punitive toward minorities. Such individuals endorsed statements such as the following: "Obedience and respect for authority are the most important virtues children should learn" and "Human nature being what it is, there will always be war and conflict." Later studies arrived at more reliable and valid measures of authoritarianism (with a particular focus on right-wing authoritarians; Altemeyer, 1988, 1994), which is perhaps quite appropriate given the right-leaning political trends of the 20th century, particularly in the United States.

Freud's exclusive focus on groups with leaders has been criticized (e.g., Billig, 1976, p. 24) and may be misplaced in the 21st century because electronic communications have created new possibilities for collective movements. For example, consider the collective movement involving Latinos in the United States in early 2006 and the mass marches of April 2006, in particular, on the issue of immigration reform. A major focus of debate among politicians, Latinos, and the general U.S. population was the status of the estimated 11 to 15 million illegal Latino immigrants in the United States. In early 2006, a collective movement of Latinos gained momentum, and marches were organized in many major urban centers. Despite the widespread success of these marches, no single leader or nationally recognized leadership group was associated with this movement. Instead of mobilization through a common leadership, Latinos had mobilized through an extensive communications network, including e-mail, cell phones, and call-in radio and television shows.

Similarly, mass communications systems, particularly the World Wide Web, have helped create international terrorist movements directed by fanatical ideologies and ideals rather than by a unified organizational structure and leadership (Moghaddam, 2006b). The ideology and "idea" of Al Qaeda, rather than direct plans and orders from Osama bin Laden and other terrorist leaders, has spread through mass communications systems to inspire terrorist attacks in different parts of the world, such as the deadly bombings in Madrid on March 11, 2004, and in London on July 7, 2005. The operations of "home grown" terrorists, such as those involved in the London bombings, is another indication that direct control by leadership is no longer essential in the age of mass communications (two of the London bombers had traveled to Pakistan and probably had some contact with Al Qaeda, but once back in the United Kingdom, they were self-directed and operating as part of an independent terrorist cell). Of course, from a Freudian perspective, it could be argued that such operations would become even more effective if leaders such as Osama bin Laden could openly communicate with their followers.

Irrespective of the direct or indirect role of the leader, a key feature of groups associated with terrorism is the threat they perceive from the outside world. Contact with outsiders seems particularly troubling for them, a topic addressed by the next theory I consider.

Terror Management Theory

> Terror management is posited to be an unconscious and ongoing defense that serves to avert the potential for terror engendered by the knowledge of mortality. (Pyszczynski, Solomon, & Greenberg, 2004, p. 55)

Terror management theory is the most influential irrationalist theory of the modern era, building on psychodynamic perspectives that assume an important role for the unconscious. The theory begins with two basic observations: (a) that like all other life forms, humans are motivated by self-preservation and (b) that humans are self-aware, and this ability leads to the recognition that every one of us will one day die. The self-preservation motive and awareness of our own morality "gives rise to potentially overwhelming terror" (Pyszczynski et al., 2004, p. 27). How we cope with this terror has important consequences.

According to terror management theory, we cope with this terror by constructing cultural worldviews that serve a death-denying function. Through our cultures, we surround ourselves with a self-protective, socially constructed reality. This includes our conceptions of the origins of life, the meaning of our existence, and ideas such as *intelligent design*, proposing that life has been intentionally created and directed by a higher being and did not evolve as proposed by the theory of evolution. Because of the protective, death-denying function of culture, we feel threatened when our cultural system is challenged: "If I believe that God created the world in 6 days and someone else believes that God created the earth out of a giant drop of milk, one of us is clearly wrong" (Pyszczynski et al., 2004, p. 29). Consequently, encountering others who are different has the potential to raise anxiety, which can then be overcome through reaffirmations of the ingroup culture.

However, the certainty of death means that no culture is powerful enough to overcome the feelings of terror in the face of immortality. The anxiety this raises is dealt with through repression and subsequent projection of fears and negative emotions onto outgroups. Thus, terror management theory gives a key role to the Freudian concept of projection as an explanatory tool. The consequence of this repression–projection process is a range of strategies, from relatively benign to destructive, for behavior toward outgroups.

The most benign of these strategies is *conversion* (i.e., when individuals abandon their own culture and adopt an outgroup culture). Pyszczynski et al. (2004, p. 30) claimed that "conversion in response to alternative conceptions of reality is extremely rare." However, is this the case? Over a million legal immigrants arrive in the United States every year. Within the first few decades of life in a new country, many immigrants are speaking English and have converted to American ways, and by the second generation, most of their children have "converted." Indeed, as we shall see in the third part of the book, conversion is integral to the policy of assimilation and the melting-pot ideology that has historically dominated in the United States. The same pattern of immigrant conversion takes place in other immigrant-receiving societies (e.g., Australia), and where it has not taken place "quickly enough," the majority group perceive it as a problem (e.g., the "problem" of Muslim immigrants in Western Europe not changing their lifestyles quickly enough). From a minority group perspective, conversion is the norm, and minorities get into trouble when they do not conform to this norm.

Derogation (i.e., belittling outgroups and dismissing their cultural systems as inferior) is the next strategy. Attitudes toward outgroups take shape among children through subtle processes influenced by the mass media as well as traditional mythologies, games, nursery rhymes, poems, and songs, such as Robert Louis Stevenson's "Foreign Children" (see Stevenson, 1998, p. 410). Whereas conversion involves us abandoning our own cultures and adopting outgroup cultures, assimilation involves outgroup members abandoning their cultures and taking on our culture—a far more preferable strategy, from the point of view of most of us. (Note: The term *assimilation* has a narrower meaning in terror management theory compared with its meaning in debates on immigration and cultural diversity, as we see in Part III of this volume.) "Why don't they do things our way?" and "Why don't they speak our language?" have become familiar questions posed by some Americans and Western Europeans who believe that outgroups should conform to Western ways. When we convert and adopt the ways of an outgroup, we are weakening our heritage group. If enough people convert, then the heritage group will eventually die. This is the fate of most minority languages when minority group members convert to using majority group languages (as discussed in chap. 1, this volume).

A more artful strategy adopted by majorities to deal with minorities and rebels and even revolutionaries has been *accommodation* (i.e., adopting some appealing aspects of the alternative culture and stripping away the threatening aspects). American society has demonstrated tremendous dynamism and flexibility in accommodating a vast array of competing and potentially threatening countercultures. Consider, for example, how Western entrepreneurs have transformed Che Guevara (1928–1967), the Argentinian born Marxist guerilla fighter, into a popular cultural symbol, now regularly shown on posters in student halls alongside 21st-century rap and rock stars.

At the opposite extreme to accommodation and conversion, which can involve "self-destruction" of the ingroup, is *annihilation* of the outgroup. Unfortunately, there is no end to historical examples of group annihilation. The most obvious examples involve the annihilation of tens of millions of native people in North and South America (Mann, 2005) as well as tens of millions of natives in Africa through the actions of Western European colonizers and settlers (Reader, 1998). Most of this killing took place in the 17th, 18th, and 19th centuries, with some attempts to adopt a more benign policy since the mid 20th century.

From a historical perspective, there is no doubt that human beings have become kinder to outgroups and less accepting of annihilation: Mass killings instigated by the likes of Genghis Khan were not condemned in the same way that mass killings by the likes of Hitler have been condemned in the modern era. Yet, at the same time, the 21st century has witnessed the rise of global terrorism and the willingness of suicide terrorists to kill themselves and as many of "the enemy" as possible. Terror management theory attempts to explain this development.

According to TMT [terror management theory], when people believe
they are objects of value in a world of meaning, they should be able to
function securely. In other words, self-esteem should serve an anxiety-
buffering function. (Pyszczynski et al., 2004, p. 39)

Terror management theory posits that *self-esteem*, "the culturally based
belief that one is a valued participant in a meaningful reality" (Pyszczynski et
al., 2004, p. 28), is essential for healthy psychological functioning. We acquire this belief by living up to the values, rules, norms, and other features of
the normative system of our culture, internalized by us through the socialization process. Through the self-worth that our cultural life gives us, we are
able to protect ourselves against the potential insecurity arising from our
knowledge of mortality. Culture enables us to see our lives as meaningful and
to see ourselves as having purpose and a wider significance rather than just
"nameless animals doomed only to die and decay" (p. 28).

Thus, terror management theory develops more specific hypotheses
about the relationship between self-esteem, mortality salience, and anxiety.
For example, with respect to the anxiety-buffering function of self-esteem,
Greenberg et al. (1992) tested the hypothesis that raising self-esteem will
lead to decreased anxiety even when the perceived threat is unrelated to the
domain in which self-esteem increased. To test this hypothesis, Greenberg et
al. gave students either negative or positive feedback about their personality.
Next, the students watched either a documentary about death or a benign
documentary. Participants who enjoyed elevated self-esteem experienced less
anxiety.

Terror management theory has served a highly valuable service by highlighting the self-protective mechanisms of cultures. This theory identifies
the fear that can arise within us when we are confronted by outgroup members who, sometimes intentionally, challenge our belief systems and cultures
more broadly. However, differences can be exciting as well as frightening.
On the one hand, tourists spend a lot of time, effort, and money to travel to
parts of the world that are new to them and to encounter other cultures. On
the other hand, and more in line with terror management theory concerns,
suicide terrorists search for outgroup members to kill them. Of course, the
fact that they also kill themselves severely tests terror management theory
assumptions that such behavior arises from a fear of death.

IRRATIONALITY AND THE MATERIALIST APPROACH

The irrationalist approach is traditionally discussed as being very different from the materialist perspective that is the focus of the next chapter.
This demarcation is fruitful in that it highlights a major difference: Irrationalist models, such as Freud's, assume that the main factors shaping inter-

group relations are buried in the unconscious. From the irrationalist viewpoint, material factors often serve as excuses for, rather than ultimate causes of, conflict, whereas from the materialist perspective, material conditions shape consciousness and serve as the impetus for conflict.

However, we must take care not to apply this demarcation between irrationalist and materialist models in a simplistic manner, because irrationality is also an underlying theme, sometimes an explicit one, in the main materialist theories. Both in classical Marxist theory and in modern psychological theories of the materialist bent, such as realistic conflict theory and system justification theory, an underlying assumption is that group members are often not consciously aware of the material factors that shape their behavior. This tradition is most clearly reflected in the concept of *false consciousness* (i.e., depicting a situation in which group members fail to correctly understand their group membership and collective interests). Such a misperception is assumed to involve unconscious processes that can be pervasive and powerful at both individual and collective levels.

IMPLICATIONS OF THE IRRATIONALIST
PERSPECTIVE FOR DEMOCRACY

The irrationalist perspective, from Freud to the authoritarian personality, has a number of important implications for democracy. The primary implication concerns the assumption of irrationality: If humans are for the most part unaware of why they think and act in particular ways, or even that they think and act in particular ways, then this calls into question the picture of the informed psychological citizen that is essential to the good working of an open society.

Democracy requires psychological citizens to be cognitively and emotionally capable of making informed choices. Such citizens are assumed to think and act rationally in terms of evaluating different choices and distinguishing between and showing preferences for particular candidates and policies on the basis of sound judgment. If psychological citizens are irrational, then they are incapable of succeeding in these tasks and sustaining a democracy.

Of course, according to the irrationalist view, the inability to sustain democracy would not be accompanied by the ability to recognize this inability. Thus, the irrationalist perspective leads us to various conspiratorial models that claim that democracy does not exist but that most people are fooled into believing there is democracy and something known as "rule by the people for the people." As we shall see in the next chapter, the conspiratorial models divide into two branches: those who believe the majority of people are doomed to remain on the irrationalist track and to continue to be ruled and fooled by a ruling elite, and those who assume the majority of people will sometime in the future break free from irrational thinking, recognize their true interests, and overpower the ruling elite.

The danger that irrationality holds for democracy was a major concern of the pioneers who established the American republic. This is strongly reflected in *The Federalist Papers* (Hamilton, Madison, & Jay, 1787–1788/1996). For example, in Federalist Paper No. 49, the people are described as "the only legitimate fountain of power" (p. 348), and the view is considered that the people should be the ultimate arbiter of disputes over the constitution and rivalries between the various branches of government. At the same time, it is noted that there is "The danger of disturbing the public tranquility by interesting too strongly the public passions" (p. 349), and there are additional warnings that repeated appeals to the people might lead to a situation in which "the passions . . . , not the reason, of the public would sit in judgement" (p. 351).

The irrationalist models also have implications for the possibility of democratic leadership, particularly with respect to threats to democracy from potentially authoritarian leadership. Because so much power and influence rests with the leader, the process of selecting and empowering leaders, and the rules limiting their actions, must be stringent.

On the one hand, the effectiveness of the group depends on the leader, and so from the irrationalist perspective, the leader is vital to group success. On the other hand, because the leader wields enormous power, it is necessary to put into place mechanisms to prevent the abuse of power. For example, presidents, prime ministers, and other heads of executive branches of government should not have the power to declare war without first providing truthful information about security threats and also getting explicit approval from other elected representatives of the legislative branch (e.g., Congress, Parliament).

However, according to the irrationalist perspective, there is a real danger that outgroups will wage war, irrespective of material conditions and objective interests of different groups. Thus, it is, first, imperative that leaders of democracies are empowered to organize effective defense for their societies. This places even greater importance on the accuracy of information used to make decisions. How real is the external threat? What level of danger is the group facing? It is of the highest importance that democracies develop more open and accurate means of addressing such questions and of evaluating the information used to make decisions in this arena.

Second, the leader's actions in displacing aggression must be carefully monitored and controlled. By mobilizing collective action against an outgroup, a leader can unleash aggressive, potentially destructive sentiments onto perceived dissimilar targets and influence people to rally around the flag. This strategy will enable the silencing of dissenting voices inside the group as well as other moves damaging to democracy. Numerous examples of this are found in modern societies. For example, following the 2003 U.S.-led invasion of

Iraq, President George W. Bush and his allies attacked *The New York Times* and other media outlets critical of the war, and these attacks reached a crescendo in June 2006, when *The New York Times* was directly accused of "unpatriotic" actions (ostensibly because the newspaper divulged "government secrets").

Third, the authoritarian personality literature suggests that we must pay closer attention to the contents of educational material and shared public narratives and guard against ethnocentrism and hate-nurturing values. For example, the narratives and literature used by Islamic fundamentalists in Saudi Arabia and Christian fundamentalists in the United States mirror one another in espousing intolerance for outgroups. The authoritarian personality literature suggests that such narratives of intolerance are associated with particular family dynamics, characterized in particular by stringent and dogmatic fathers.

Fourth, terror management theory suggests that when organizing for intergroup contact, there is an urgent need to educate each group about beliefs, values, and normative systems other than their own. That is, there is a need to introduce other alternative normative systems in a nonthreatening way, to point out similarities with their own system, and to guide people to recognize a common core.

More broadly, the irrationalist perspective suggests we need to educate citizens to be far more critical in distinguishing between the rationalization of behavior and rational behavior, particularly when assessing politicians. Even in democracies, political leaders wield enormous power to maneuver their nations into war, resulting in large-scale death and destruction. The irrationalist perspective highlights the high probability of this behavior and the need to seek remedies at the societal level rather than just at the level of individuals.

4

THE MATERIALIST VIEW: FROM REALISTIC CONFLICT THEORY TO EVOLUTIONARY PSYCHOLOGY

The theories considered in this chapter share a foundational proposition: Material factors either internal or external to the individual determine intergroup relations. Factors external to individuals include their positions in the production process and the material conditions in which they live, scarcity of resources, population size, and the rate and direction of ecological change. Factors internal to the individual include genetic characteristics.

A second common theme in most of the materialist theories is the assumption that people remain for the large part unaware of the determinant role of material factors in their lives; in this way, there is a link between the materialist theories considered here and the irrationalist theories discussed in chapter 3 of this volume. Material factors are assumed to serve as a hidden external hand (as in the case of realistic conflict theory) or a whispering within (as in the case of evolutionary psychology) that gives direction to thought and action. However, several of the theories also propose that when people become aware of the role of material factors, their awareness fundamentally changes intergroup relations from unjust but harmonious relations to intergroup conflict and, finally, to just and fair intergroup relations. For example, the classic Marxist position is that the evolution of class consciousness eventually leads to class conflict, revolution, and change toward a more just society.

MARX, PARETO, AND THE BROADER MATERIALIST THESIS

> Social movements of oppressed and excluded groups have . . . asked why extension of equal citizenship rights has not led to social justice and equality. Part of the answer is straight-forwardly Marxist . . . economic life is not sufficiently under the control of citizens to affect the unequal status and treatment of groups. (Young, 1989, p. 250)

Any account of the materialist thesis, in its modern manifestation at least, must begin with the ideas of Karl Marx (e.g., Marx, 1852/1979; Marx & Engels, 1848/1967). This should not be a controversial or surprising assertion. What is perhaps controversial and surprising to most modern readers is my assertion that a discussion of Marx in this context should proceed hand in hand with a discussion of the Italian scholar Vilfredo Pareto. Relative to Marx, Pareto (1935) remains neglected (outside certain narrow specialties; e.g., Meisel, 1965), perhaps because his intergroup model is not to the liking of our modern academic sensibilities. Besides, Pareto has been tainted by the association of some versions of his ideas with the fascist movement in the early half of the 20th century.

However, it does not serve scholarly inquiry well to neglect Pareto, because his is the gloomy voice of realism that reminds us of the course of history as it has been so far rather than the course of history many of us would prefer. In this sense, Pareto's seemingly negative outlook on the perpetuation of cycles of intergroup inequalities and conflicts remind us of a similar gloom associated with Freud's perspective that we can bind people together in love as long as there are some left over to hate (as discussed in chap. 3, this volume).

Marx and Pareto on History

Whereas Marx (e.g., Marx, 1852/1979; Marx & Engels, 1848/1967) saw intergroup relations as progressing along historical, evolutionary paths to a final "ideal" destiny of a classless society without a centralized power, Pareto (1935) proposed that history proceeds in cycles and that inequality and the rule of the powerful is universal and everlasting. Thus, the end point of societal evolution as postulated by Marx and Pareto is very different in this crucial respect.

However, in another respect this end point is assumed to be the same: Both Marx and Pareto saw the course of societal evolution to be fixed and inevitable. Just as Marx saw it as inevitable that class conflict, class consciousness, and a proletariat revolution would lead to a classless society, Pareto saw it as inevitable that the elite would always rule and inequalities would always continue in human societies. This deterministic feature of social movements described by Marx and Pareto is unfortunate because, like all other deterministic movements that insist that the end of history must be this way or that (e.g., Fukuyama, 1992), they are both nonfalsifiable and highly unlikely. The only certainty about human societies is the uncertainty of their futures.

Another subtle similarity between Marx and Pareto is that they were both utopians—Marx being famously recognized as such by Popper (1966). The Marxist classless society is perhaps easy to recognize as utopian, but Pareto was also utopian in his vision of elite circulation saving a society—an outcome that is plausible but in practice is not achieved (hence, Pareto's comment about history being a graveyard of the aristocracy).

In contemporary language, Marx saw the world as characterized by a clash of social classes rather than of civilizations. From a psychological perspective, this clash of social classes evolves in six steps. First, human society reaches a level of technological development that allows for the production of a surplus. The surplus is initially achieved through the transition from hunting–gathering societies to settled agricultural societies, and later the surplus increases dramatically through industrialization.

Second, a powerful ruling group monopolizes the surplus and uses it to establish and control a central authority, a military, and a dominant culture, including political ideologies and religious belief systems. The dominant cultural system and the state takes shape to reflect the interests of the ruling group, with both the rulers and the ruled justifying societal conditions through reference to their shared culture. At this stage, people do not recognize their true class memberships or interests. The appropriation of culture through socialization practices means that the disadvantaged people who are ruled justify the dominant position of those who rule over them. Similarly, the ruling class interprets existing power and resource inequalities as fair and "natural."

Third, there is a transition from feudalism to capitalism, with capitalists owning the means of production and proletarians selling their labor as a commodity on the market. Initially, the members of each class continue to experience false consciousness (i.e., the inability to recognize their true class membership and interests). Thus, proletarians fail to see that they belong to a class with interests that oppose the capitalist class. In Freudian terms, social classes are acting irrationally, meaning that they are not aware of their real actions and interests.

However, as class divisions become increasingly deeper and clashes between the classes grow more intense, class consciousness gradually emerges out of increasingly intense class conflict. A vanguard of the proletariat, which includes intellectuals and disenchanted capitalists, help in this process of raising class consciousness. Consequently, intergroup relations enter a fourth stage of the proletariat revolution and the eventual toppling of the capitalist class. Thus, the proletariat stops acting irrationally and accurately recognizes motives, actions, and interests.

The fifth and sixth stages involve the establishment of the dictatorship of the proletariat and, finally, the gradual evolution of a classless society and the dissolution of the central government, respectively. The dictatorship of the proletariat establishes the material conditions that enable a new consciousness to emerge so that people learn to work for the good of the collectivity and to dedicate themselves to a greater collective good than the pursuit of personal profit.

The gradual evolution of this new consciousness means a decreasing need for a central authority, which, after all, always served the primary purpose of maintaining inequalities by force. The final point of this evolution is the complete disappearance of a central authority in a classless society, in which everyone owns everything through the collective ownership of society.

The idea that people would one day be able to achieve a consciousness that makes a central government redundant seems far removed and even "foreign" to many of us. However, this is not an idea unique or original to Marx; idealists of different stripes have lauded this idea throughout the ages. Those who see such a "European" idea as antithetical to the American spirit should recall that Henry Thoreau (1849/2003), the most American of thinkers, began his essay "Civil Disobedience" in this way:

> I heartily accept the motto,—"That government is best which governs least;" and I should like to see it acted up to more rapidly and systematically. Carried out, it finally amounts to this, which also I believe—"That government is best which governs not at all;" and when men are prepared for it, that will be the kind of government which they will have. (p. 265)

Marx and Thoreau would not have agreed on the course of events leading to people being prepared for a government that "governs not at all," but they both saw the disappearance of central government as an ideal end goal—a goal also adopted by modern Libertarians (Boaz, 1997). Nor is the idea of collective ownership unique to Marx; Sir Thomas More (1478–1535), who literally lost his head because of his devotion to conservative Catholic tradition, conceived of a utopia in which there was no private property.

A subtlety of the Marxist intergroup model is that false consciousness is not exclusive to any one class and emerges from the relative position of people in the production process, not out of a conscious conspiratorial strategy by capitalists to "fool" the proletariat. Thus, in a sense, both capitalists and proletariat buy into the false picture of the intergroup situation, but whereas the capitalists are perceiving the world in a way that serves their own class interests, the proletariat are endorsing a picture of the world that extends the exploitation of their own class (just as most women in Western societies prior to the "liberation" movements of the late 20th century endorsed traditional gender relations and thus the superior position of men).

Pareto's Vision

Pareto (1935) presented a model of intergroup relations that agrees with much of Marx's (1852/1979; Marx & Engels, 1848/1967) first four stages: He too accepted that a minority, the "elite" as he termed them, control the surplus produced by the masses (i.e, the nonelite). He accepted that the elite manufacture ideologies to justify the existing inequalities. Pareto also argued that a vanguard—or a "counter-elite," to use his term—effects the mobilization of the nonelite (i.e., the "proletariat," in Marx's terminology) to rise against the elite. However, from here Pareto turned sharply away from Marx and foresaw a very different future for the revolution.

The sources of the different directions taken by Marx and Pareto are in large part their assumptions about the factors that shape human social arrangements. Marx saw material conditions and relations in the production process as the determining factor—the clear expectation being that social arrangements and human consciousness would change as material conditions changed. For Pareto, the key factor shaping social systems lies within individuals and has to do with natural variation in abilities:

> Let us assume that in every branch of human activity each individual is given an index which stands as a sign of his capacity, very much the way grades are given in the various subjects in examinations in school. The highest type of lawyer, for instance, will be given 10. The man who did not get a client will be given 1—reserving zero for the man who is an out-and-out idiot. . . . And so for all branches of human activity . . . so let us make a class of the people who have the highest indeces in their branch of activity, and to that branch give the name "elite." (Pareto, 1935, Vol. 3, pp. 1422–1423)

Whereas Marx saw an evolutionary process with an inevitable end point—the classless society—Pareto saw a cyclical process, with the inevitable continuity of elite rule. The counterelite leads the nonelite to topple the current elite, but after the elite have been defeated, the counterelite rules as the new elite and continues the system of inequalities. The new elite can give its regime a new title, such as *democracy, communism, capitalism, socialism, fascism,* or *Islamic Republic.* New slogans are adopted, such as *freedom, equality,* and *equal opportunities.* However, these labels and slogans are merely screens behind which the new elite carries on the exploitation of the nonelite.

Pareto saw history as the "graveyard of the aristocracies" (1935, Vol. 3, p. 1430) because each new elite eventually makes the same mistake as the old elite it succeeded: By practicing nepotism and refusing to allow talented nonelite members opportunities to rise and join their ranks, established elites bring about their own downfall. As talented members of the nonelite become more and more frustrated by the "glass ceiling" that pushes down on them, they use their talents to mobilize the nonelite and start a new mass movement to destabilize the system. The consequence of closing the system and not allowing circulation was clarified by Plato (1987) in *The Republic* 2,500 years ago:

> You are, all of you in this community, brothers. But when god fashioned you, he added gold in the composition of those of you who are qualified to be Rulers . . . silver in the Auxiliaries, and iron and bronze in the farmers and other workers. Now since you are all of the same stock, though your children will commonly resemble their parents, occasionally a silver child will be born of golden parents, or a golden child of silver parents, and so on. Therefore the first and most important of god's commandments to the Rulers is that in the exercise of their functions as Guardians their principal care must be to watch the mixture of metals in the character of their children. If one of their own children has traces of bronze or iron in its make-up, they must harden their hearts, assign it its proper value, and degrade it to the ranks of the industrial and agricultural class where it properly belongs: similarly, if a child of this class is born with gold or silver in its nature, they must promote it appropriately to be a Guardian or an Auxiliary. And this they must do because there is a prophecy that the State will be ruined when it has Guardians of silver or bronze. (Book III, 415b, c, d)

Thus, Plato preceded modern theorists, by a mere 2,500 years or so, in predicting the eventual collapse of societies that are not open and refuse to allow circulation of talent.

CLASSIC THEMES AND MODERN RESEARCH

From the writings of Marx (1852/1979; Marx & Engels, 1848/1967) and Pareto (1935) there emerge a number of major "classic" themes that are also present in modern materialist theories and empirical research on intergroup relations. The first theme is that a ruling minority controls most of the key resources in society and uses this monopoly to manufacture ideology and shape culture to further serve its own interests. In the sections that follow I discuss this theme in relation to resource mobilization theory, social dominance theory, and system justification theory. The second theme is that by allowing some level of openness and circulation of talent in society, the dominant group extends its own rule, which I examine later in this chapter in relation to the five stage model and research on social mobility and tokenism. The third theme is that of conflict arising out of differing material interests, which I discuss in relation to realistic conflict theory. Finally, I consider evolutionary psychology through the fourth theme of competition for scarce resources.

MONOPOLY OF CULTURE AND RESOURCES: RESOURCE MOBILIZATION THEORY, SOCIAL DOMINANCE THEORY, AND SYSTEM JUSTIFICATION THEORY

The idea that a small band of people, labeled *elite* or *capitalist* or *ruling class* or simply *the rich*, shapes values, attitudes, ideas, ideology, and culture more broadly is found in a variety of theories. The aspect of this idea that is of most direct interest to psychologists is that through the control of material resources the rich can shape psychological experiences, including how satisfied or deprived people feel about their situation and the way they are being treated, particularly in terms of fairness. The most direct manifestation of this idea is found in *resource mobilization theory* (McCarthy & Zald, 1977), which maintains that social movements can be launched through the mobilization of resources (which include intellectual and human as well as material resources). *Social dominance theory* (Sidanius & Pratto, 1999) and *system justification theory* (Jost & Banaji, 1994) are more focused on the psychological processes that are at the source of intergroup inequalities and that enable their continuation.

Resource Mobilization Theory

Do you have in front of your home a gleaming sports car standing ready for you to jump into and speed away? Do you have a beach house you can go to for exotic holidays? Is there a swimming pool and tennis court on the grounds of your house? The vast majority of us do not have such luxuries, but at the same time, we do not feel particularly deprived as a result of not having them. However, what if we received a stream of messages to persuade us that it is both possible and right that we should have such luxuries; that, indeed, although such luxuries have seemed out of reach, if we mobilize as a group we will be able to achieve these legitimate rights? These messages persuade us that you and I could and should have sports cars and beach houses, as a right. Could we be led to become angry about not having what we previously saw as luxuries but now see as necessities? Yes, we could, according to a theory that raises new questions about the relationship between material resources and psychological experiences.

What factors are most important in creating social movements and change? What is it that "fires up" people to act for change? Is it psychological experiences and perceptions, such as feelings of anger, deprivation, and the perception of being treated unjustly? Is it heated frustrations and feelings of injustice that power and direct social movements? Although this idea has intuitive appeal, psychologically based interpretation of social movements has been seriously challenged by resource mobilization theory, contending that psychological factors can be shaped by material conditions and the mobilization of resources (McCarthy & Wolfson, 1996; McCarthy & Zald, 1977).

Of course, it is not a contentious or a new claim that resources are important in social movements, both national and international (United Nations, 2005). However, resource mobilization theory has created debate (see McAdam, 1999; Tarrow, 1998) because it depicts the controllers of resources as capable of using psychological factors to shape a *social movement*, that is, "a set of opinions and beliefs in a population which represents preferences for changing some elements of the social structure and/or reward distribution of a society" (McCarthy & Zald, 1977, pp. 1217–1218). The organizational analogue to a social movement is a *social movement industry*, which typically incorporates a number of *social movement organizations* (i.e., formal organizations that attempt to implement the goals of a social movement; see also Lofland, 1996). *Constituents* provide resources to social movement organizations. For example, the broad social movement labeled *the women's movement* had an analogous social movement industry with numerous social movement organizations—the most important perhaps being NOW (i.e., the National Organization for Women)—and constituents ranging from individual women and men to major political and business organizations.

From the resource mobilization theory perspective, there are always, in all societies, numerous bases on which injustices could be socially constructed and made the focus of political attention. For example, consider the situation of women. Why did the "liberation" of women speed up in the post–World War II era? Women had been living as second-class citizens for at least thousands of years prior to the 20th century. Why did the liberation movement not come about in the 11th century or the 16th century or the 18th century? Is it because women enjoyed a more equal status during earlier eras? Not at all; women were just as badly off, and perhaps treated even worse, in the past. It is not the actual plight of women that is the original source of their collective liberation action in the second part of the 20th century, but rather it is the material interests of the elite with resources.

After World War II, the major owners of capital in the United States and other Western industrial societies recognized that women were needed for work outside the home. Given the labor needs of modern industry, it was now seen as inefficient to keep half of the potential workforce out of the job market. This inefficiency came under the spotlight at a time of Cold War rivalry between capitalist and communist systems, as represented by the United States and the former Soviet Union. Western capitalism would be better equipped to win the Cold War when women took on job responsibilities outside the home, as they had done in the Soviet empire. Consequently, it was now seen to be in the interests of people who controlled resources to mobilize women to work outside the home, and therefore, resources were mobilized to open up new educational and employment opportunities for women.

Thus, from the perspective of resource mobilization theory, the timing and nature of the women's liberation movement can be better explained by referencing the interests of the capitalist elites who controlled resources in the 20th century and the competition between capitalist and communist systems, rather than the feelings of deprivation and other psychological experiences of women. The nature of the production process in the late 20th century and Cold War competition created an economic need for women to work outside the home so as to maximize production potential. Resources were mobilized to highlight and increase feelings of deprivation and injustice among women in the capitalist West, particularly through the media as well as educational and political systems. Powerful political groups channeled these feelings of anger and frustration into political and social action, which lead to equal rights legislation and more educational and employment opportunities for women. The result is that by the 21st century, women in Western capitalist societies were successfully competing with men in the educational arena (Smallwood, 2003), and it is now the norm for married women to work outside the home.

Resource mobilization theory, then, accepts that feelings of deprivation, perceptions of injustice, and other psychological experiences are important in social movements. However, the theory contends that those who control resources can shape psychological experiences and influence the situation so that a particular group feels less or more deprived, less or more unjustly treated, and so on. In summary, psychological experiences are seen to be determined by material resources.

Social Dominance Theory

> In describing how "well" group dominance works as a system and in reminding people that group dominance is one of the most predominant forms of social organization, we might also appear to be justifying social dominance. However, rather than trying to support and justify social inequality, our personal political biases are decidedly egalitarian. (Sidanius & Pratto, 1999, p. 309)

> Rather than being an endorsement of oppression, social dominance theory can be seen as a *prerequisite* to morally driven intervention. (Sidanius, Pratto, van Laar, & Levin, 2004, p. 862)

In its relatively short history, social dominance theory (Sidanius & Pratto, 1999) has generated considerable controversy and attracted particularly heated criticisms of both theoretical (e.g., J. C. Turner & Reynolds, 2003) and empirical (e.g., Guimond, Dambrun, Michinov, & Duarte, 2003) bases, leading its proponents to make extraordinary efforts to explain and defend their political positions (see also Sidanius et al., 2004). Why should a psychological theory of intergroup relations generate so much heated debate? The basic reasons can be better understood by looking back at the experiences of a much earlier theory, put forward by Pareto (1935), with which social dominance theory has important similarities. Like Pareto's elite theory, social dominance theory highlights the "universal" nature of stratification and group-based inequalities. The result is that, like Pareto's *elite theory*, social dominance theory is interpreted by some as condemning humans to inevitable group-based inequalities. Social dominance theory seems particularly susceptible to this criticism in large part because of its reliance on evolutionary theory. This reliance has led critics to interpret social dominance theory as arguing that "hierarchy and inequality are genetically mandated at either the individual or species level" (Jost, Banaji, & Nosek, 2004, p. 912).

Because social dominance theorists have apparently been misunderstood by critics, we must take special care in our assessment of their actual claims. The theory has three starting assumptions. First, hierarchies based on age and sex are universal and common to all societies, but only surplus-producing social systems are characterized by hierarchies based on "arbitrary-set" systems that are malleable and vary across cultures (e.g., ethnicity, class, religion). Second, "most forms of group conflict and aggression (e.g., racism, ethnocentrism, sexism, nationalism, classism, regionalism) can be regarded as different manifestations of the same basic human predisposition to form group-based social hierarchies" (Sidanius & Pratto, 1999, p. 38). Third, human social systems are influenced by one set of forces pushing toward, and a second set pushing against, greater group-based social inequalities.

Social dominance theory has three aspects that are particularly controversial. First, the claim that there is a "human predisposition" to form group-based social hierarchies is not treated by social dominance theory as a description of a malleable, socially constructed social arrangement. Rather, it is described as arising in part from "temperament," thus proposing that this human predisposition is partly inbuilt and relatively fixed. This feature of temperament arose out of evolutionary processes, and more broadly, "the evolutionary perspective suggests . . . that humans will tend to live in group-based and hierarchically organized social systems" (Sidanius & Pratto, 1999, p. 54).

The implication is that group-based inequalities are part of our evolutionary heritage. (Again, this is the kind of claim that serves as a red flag for thinkers who prefer to believe that the present social arrangements can and should be changed to achieve greater equality and fairness.) In this way, social dominance theory seems to be dismissing as "impossible" or "utopian" plans for egalitarian societies, despite claims by Sidanius and others that "our personal political biases are decidedly egalitarian" (Sidanius & Pratto, 1999, p. 309).

The insistence by social dominance theorists that temperament and evolutionary sources are in large part responsible for existing group-based inequalities is not matched by their research efforts. None of their major research studies examine the role of temperament or evolutionary sources.

A second area of acute controversy is the social dominance theory claim that the roots of gender differences in behavior and psychological functioning are differences in the best possible strategies available to women and men for reproductive success. The theory retreads a path well-worn by evolutionary psychologists (see Moghaddam, 2005a, chap. 19): Women can have fewer offspring than men, and so their best reproductive strategy is to invest more highly in the fewer offspring they have. To maximize investment in fewer offspring, females will be more selective in their choice of mates and will seek males who have resources and are willing to invest exclusively in them and their children.

Men will seek to reproduce through quantity by having access to more females and having more offspring rather than by investing in a smaller number of offspring with one partner. Further, men will attempt to accumulate and monopolize resources and to usurp the productions of other men so as to beat the male competition for access to women. This will result in resource inequalities between men, with more powerful men monopolizing resources. Consequently,

> female selection of high-status mates and male attempts to monopolize social and political resources may lead to the creation of exploitative social, economic, and political systems in which patriarchy and arbitrary-set stratification among males are assortative: adaptive for those who enjoy more social and economic resources and power, and maladaptive for those who do not. (Sidanius & Pratto, 1999, p. 265)

These claims have been met with incredulity and passionate rejection by critics, feminists among them, of course. Critics point out that the social dominance account does not match the particular situation of women and men in the 21st century, including the availability of contraceptives and the academic and professional advances of women that allow them to independently accumulate resources and not rely on men as sole wage earners.

In the contemporary Western world characterized by dual career families, couples adopt the strategy of *bipartisan investment* (i.e., women and men cooperate to maximize the chances of offspring success). In most cases, men do not abandon their children, because they are aware that if they do, their offspring have a lower chance of success. Thus, critics contend, gender relations are far more malleable and context-dependent than social dominance theorists claim, and gender-based hierarchies can be ended (for a response to criticisms of social dominance theory related to gender, see Sidanius et al., 2004, pp. 859–861).

A third area of controversy revolves around a measure associated with social dominance theory titled the Social Dominance Orientation: a "very general individual differences orientation expressing the value that people place on nonegalitarian and hierarchically structured relationships among social groups" (Sidanius & Pratto, 1999, p. 61). The Social Dominance Orientation Scale has changed with respect to the number and content of items over the years (see Rubin & Hewstone, 2004, p. 836), but in terms of one central feature, it remains the same: Irrespective of the groups involved and the reasons for a person supporting inequality, the measure focuses on how much people endorse statements about intergroup inequality. This measure is not integral to the theory but has become a focus of debate because it has been used in studies conducted to test the theory.

A close examination of the items on the Social Dominance Orientation Scale suggests they address attitudes toward several different issues. For example, items such as "It's probably a good thing that certain groups are at the top and other groups are at the bottom" and "To get ahead in life, it is sometimes necessary to step on other groups" (Sidanius & Pratto, 1999, p. 67) seem to measure attitudes toward group-based dominance, whereas items such as "All groups should be given an equal chance in life" and "We should strive to make incomes as equal as possible" (Sidanius & Pratto, 1999, p. 67) seem to measure attitudes toward equality (see also Jost & Thompson, 2000).

Moreover, it seems misleading to refer to the Social Dominance Orientation as a "personality" measure (Pratto, Sidanius, Stallwarth, & Malle, 1994) because this implies it measures some context-independent psychological features of the individual. Instead, research suggests the Social Dominance Orientation measures context-dependent attitudes (Levin, 2004). Besides, the use of personality measures to explain intergroup relations leads to the additional problem of explaining changes in behavior across contexts by referencing a stable individual disposition (Rubin & Hewstone, 2004, p. 837).

More serious than the charge that the Social Dominance Orientation Scale measures several different constructs is the charge that this individual-difference measure reflects the reductionist nature of social dominance theory (Schmitt, Branscombe, & Kappen, 2003). Indeed, it was probably a strategic mistake for Sidanius and his colleagues to put forward the Social Dominance Orientation as the principal measure in their research on social dominance theory, because it opens the theory up to the charge that it explains intergroup relations on the basis of an individual-difference variable.

Despite these shortcomings, the Social Dominance Orientation has proven very useful in highlighting intriguing attitudinal differences across majority and minority groups: Whites and other majority group members have been found to more strongly endorse intergroup inequalities than do African Americans and other minorities (e.g., Pratto et al., 1994; Sidanius, Levin, Liu, & Pratto, 2000). Moreover, certain institutions, such as the police force, have been found to be staffed by people who endorse group-based inequalities more strongly than does the general public (Sidanius, Liu, Pratto, & Shaw, 1994). An implication is that majorities serve their own interests in part by establishing institutions that support group-based inequalities. Of course, this is not a novel claim, but as I discuss later, social dominance researchers have generated some novel evidence in support of it.

Social dominance theory has also served a highly useful purpose by highlighting different patterns of identification among minority and majority groups. The theory suggests that majority groups (e.g., Whites in the United States and Western Europe) will identify more strongly with common identity that can encompass all groups (e.g., national identity), whereas minority groups (e.g., ethnic minorities in the United States and Europe) will identify more strongly with communal identity that encompasses a specific local group (e.g., African American identity).

This distinction is important because common identity (e.g., based on nationalism) tends to be associated with the status quo, existing inequalities, and thus the perpetuation of majority group dominance, whereas communal identity tends to be associated with ingroup interests. With regard to rights and duties (Finkel & Moghaddam, 2005), by citing common identity, the majority group is able to invoke duties to serve the status quo; likewise, by citing communal identity, minority groups are able to invoke the rights of the minority ingroup to act on the basis of their distinct interests, which inevitably conflict with the interests of the majority group. Related to this, social identity theory (Tajfel & Turner, 1979) and other perspectives (e.g., Moghaddam & Riley, 2005) suggest that the perceived stability of the sociopolitical system is an important factor in these processes: Minorities are far more likely to identify strongly with communal rather than common identity when they perceive greater instability and change.

The higher priority given by majority groups to common identity could be interpreted as being in line with findings that the more educated and affluent elite tend also to support democratic values, nonconformity, and civil liberties in general (see the review by Sullivan & Transue, 1999). Such support for civil liberties was essential in the political progress made by women, ethnic minorities, and gay men and lesbians, particularly since the 1960s. Members of the majority group, it could be argued, see policies of inclusiveness as strengthening the entire system and the common identity—as long as their own superior status is maintained.

Thus, if we set aside the claims social dominance theory makes about there being an evolutionary basis to (a) group-based inequalities and (b) assumed gender differences, the theory boils down to some sensible tenets, most of them emanating from Marx (e.g., Marx, 1852/1979; Marx & Engels, 1848/1967) and Pareto (1935). First, societies are characterized by stratification and group-based inequalities. Second, the theory sees individual and institutional discrimination, and the ideologies and "legitimizing myths" people share to justify discrimination, as helping to maintain group-based inequalities. Third, groups enjoying greater power are influenced by dominant ideologies to behave in their own interests more than do less powerful groups, and this *behavioral asymmetry* helps to perpetuate group-based inequalities.

Even this stripped-down version of the theory seems pessimistic because the future it points to is more in line with Pareto's vision of everlasting group-based inequalities than Marx's utopian egalitarian society. In defense of this "pessimistic" outlook, I should point out that with divisions between rich and poor becoming even greater in the United States and much of the world (R. Frank & Cook, 1995; Wade, 2004), it seems that the more "gloomy" predictions of Pareto and social dominance theory have proven more accurate, so far at least. Whereas social dominance theory views intergroup inequalities as having strong evolutionary roots, the next theory we explore views intergroup inequalities as ideologically founded and malleable.

System Justification Theory

> A system justification perspective helps to understand why people who are economically disadvantaged often oppose income redistribution . . . , why women accept gender stereotypes and conventional definitions of sex roles . . . , and why so many members of disadvantaged groups reject egalitarian alternatives to the *status quo*. (Jost et al., 2004, p. 908)

Why do economically deprived people continue to put up with and even strongly support existing social arrangements, even in the United States, where group-based inequalities have been increasing in the 21st century and the very rich are increasing their share of wealth while the poorest are dropping further behind (Ehrenreich, 2002)? This question has come to the forefront in liberal American consciousness, as reflected in popular books such as *What's the Matter With Kansas*, in which T. Frank (2005) described how the residents of Kansas, an economically deprived state, seem to vote against their own economic interests by supporting right-wing political candidates. The classic Marxist assessment leads to a focus on *false consciousness*: the idea that the economically deprived are socialized by the dominant ideology to remain blind to their social class membership as well as the conflict between the interests of their class and the ruling class. A number of psychological theories, notably cognitive dissonance theory (Festinger, 1957) and the just-world hypothesis (Lerner, 1980), help to explain how people adopt those particular narratives that justify the existing social order.

Cognitive dissonance theory proposes that people are motivated to resolve inconsistencies between their thoughts, feelings, and actions and to rationalize their actions. An impressive body of evidence has accumulated since the mid 1950s in support of the counterintuitive idea that under certain conditions people who are given less rewards for work, are mistreated by authorities, and are generally treated as second-class citizens will show *greater* support for the arrangements they find themselves in (see discussions in

Harmon-Jones & Mills, 1999). The explanation provided by cognitive dissonance theory revolves around intrapersonal cognitive-motivational processes involving a need to avoid the anxiety arising from incongruent thoughts, feelings, and actions. For example, "John" justifies his low wages by convincing himself that although his rich boss has scores of mansions, planes, and fleets of cars, his family life is much richer in nonmaterial ways and he is blessed (with a happy family life, good friends, etc.) compared with his boss.

However, the dissonance associated with being in a disadvantaged position can be resolved in alternative ways (Jost, Pelham, Sheldon, & Sullivan, 2003, p. 16). From among the many possible narratives, why is it that John adopts a narrative that legitimizes the present group-based inequalities? One reason is that the dominant ideology, shaped by the ruling elite, endorses some narratives and not others; for example, it endorses narratives that give priority to individual action (e.g., "I could have become like my boss if I had worked hard enough and was sufficiently talented) but not collective mobilization (e.g., "We poor, disadvantaged people should take united action against the bosses and claim an equal share of resources").

A similar emphasis on intrapersonal cognitive-motivational factors is used by the *just-world hypothesis*, suggesting that system legitimization arises because people are motivated to adopt narratives that depict the world as just and fair (Hafer, 2000; Olson & Hafer, 2001). The source of such narratives is the dominant ideology, which preserves the status quo. In capitalist societies, this is achieved by blaming individual victims rather than social systems. For example, when the factory workers learn that John has been fired, they are likely to adopt victim-blaming narratives (e.g., "John should have worked harder"), rather than system-blaming narratives (e.g., "In the present economic arrangements, workers are hired at the cheapest price possible and discarded whenever profits demand it").

The Marxist idea of false consciousness and the psychological theories of cognitive dissonance and the just world provide the launching pad for system justification theory (Jost & Banaji, 1994), which attempts to be expansive by tackling behavior at the levels of the individual, the group, and the social system (i.e., the existing intergroup arrangements and the ideology that upholds it). People are motivated toward three levels of justification: (a) *ego justification* (individual level), or the need to maintain a favorable self-image and to justify one's thoughts and actions; (b) *group justification* (group level), or the need to maintain a favorable ingroup image and to justify the ingroup's ideas and actions; and (c) *system justification*, or the need to justify and legitimize "existing social arrangements . . . even at the expense of personal and group interest" (Jost & Banaji, 1994, p. 2).

According to system justification theory, in almost all circumstances the system justification motive is stronger than motives for ego and group justification. This is why there are so few collective movements to change the existing system and why revolutions are rare. Even major labor strikes seldom happen. People generally appropriate and use as their guides those narratives that justify the present intergroup arrangements as just and fair.

Jost and his colleagues produced an impressive array of studies to demonstrate system justification (Jost & Burgess, 2000; Jost & Hunyady, 2002; Jost & Kay, 2005; Jost, Pelham, & Carvallo, 2002; Jost, Pelham, et al., 2003; Jost & Thompson, 2000; Kay, Jimenez, & Jost, 2002; Kay & Jost, 2003; Kay, Jost, & Young, 2005). Their methodological approach was in line with the turn toward implicit social cognition (Greenwald & Banaji, 1995) and explorations of how people can be influenced by thoughts and feelings of which they themselves are not conscious. The source of such thoughts and feelings is the ideology dominant in society (shaped in large part by the ruling group); for example, this ideology influences stereotypes of minority groups.

Research by Steele (1997) has demonstrated how gender and racial stereotypes can serve as a "threat in the air" so that even a subtle reminder of gender or race stereotypes can influence women and African Americans to underperform without being aware that their performance has been detrimentally impacted by stereotypes. Jost and his associates explored how so-called threats in the air can lead minority group members to endorse the existing system.

In the research of Jost and his associates, the threat in the air is a threat against the system, such as in the shape of stereotypes that do not support the system. Research has shown that when participants are exposed to "complimentary" stereotypes, such as "poor as happy" and "rich as miserable" or "poor as honest" and "rich as dishonest" or "women as considerate" and "men as assertive," they are more prone to justify the system than when they are exposed to "noncomplimentary" stereotypes, such as "poor as unhappy" and "rich as happy" (Jost & Kay, 2005; Kay & Jost, 2003). It seems that a distribution of positive features among groups leads to a perceived compensation for actual power and resource group-based differences. Thus, the world is "fair" after all, because although the rich have more material resources, the poor are happier.

This view of the "world as fair" is maintained in part by putting down winners on traits that are not causally relevant to the outcome and lauding losers on traits that are not causally relevant to the outcome (Kay et al., 2005). Therefore, at the same time that the system is justified, rewards are distributed in an apparently more even manner so that, for example, powerful people are described as more intelligent but less happy, and overweight people are deemed more lazy but also more sociable. In a study that would surely please Wall Street analysts, profitable companies were found to be judged more ethical than unprofitable companies (Jost, Blount, Pfeffer, & Hunyady, 2003). Such system justification trends tend to be heightened when the social system is perceived to be under threat, such as when Americans are exposed to descriptions of a decline in the status of the United States.

The emphasis placed by Jost and his colleagues on people actively justifying the system, as well as on the lack of change in the system, has led some critics to argue that system justification theory does not give enough attention to social change and collective minority movements for change (e.g., Huddy, 2004, p. 953). After all, change does come about, and even major revolutions do happen. At some stage, a tipping point is reached so that motivations for ego- and group-justification overwhelm motivation for system justification.

From a system justification perspective, this tipping point is seldom reached and systems continue to be justified because of an array of (a) cognitive factors such as cognitive consistency and cognitive conservativism, attributional simplicity, uncertainty reduction, and epistemic needs for structure and closure; (b) motivational factors such as the fear of equality, illusion of control, and the belief in the just world; and (c) structural and ideological factors such as political socialization and control of rewards and punishments by the ruling group (Jost, Pelham, et al., 2003, p. 15). This "big picture" approach is at once the strength and weakness of system justification theory: It is exclusive and expansive in its scope, but resource limitations mean that only a few of its aspects—critics would contend the minor ones—can be tested using experimental methods.

SOCIAL MOBILITY AND TOKENISM: THE FIVE-STAGE MODEL

The puzzle of how a sociopolitical system characterized by enormous group-based inequalities survives and is even supported by those who are at the "bottom of the food chain"—the economically deprived—is at the heart of a number of materialist theories (as discussed previously, in the case of system justification theory; Jost & Banaji, 1994). In addressing this puzzle, the role of individual mobility has been highlighted by Marx (1852/1979; Marx & Engels, 1848/1967) and other classical theorists but also by modern theorists. The *five-stage model* (D. M. Taylor & McKirnan, 1984) is similar to classical theories in its grand scope, but it rests on a foundation of modern psychological concepts such as social attributions, giving particular attention to the role of tokenism.

The five-stage model divides people into advantaged and disadvantaged groups (similar to social dominance theory in its assumption about the pervasiveness of group-based inequalities; Sidanius & Pratto, 1999) and proposes that there are five distinct stages in intergroup relations. At Stage 1, group formation is based on ascribed characteristics, such as race or sex, and there is no mobility between groups. Group members compare themselves with others within their own group, and group-based inequalities are explained in terms of group characteristics. An example is the relationship between U.S. slave owners and slaves during the 18th century in the southern United

States. At Stage 2, group membership is still the basis for individual status and power, but people now assume that the determining factors in their power and status are individual characteristics. Stage 3 is characterized by attempts at individual mobility, particularly by the most talented members of the disadvantaged group, who compare themselves with the members of the advantaged group (rather like when talented African Americans compare themselves with Whites in the United States).

The deciding factor in what happens next, in the transition between Stage 3 and Stage 4 is the permeability of the advantaged group. If talented members of the disadvantaged group are not permitted to move up individually to the advantaged group, at Stage 4 they will engage in consciousness-raising among disadvantaged group members toward achieving collective action, which takes place in Stage 5. However, if the advantaged group proves to be permeable, then talented disadvantaged group members will move up individually (their original preference) and join the advantaged group as the strongest advocates of the fairness of the social order.

Having succeeded in the system, talented individuals who move up from the disadvantaged group to join the advantaged group uphold the view that one's position in the social hierarchy is based on individual characteristics, particularly talent and drive. These individuals serve as "tokens," symbolizing the "success" and "openness" of the system.

In support of the five-stage model view about the power of tokenism, experimental studies show that even when there is only a very slim chance of moving up to join the advantaged group, disadvantaged group members prefer to adopt individual action to help themselves rather than collective action to help all members of the disadvantaged group (Lalonde & Silverman, 1994; Wright, Taylor, & Moghaddam, 1990). Of course, the five-stage model is following Pareto (1935), discussed earlier in this chapter, in its proposition that talented disadvantaged group members prefer to move up individually and only attempt collective action when their personal path to progress is blocked. The power of tokenism is particularly evident in the United States, where the American Dream suggests that anyone can "make it" as long as they have the required personal merits; although America is a *Winner Takes All Society* (R. Frank & Cook, 1995), the American Dream narrative tells everyone they could be the next winner.

MATERIAL INTERESTS SHAPE CONFLICT:
REALISTIC CONFLICT THEORY

Social dominance theory (Sidanius & Pratto, 1999), system justification theory (Jost & Banaji, 1994), and the five-stage model (D. M. Taylor & McKirnan, 1984) all give importance to the impact of material factors on intergroup relations by examining the tendency of people to (a) endorse group-based inequalities (i.e., social dominance theory), (b) justify group-based inequalities (i.e., system justification theory), and (c) give priority to individualistic mobility strategies (i.e., the five-stage model; D. M. Taylor & McKirnan, 1984). These theories assume that the control of resources allows the ruling elite to shape ideology and create false consciousness so that disadvantaged groups endorse a system that works against their material interests. However, a far more direct adoption of the materialist thesis in psychology is found in *realistic conflict theory*, particularly as championed by the brilliant Turkish American psychologist Muzafer Sherif (1906–1988).

Sherif (1966) argued that the psychological characteristics of groups in interaction, such as their attitudes toward one another, are determined by the "functional relations between groups" (p. 63). People are self-centered and attempt to maximize their rewards. In the intergroup context, this means that people are favorable toward and cooperate with outgroups that share their material interests but are negatively disposed toward and compete against outgroups that have opposing material interests. In a series of publications, Sherif discussed field studies designed to demonstrate how material conditions determine the psychology of intergroup relations (Sherif, 1951, 1966; Sherif, Harvey, White, Hood, & Sherif, 1961; Sherif & Sherif, 1953, 1969; Sherif, White, & Harvey, 1955).

Sherif (1966) conducted his field studies in summer camps, with participants who were 11- or 12-year-old, healthy, White, Protestant, middleclass boys and who had no prior ties to one another. The uniformity of the participants in terms of key criteria, including sex, age, religion, and ethnicity, meant that Sherif was able to create intergroup differences without having to consider "naturally" existing differences.

Sherif (1966) first established functional relations within and between groups, then examined how functional relations determined the characteristics of groups and intergroup relations. Throughout the studies, Sherif and his associates played the role of summer camp personnel. He defined a group as a number of individuals who have stable role and status relations with one another and who share values and norms that regulate their attitudes and behavior (1966, p. 12). Intergroup relations occur when "individuals belonging to one group interact, collectively or individually, with another group or its members *in terms of their group identification*" (p. 12).

It is important to note that like Tajfel and Turner (1979, 1986; social identity theory) and other theorists of the identity tradition (see chap. 5, this volume), Sherif (1966) conceived that intergroup relations take place when people interact in terms of their group identification. However, realistic conflict theory views identification with a group as arising from functional relations.

There were four basic stages to Sherif's (1966) field studies. During Stage 1, *friendship formation*, the boys arrived in the summer camps and got to know one another. Having noted the friendship patterns that emerged in Stage 1, Sherif separated "best friends" and made sure they were placed in two different groups during Stage 2, *group formation*. Stage 3 involved *intergroup competition* through games such as tug-of-war. Very quickly the attitudes of the boys hardened against outgroup members, and former best friends were now "the enemy." Each group developed norms and rituals, and group cohesion and support for aggressive leadership increased as the boys faced a competitive outgroup.

Intergroup competition for scarce resources, such as material prizes and social status, had led to negative intergroup attitudes and conflict. The question now was, would Sherif be able to reverse this destructive course of events and create peaceful intergroup relations again? He did achieve this unlikely feat by introducing *superordinate goals*, these being goals that all groups want to achieve but that can only be achieved through the participation of all groups. For example, the experimenters created a situation in which the truck bringing food to the summer camp "broke down," and because both groups of boys needed food, they cooperated to pull the truck into the camp. After several such collaborative efforts, the boys once again set aside their intergroup antagonisms and essentially merged into one group.

Sherif's (1966) field experiments have served as powerful illustrations of how intergroup conflict can arise and how it can be ended. Rather like the prison simulation of Zimbardo (2007), which demonstrated that psychological normal citizens can become aggressive and harmful when placed in a social role that "demands" such behavior, Sherif's field experiment points to possible, rather than inevitable, narratives and storylines followed in conflict situations. Attempts to replicate Sherif's summer camp experiment (e.g., Diab, 1970) and Zimbardo's prison simulation (e.g., Reicher & Haslam, 2006) have not been successful—but in these cases the emphasis on replication is misleading. Sherif and Zimbardo pointed to the destructive path that could, but not necessarily will, be taken in certain contexts.

COMPETITION FOR SCARCE RESOURCES: EVOLUTIONARY THEORY

Since the publication of Darwin's (1809–1882) revolutionary work *On the Origin of Species by Means of Natural Selection* (1859/1993), *evolutionary theory* has, in different ways, been influential in assessing and interpreting intergroup relations. In the late 19th and early 20th centuries, before the genetic research of Gregor Mendel (1822–1884) became widely known, evolutionary ideas were used by so-called social Darwinists to justify group-based inequalities and a picture of society as hierarchically arranged through a struggle for existence (see Moghaddam, 2005a, chap. 19). The unit of analysis was taken to be the individual, and it was assumed that although there is some variation within racial groups, there is far greater variation between racial groups, such as between Whites and Blacks. According to this thinking, some groups are "naturally superior," and that is why, for example, "the sun never sets on the British Empire."

Breakthroughs in genetic research brought about a fundamental shift over the course of the 20th century, from a focus on the individual to the gene as the basic unit of analysis (best exemplified by Dawkins, 1989). As Allen and Chagnon (2004) put it,

> The new biological theory persuasively argued that all social interactions had potential reproductive consequences. . . . Favoring and disfavoring neighbors in social interactions had reproductive implications because it could potentially be a way to spread your own genes, a radical new twist to Darwinian theory. (p. 40)

According to this "selfish gene" view, genes use persons as convenient vehicles so that "winning" genes get passed on and survive across human generations. Given that the main theme of evolution is competition between genes, it is implied that humans who carry similar genes will—influenced by a "whispering within"—be more prone to cooperate with one another, and those who have dissimilar genes will compete and fight.

This evolutionary perspective has become highly influential in the explanation of social behavior, generally, and intergroup conflict, specifically (e.g., Schaller, Simpson, & Kenrick, 2006). In a seminal volume in this tradition, Van den Berghe (1987) articulated the approach in this way:

> Ethnic and racial sentiments are extensions of kinship sentiments. . . .
> There exists a general behavioral predisposition, in our species as in many others, to react favorably toward other organisms related to the actor. The closer the relationship is, the stronger the preferential behavior. (pp. 18–19)

The pattern of intergroup aggression evident in Bosnia, Sudan, and other regions in the early 21st century involving the killing of outgroup males and the raping of outgroup females is interpreted as fitting this so-called selfish-gene pattern. It is argued that groups who enjoy greater power will use their influence to monopolize access to females and thus gain greater reproductive success. For example, Chagnon (1997) discussed two relatively powerful villages among the Yanomamo, inhabitants of jungles in southern Venezuela and Northern Brazil, in this way:

> Both groups had frequently taken advantage of their relatively large sizes to coerce smaller groups around them, getting more women from them than they return in marriage alliances. There are, as a consequence, many women in both groups who have either been forcibly abducted from weaker neighbors or coerced from them by hard bargaining in putatively friendly alliances. Both groups have large numbers of . . . men who have killed other men. (p. 210)

IMPLICATIONS OF MATERIALIST THEORIES FOR DEMOCRACY

The materialist theories have profound implications for democracy. On the one hand, the materialist theories view the outcomes of democratic practices (e.g., election results) as determined by material conditions. The basic idea is that those who control the resources can, to a large extent, determine the outcomes of elections. For example, the candidates who can raise the greatest "election war chests" (i.e., by collecting money from supporters or using multimillion dollar contributions from friends, family members, and themselves) are most likely to win presidential elections in the United States. On the other hand, from a materialist perspective, those who gain power through democratic practices also control resource allocation and decide who gets the money. For example, by becoming the President of the United States, it is possible to influence, in important ways, how government resources are allocated between competing groups, such as military contractors, religious organizations, low-income workers, and so on. In the language of justice research (Tyler & Huo, 2002), materialist theories view both *procedural justice* (i.e., the processes through which resources are allocated) and *distributive justice* (i.e., the end result of the resource allocation process) as largely shaped by material factors.

Material Resources Determine Outcomes of Democratic Practices

Why are presidential candidates in the United States (and, increasingly, other Western democracies) so highly focused on fundraising? Materialist theorists would argue that the reason is clear: Candidates who gain access to the largest election war chests also have the greatest possibility of influencing election outcomes. Those who have access to fewer resources are less influential and less successful in elections.

However, an objection could be raised given that in democracies it is the voters who decide election results, and at the voting booth the vote of a poor person counts as much as the vote of a rich person. We need to step back and ask ourselves these questions: How equal are the rich and poor as voters? Is this another case of some people being more equal than others? For example, if "Joe" works for a corporation owned by "Dorothy," rents a house owned by Dorothy's husband, and owes money to a bank presided over by Dorothy's uncle, can Joe and Dorothy enjoy equal democratic rights? Well, they do enjoy equal rights in the sense that they each have one vote to cast in political elections, but there are enormous differences in how much influence Joe and Dorothy enjoy in how voting decisions are made in the country, in how elected officials legislate, and so on. System justification theory (Jost & Banaji, 1994) is the modern theory with the most direct implications here: Greater group-based inequalities mean that dominant groups can more effectively manufacture and propagate an ideology that furthers their own interests and thwarts genuine democracy.

If material conditions shape social relationships and consciousness, as the materialist theories influenced by Marx (e.g., Marx, 1852/1979; Marx & Engels, 1848/1967) claim, then those who control resources have tremendous influence on how voters think and act. Through the control of resources, the rich can shape discussions, create controversies, manufacture discontent or satisfaction over issues, and make or break candidates. From this perspective, psychological functioning is dependent on and shaped by material conditions.

Other materialist theories, particularly resource mobilization theory (McCarthy & Zald, 1977), also endorse the view that extreme group-based resource inequalities, characteristic of 21st-century United States (and, increasingly, the United Kingdom), lessen the quality of democracy. This is because those who monopolize resources can create social causes and social movements, similar to the situation in the marketplace in which those with enough resources can create new fashions and fads to increase product sales. Just as we suddenly find every child yearning to buy more and more "Live Strong" wristbands or the latest hard-to-find computer games, a "need" is created and made popular in association with certain causes, such as the need to end the inheritance tax (repackaged as the "death tax" by the Republican Party under the leadership of President George W. Bush).

Election Winners Control Resources

A number of the materialist theories, from classic elite theory (Pareto, 1935) to modern evolutionary-based approaches (e.g., social dominance theory; Sidanius & Pratto, 1999), point to what seems to be the rigidity, continuity, and universality of group-based inequalities. All major societies are stratified and characterized by inequalities in material resources. From a materialist perspective, the situation in democracies is no different in terms of the prevalence of group-based inequalities. Those who enjoy superior access to resources win elections in democracies, and by winning elections they ensure continuity in superior access to resources. The most we can do to support democratic ideals is to implement policies designed to ensure that children have at least a minimal level of equality of opportunity, accepting that the playing field will never be completely level.

Materialist theories imply that group-based inequalities are more likely to be seen as fair and "democratic" when society is seen as meritocratic and open. That is, individual mobility should be seen to be possible. There is a strong tradition in materialist theories, influenced by Marx (e.g., Marx, 1852/ 1979; Marx & Engels, 1848/1967), to give importance to the subjective, perceived nature of mobility: It is not how many people actually make their way up to the top but how the tokens who make it to the top are perceived.

The five-stage model (D. M. Taylor & McKirnan, 1984) gives particular importance to how those who are allowed to move up from the lower strata to join the elite group become the strongest supporters of the sociopolitical system: They not only symbolize that the system works but function as spokespersons in favor of the system. And here we get to another vital link between the materialist theories and democracy: Democratic procedures can provide avenues for social mobility so that the likes of Ronald Reagan and Bill Clinton, who came from middle class families but made it to the White House, can serve as symbols of the openness of the sociopolitical system—even when group-based inequalities continue to increase.

The perception of meritocracy and openness is a vital feature of democracies, and it is central to the American Dream, with its associated values of self-help and individual responsibility. As we shall see in Part III (i.e., chaps. 7 and 8, this volume), at the heart of the American experience of managing diversity is the assumption that anybody can make it in America. This assumption keeps the spotlight on individual mobility and personal aspirations and overlooks group-based inequalities that make American society a very uneven playing field.

5

IDENTITY: FROM SOCIAL IDENTITY THEORY TO OPTIMAL DISTINCTIVENESS THEORY

Identity has become the dominant theme in intergroup relations since the late 20th century. In both academic research and public discourse, locally and globally, identity is now the main theme of discussions on collective life, diversity, and multiculturalism. Of course, the term *identity* has been ascribed very different meanings by different authors (a point made by several observers; e.g., Breakwell, 1986, p. 10). My aim here is not to review the range of definitions or the various attempts to clarify differences between terms such as *identity* and *self* (for a related discussion, see Harré, 1984) but only to note the enormous diversity of perspectives on *identity* (see Ashmore & Jussim, 1997; du Gay, Evans, & Redman, 2000; Hoover, 2004; Tesser, Felson, & Suls, 2000). In the present discussion, by *identity* I mean what sort of person a human being believes him- or herself to be. My approach to understanding identity is to focus on the self-reflective tendencies of humans.

Identity is made possible by a theory a person holds that answers the question "What sort of person am I?" The link with groups arises because in almost all cases people respond to the question "What sort of person am I?"

by referring to memberships in groups and providing information such as "I am a liberated female," "I am a Christian," "I am an active member of the football club," "I am a Muslim," "I am a serious student," "I am a patriotic American," "I am a peace-loving Canadian," "I am a conservative Englishman," "I am a White conservative," "I am a Jew," "I am a devoted family member," and so on.

The particular group memberships given priority by individuals in describing themselves depend on distinctiveness in context; the more distinctive a characteristic, the more likely it will be cited. For example, an African American is more likely to give priority to describing him- or herself as an African American if he or she is in a predominantly White school, and a female is more likely to describe herself by first referring to gender if she is in a male-dominated law firm (McGuire & McGuire, 1981).

Identity not only is based on information but also involves emotions, often very strongly experienced ones. For example, membership in a national group (e.g., "I am American") can be associated with patriotism and a strong sense of pride (e.g., "America is the sole superpower"), but it might also be associated with an emotion such as embarrassment (e.g., "What a mess we made at Abu Ghraib prison in Iraq").

EXPLAINING THE NEW FOCUS ON IDENTITY

The new focus on identity, reflected in the enormous literature on the self and identity (see the review in Moghaddam, 2005a, chap. 14) is due to a number of factors, three of which are discussed in the sections that follow.

Globalization and Identity

Consider the following two cases:

Case 1
   "Ahmed" is a 30-year-old Indian father of three children and is married to one of his relatives who lived in a neighboring village. Ahmed lives in the same village where he was born, surrounded by his extended family and 2,000 other villagers who are mostly familiar to him. Ahmed has rarely left the village for more than a week, and he will probably live on the same plot of land, first acquired by his great grandfather, for the rest of his life.

Case 2
   "Krishno" is a 36-year-old father of three. His family is Indian, but he was born in Kenya and lived the early years of his life in Bahrain, where his family set up as traders. When he was a teenager, Krishno moved with his family to Canada and then to the United States, where he went to college. When Krishno was working in New Jersey, he met and mar-

ried "Chandra" and then moved with her to California, where they now live with their children.

In Case 1, Ahmed is surrounded by people who have known him all of his life. He is seldom meeting people who do not know him and his family. He rarely has to explain who he is and where he comes from. The issue of identity is not often raised in his everyday social interactions. In Case 2, however, geographical mobility and life in major urban centers means that Krishno is often meeting people who ask questions about his identity, such as "Where do you come from?" "What kinds of traditions do your people follow?" and "Who do you identify with? Do you think of yourself as American or Indian or something else?"

Globalization and the vast movement of people, goods, and services around the world is leading to greater contact between individuals from groups that had rarely come into contact before (see the readings about globalization and different cultural groups in Spindler & Stockard, 2007). For example, 500 years ago people from India did not have contact with North Americans, but in the 21st century, such contact is now commonplace. Increased intergroup contact is leading to a greater focus on identity, as individuals from different groups present themselves to one another and explain "the kinds of persons they are."

Mass Media and Identity

Just as new questions are raised about identity when people move from place to place and interact with "strangers," particularly outgroup members, such questions are also raised through the influence of the global mass media. Ahmed has lived in the same village all of his life, but now the village has television, bringing images of the consumer life he could enjoy, the many places he could visit, and the countless alternative life narratives he could follow. The mass media presents new possibilities and raises questions for Ahmed: What kind of a person could he (and his children) become, given all the choices out there—choices he never knew existed?

Central to the influence of the mass media is advertising, which changes our ideas about the goods and services we need to live the kind of life we now desire. Ahmed used to walk everywhere, as his ancestors had always done in his village. However, advertising changed his ideas so that he came to see it as essential that he have a bicycle, and now he would like one day to have a motorbike and perhaps even a van. How could a farmer like him live without a van? His ideas changed about the sorts of things that are essential to his identity—just as advertising and "choice" in the West change our ideas about what we need: "An American now enjoys a choice of 50,000 food products, compared with only 100 as many a [sic] centuries ago" (N. Myers & Kent, 2004, p. 123).

Minority Mobilization

Other reasons for the increased salience of identity are efforts at collective mobilization by various minority groups in both Western and non-Western societies, particularly those based on ethnicity. There are sharply differing views as to why ethnicity is proving to be so potent in mobilizing people. On the one hand, ethnicity is seen to be "in our blood" and fixed (Worchel, 1999); on the other hand, ethnicity is viewed as flexible, "a mode of identification, not a categorical identity" (Jowitt, 2001, p. 27). Irrespective of these differences, there is general agreement that the ethnic mobilization often associated with intergroup conflict is global, for example, as reflected by ethnopolitical conflict in different parts of the world (Chirot & Seligman, 2001).

Rather than diminish ethnic allegiances, modernization has, in many cases, led to increased ethnic mobilization. The case of China is particularly instructive because of its rapid economic growth—about 10% per annum in the 1st decade of the 21st century—and rapid urbanization. Advertising in China is now nationwide: "China now has an extensive network of television stations and a proliferation of cable and satellite services, resulting in a TV-based 90% market penetration rate in urban households" (N. Myers & Kent, 2004, p. 114). However, the emergence of one large consumer market in China has not melted away local allegiances; indeed, in an insightful assessment of identity in China, Gladney (2007) concluded the exact opposite: "China is now seeing a resurgence of local nationality and culture, most notably among southerners such as the Cantonese and Hakka" (p. 54).

In Western societies, in addition to various ethnic movements (involving Blacks, Latinos, etc.), since the 1960s there have been collective movements based on reconstructed identities, such as feminine identity and gay male and lesbian identity. The emphasis of these groups has been on their collective rights, and the demand for collective rights has been associated with a reconstruction of collective identity. For example, the feminist movement has involved women defining themselves in new, positive ways (Moghaddam, 2005a, chap. 17). The struggle to reconstruct minority-group identities reflects what seem to be certain basic "identity needs," and these are addressed particularly in *social identity theory* (Tajfel & Turner, 1979, 1986).

SOCIAL IDENTITY THEORY

> There is a powerful trend, to be seen virtually all over the world, aiming at the preservation or the achievement of diversity, of one's own special characteristics and "identity." (Tajfel, 1978a, p. 2)

The emergence and widespread international influence of social identity theory (Tajfel & Turner, 1979, 1986; see readings in Postmes & Jetten,

2006; Worchel, Morales, Páez, & Deschamps, 1998) is best understood in the context of two wider movements that gained momentum from the late 1960s. The first is the movement among various groups (e.g., women, ethnic minorities, gay men and lesbians), within and across nations, to reconstruct their identities. This movement highlighted group mobilization and group identities, presenting researchers the challenge of explaining new collective movements. A second movement that influenced social identity theory involved the research effort to achieve nonreductionist explanations of social behavior and societal trends (see readings in Israel & Tajfel, 1972). Intergroup conflict, war, genocide, and other such problems were to be explained by researching contexts and the characteristics of collective life rather than the characteristics of individual personalities.

The roots of social identity theory are found in Tajfel's (e.g., Tajfel & Wilkes, 1963) earlier research, evolving out of the "new look" cognitive approach of the 1950s (G. A. Miller, Galanter, & Pribram, 1960) on the categorization of nonsocial stimuli (discussed in chap. 2, this volume). Tajfel postulated, and research eventually corroborated, that categorization leads to minimization of differences within groups and exaggeration of differences between groups. Given that the "mere" categorization of nonsocial stimuli led to such dramatic consequences, what would be the consequence(s) of the categorization of social stimuli? There was already some research evidence suggesting that even the arbitrary assignment of individuals to social categories (Rabbie & Horwitz, 1969) and the mere awareness of the presence of another group (Sherif, 1966) could lead to ingroup favoritism. However, Tajfel's group was the first to systematically strip away all the usual characteristics of group affiliation (e.g., familiarity, leadership, similarity, common goals) to test the influence of mere social categorization that individuals assigned to a "minimal category."

Tajfel and his research associates developed what became known as the *minimal group paradigm* (see D. M. Taylor & Moghaddam, 1994, chap. 4), a laboratory experimental procedure designed to place individuals in groups that have as little significance as possible for those assigned to a group. In the first part of the experiment, participants would carry out a trivial task such as estimating the number of dots flashed on a screen. The participants would then be given feedback telling them that they have been placed in one of two groups—Group X or Group Y—based on their response on the trivial task. Next, the participants were asked to allocate points to the members of Groups X and Y, using a number of matrices designed to identify different trends in point allocation (such as bias in favor of the ingroup or outgroup, maximum joint profit, and maximum differentiation).

The key features of the minimal group paradigm experimental situation are as follows: (a) participants do not know the identities of those in the ingroup or the outgroup; (b) participants have not had, and do not expect to have, contact with the members of the ingroup or the outgroup; (c) participants will not receive any of the points they allocate; (d) the basis for Groups X and Y is a trivial task, selected to be "minimal"; (e) the basis for social categorization is not linked to the points to be allocated; and (f) a variety of different strategies, including fair and discriminatory options, are available to make allocations. The first laboratory experiments using this procedure established that even social categorization on the basis of a minimal criterion can lead to bias in favor of the ingroup (Tajfel, 1970; Tajfel, Flament, Billig, & Bundy, 1971), a finding that has proved robust (D. M. Taylor & Moghaddam, 1994, chap. 4).

Early interpretations of findings from the minimal group paradigm assumed a "generic norm" of ethnocentrism (see Tajfel et al., 1971), a trend already highlighted through cross-cultural studies (LeVine & Campbell, 1972). However, by the mid 1970s Tajfel and his colleagues had moved toward a more sophisticated account of intergroup relations, generally, and findings from the minimal group paradigm, specifically. This new account became known as social identity theory (Tajfel & Turner, 1979, 1986) and has proved to be enormously successful in stimulating research (R. J. Brown, 2000; Ellemers, Spears, & Doosje, 1999; Postmes & Jetten, 2006).

Five Basic Tenets of Social Identity Theory

A major reason for the considerable international influence of social identity theory (Tajfel & Turner, 1979, 1986; see readings in Worchel et al., 1998) is that the theory leaves room for cultural variations (Moghaddam, 2006c) but at the same time presents substantial and specific postulates.

Identity Motivation

The starting premise of social identity theory (Tajfel & Turner, 1979, 1986) is that individuals are motivated to achieve a positive and distinct identity. On the one hand, this is a universalist claim because it assumes all humans are motivated in this same way. On the other hand, this claim leaves ample room for cultural variations to play a role because the theory does not specify the criteria according to which a positive and distinct identity will be sought.

The minimal group paradigm (Tajfel et al., 1971) provides strong evidence that just about any criterion for social categorization can be used by group members to construct a positive and distinct identity for themselves. How one estimates dots that are flashed on a screen, how one sees ambiguous colors on slides, and what one's preferences are for different abstract paintings are among a wide range of criteria shown to serve as a basis for intergroup bias and differentiation. Indeed, when there is only one criterion for social categorization, a criterion that is considered trivial in a real-world context can have the same influence on intergroup relations as a criterion that is considered important (Moghaddam & Stringer, 1986).

Of course, it is not the objective importance and meaning of criteria for categorization but the cultural meaning that is influential in intergroup relations. Certain criteria become carriers, serving to give meaning to and propagate the significance of intergroup differences (Moghaddam, 2002). Consider, for example, the use of skin color to categorize people: On an objective basis, there is no reason why skin color should be a more important criterion for social categorization than something like height or ear length—and indeed, there is evidence that in some societies height and ear length have served as more important criteria than skin color (see chap. 2, this volume). The plasticity of the basis for social categorization implies that those with the greatest power can manufacture and ascribe meaning to intergroup differences in ways that serve their own interests (see the related discussion on Veblen, 1899/1953, in chap. 2, this volume).

Centrality of Social Identity

Imagine you are attending a job interview and introducing yourself to some potential new colleagues. Typically, they would want to know your name, your training, where you previously worked and lived, and perhaps something about your interests. As you present yourself, you are hoping that your potential new colleagues gain a positive impression of you. For example, when you tell them that as part of your training you took courses in psychology, you hope they will say something like, "That will be very useful in this organization!" (rather than "Oh, what a waste of time!"). When they learn where you went to school, you hope they will say, "That's a very good school" (rather than "That's too bad!").

Social identity theory (Tajfel & Turner, 1979, 1986) postulates that the need for a positive and distinct identity will lead individuals to want to belong to groups (e.g., a professional group, a school, a sports team; see Baumeister & Leary, 1995, for a review of research on the "need to belong") that enable their members to fulfill their identity needs. The theory gives highest importance to group memberships and defines *social identity* as "that part of an individual's self-concept which derives from his knowledge of his membership in a social group (or groups) together with the value and emotional significance attached to that membership" (Tajfel, 1978b, p. 63).

Social identity theory allows room for cultural variation in how many groups a person belongs to and how strong the individual's emotional attachments are to these groups. Related to this is the distinction between *monogroup societies*, in which "membership in one group dominates life and fundamentally influences the behavior of all or most individuals in that society in all domains" (Moghaddam, 2006c, p. 160) and *multigroup societies*, in which "the influence of membership in many different groups with diverse characteristics has different levels of influence on the behavior of different individuals" (p. 160). Examples of monogroup societies are Saudi Arabia and the Islamic Republic of Iran, where government policies have created a situation in which religious affiliation is the most important group membership and one that influences all other aspects of individual and collective life. Western countries are closer to being multigroup societies, although there are exceptions. For example, Quebec, Canada, could be argued to be closer to a monogroup society because affiliation as a French or an English Canadian dominates and influences behavior in most domains.

Democracies tend to be multigroup societies, and political parties in democracies face the challenge of attracting support from groups with widely different identities and priorities. This task is made easier if a political party can appeal to a common core set of values that can attract and mobilize a large number of different groups. For example, at the turn of the 21st century the Republican Party of the United States managed to harness the energy and support of many different groups through an appeal to what it termed *core Christian values*. In this sense, national political parties attempt to influence voters to act as if they are in monogroup rather than multigroup societies.

Assessing Social Identity Through Social Comparisons

We come to understand our own situations by comparing ourselves with others: The centrality of social comparisons in our everyday lives has been a theme of research for over half a century (Festinger, 1954). However, it is not just as individuals that we make social comparisons; it is also as group members. The nature of the social comparisons we make are influenced by both our perceptions of our group memberships (see readings in Abrams & Hogg, 1999) and the particular group goals we adopt (D. M. Taylor, Moghaddam, & Bellerose, 1989). For example, when we see ourselves as a member of a disadvantaged group and our goal is to make demands for change and better treatment for our group, then we are inclined to compare ourselves with "better off" groups and to highlight our relative deprivation (D. M. Taylor et al., 1989). We declare, "Look at the members of that other group! They do the same work as us but enjoy higher wages and better working conditions. That's not fair!"

Women and ethnic minorities have used this strategy of making upward social comparisons, particularly since the 1960s. However, notice that in order for this strategy to be effective, others have to agree that the minority group making the upward comparison has the right to do so. For example, today, in the early part of the 21st century, when women sales personnel compare their salaries with those of men doing the same job, this is accepted as legitimate, whereas in the early part of the 20th century, such a comparison would have been seen by most people as unjustifiable. A century ago in Western societies, and even now in many traditional societies, women were not seen to have the right to compare themselves with men.

Because social comparison processes have such a powerful influence in intergroup relations, the ability to influence social comparison targets is of the highest importance. This ability is part of the enormous advantage enjoyed by those who control resources and the media, as suggested, in particular, by system justification theory (Jost & Banaji, 1994), and Marx (1852/1979; Marx & Engels, 1848/1967) and Pareto (1935) before that. To mobilize a minority group, leaders must persuade minority group members that their rights are being violated and it is legitimate for them to compare their situation upward with those who enjoy these rights (Moghaddam, 2004). For example, in 2006 the federally mandated minimum wage in the United States was such that those who worked full time but earned minimum wage were still living below the poverty line. However, the mainstream American media has neglected the tens of millions of people living below the official poverty line and has implicitly treated them as a group outside the range of social comparison.

Availability of Cognitive Alternatives

Group members who are satisfied with their social identity will attempt to preserve the status quo or to improve their situation. Far more interesting, theoretically, are group members who are dissatisfied with their social identity, and the thoughts and actions of this group are the main focus of social identity theory (Tajfel & Turner, 1979, 1986). Tajfel and Turner postulated that the strategies that these "dissatisfied" minority group members adopt depend on whether they perceive the present situation to be (a) stable and (b) legitimate.

Once again, social identity theory points to the importance of the normative system dominant in society and to the kinds of system justification ideologies highlighted by more recent theories (Jost & Banaji, 1994). What factors influence the extent to which people see a social system as legitimate and stable? The influence of authority figures is highly important (e.g., as suggested by the research of Milgram, 1974, on obedience to authority; see also Moghaddam, 2005a, chap. 16), as is the role of the media, in shaping norms that regulate everyday lives (Moghaddam, 2005a, chap. 15).

An interesting similarity between the United States and Islamic societies is the high power and influence of religious leaders, compared with lower religious influence in most of Europe, Canada, and Australia. A Marxist interpretation, based on the idea that religion serves as the opium of the people, is that as the largest capitalist nation, the United States "needs" religion to maintain stability by persuading the masses that American society is fair. An alternative interpretation is that the United States was founded by pilgrims escaping religious persecution and has always had a tradition of high religiosity (for alternative interpretations for societal differences in religiosity, see Pippa & Ingelhart, 2005).

Social identity theory leaves room for cultural variations in the factors that influence group members to perceive society to different degrees as stable and legitimate. In some societies religious leaders can influence perceptions, in other societies scientists and writers have more influence, and it may be that at a global level movie stars and pop musicians are also gaining influence. Alternatively, materialist theories would contend that underlying all these different sources of influence there is a common factor: Those who control resources can mobilize religious, political, and pop-culture movements to influence how legitimate and stable people see the world.

Strategies for Improving Social Identity

Social identity theory (Tajfel & Turner, 1979, 1986) postulates that minority group members who perceive their social identity to be inadequate have a variety of options for trying to improve their situation, ranging from normative individualistic options to nonnormative collective options. Individualistic strategies include making intragroup comparisons (e.g., ethnic minority members comparing themselves only with other ethnic minorities), giving priority to trying to move up individually to a higher status group (e.g., a woman becoming the first partner at her law firm), and redefining ingroup characteristics as positive (e.g., "Black is beautiful"). Such individualistic strategies are normative, in the sense that they do not alter the intergroup balance of power. Indeed, those individuals who manage to climb up and join an advantaged group tend to be strong supporters of the system (as predicted by the five-stage model discussed in chap. 4, this volume; see also D. M. Taylor & McKirnan, 1984).

In contrast, collective options tend to be nonnormative, in the sense that they do alter the intergroup balance of power. The strategy with the most serious consequences for the sociopolitical system is *direct challenge*, whereby a minority group directly challenges the majority group and attempts to change intergroup power relations. It is in the interests of majority groups to direct minority group members toward individualistic strategies and away from collective strategies. Ideologies that endorse individualism, self-help, and personal responsibility serve such a system justification purpose.

Culture plays a central role in the strategies preferred by minority group members who experience inadequate social identity. For example, in the United States, the American Dream ideology upholds a picture of American society that is open and presents every talented and hard-working person opportunities for success. The American Dream suggests that everyone can make it, and if anyone does not make it, it is because of their own personal inadequacies. In this cultural context, people are taught to give priority to individual responsibility, self-help, and personal effort. There is far less emphasis on getting ahead as a group member.

Collective Identity Model

We should not leave this discussion of social identity without confronting the thorny puzzle of how personal and collective identity evolves in the developing child, a question that is not addressed by social identity theory (Tajfel & Turner, 1979, 1986) but has been tackled in D. M. Taylor's (2002) *collective identity model*. The traditional view is that self-identity and self-esteem are primary, and as the child grows, there later evolve collective identity and collective esteem. Social identity theory seems to accept this traditional view by describing social identity as a component of personal identity. However, D. M. Taylor (2002) turned this picture of the world on its head and argued that collective identity "is rationally and psychologically primary" (p. 41), and that "without a collective identity, the individual has no clearly established template upon which to articulate a personal identity or personal self-esteem" (p. 40). According to D. M. Taylor, a major reason for the poor academic performance and low motivation of minority group students is the lack of healthy collective identity among these groups, resulting in collective demotivation (see D. M. Taylor, 2002, chap. 7). However, if we adopt D. M. Taylor's model, a fundamental challenge remains: How does the infant become aware of collective identity? Are we expected to believe that, for example, an infant born into an ethnic minority family becomes aware of ethnic identity prior to self-identity?

A possible solution is provided through debates concerning *intersubjectivity* (i.e,. how infants come to know other minds) and *interobjectivity* (i.e, how individuals come to know social reality as objectified by their group culture; Moghaddam, 2003). A novel answer to the puzzle of intersubjectivity is that infants come to know other minds through the objectifications of their cultural group (i.e, through interobjectivity). It is not that infants become aware of their ethnic and other group memberships but that they come to know the world through the socially constructed world of their culture, which comes to represent for them objective reality. This includes narratives of how they are different from others, collectively and individually.

DISTINCTIVENESS THEME

Social identity theory (Tajfel & Turner, 1979, 1986) posits a need for a distinct as well as a positive identity. The idea of a need for distinctiveness has been explored very creatively by research programs led by Gerard Lemaine in France, Marilyn Brewer in the United States, and John Turner in England and Australia. In a study involving children in summer camps, Lemaine, Kastersztein, and Personnaz (1978) created situations in which two groups of children competed in a hut-building contest. The characteristics of the two groups were very similar, except that one group was disadvantaged in the resources it had available to build a hut. The disadvantaged group first "closed their frontiers" to try to prevent the advantaged group from realizing their plan of action; then they set out to differentiate and score points in alternative ways such as creating a garden behind the hut. In another study, students wrote job applications, competing against other applicants who either were similar to them or enjoyed advantages, such as being from a more prestigious academic institution, on some criteria relevant to the application. Students competing against advantaged applicants wrote letters in which they differentiated between themselves and their competitors. They did this by highlighting those characteristics, such as experience, that set them apart and by introducing alternative criteria that could not be easily used to evaluate them comparatively.

Identity needs have evolutionary functions (discussed in greater detail later in this chapter), their immediate source being social demands of particular cultural groups. Of course, cultural systems influence the particular ways in which identity needs are manifested. For example, a need for positive social identity may lead a woman to position herself as a "liberated feminist" in Culture A, but the same need may lead a woman to position herself as a "traditional homemaker" in Culture B. Such surface cultural differences, however, should not distract us from the deeper similarity in evolved needs (see the related response of Sedikides, Gaertner, & Vevea, 2005, to Heine, 2005).

Whereas Lemaine explored the behavioral strategies adopted by group members to differentiate between the ingroup and the outgroup to maintain a positive social identity, I now turn to research programs that have focused more on cognitive strategies.

SELF-CATEGORIZATION THEORY, OPTIMAL DISTINCTIVENESS THEORY, AND THE COMMON INGROUP IDENTITY MODEL

> Cognitive representations of the self take the form of self-categorizations, in which the self and certain stimuli are cognitively grouped as identical in contrast to some other group of stimuli. Self-categorizations vary in their level of inclusiveness and are organized hierarchically. (J. C. Turner, Reynolds, Haslam, & Veenstra, 2006, pp. 13–14)

> Social identity is driven by two opposing social motives—the need for inclusion and the need for differentiation." (Brewer & Gaertner, 2004, p. 307)

> The development of a common ingroup identity does not necessarily require each group to forsake its less inclusive group identity completely. (Gaertner & Dovidio, 2005, p. 629)

Implicit in social identity theory (Tajfel & Turner, 1979, 1986) is a tension between personal identity and social identity of individuals who emphasize their personal characteristics and stand outside of groups as opposed to those who want to "belong" and to be accepted as group members. Of course, this tension is pervasive in much of 21st-century life: Consider, for example, advertising that makes me feel unique and special when I buy Product X at the same time that I know (if I stop to think about it) that millions of others are also using Product X and are, in this respect, exactly like me. Two research programs that have addressed this personal–group tension emerge out of *self-categorization theory* (J. C. Turner et al., 1987, 2006; Turner & Oakes, 1989; J. C. Turner & Onotaro, 1999) and *optimal distinctiveness theory* (Brewer, 1991; Brewer & Gaertner, 2004; Brewer & Gardner, 1996; Brewer & Roccas, 2001).

Self-categorization theory has its roots in J. C. Turner's (1982) earlier explorations of the personal identity–social identity tension as related to social identity theory developments, but it has evolved to encompass the self and personality more broadly (J. C. Turner et al., 2006). It is proposed that self-categorization is an infinitely malleable, dynamic cognitive strategy through which the self can be categorized in contrast to many different entities—such as other individuals within a group—or as part of an ingroup that stands in contrast with outgroups, which can be as large as "society" or even "humanity." Self-categorization is a continuous process, changing with variations in context and frames of reference (in terms of fluidity, it is somewhat akin to the "psychological field" in Gestalt psychology; Ellis, 1959). However, inherent in self-categorization processes is a tension between personal identity and social identity, of standing apart and merging in, so that "in general the more salient is personal identity the less salient will social identity *tend* to be and *vice versa*" (J. C. Turner et al., 2006, p. 15).

Whereas self-categorization theory highlights the inhibition of certain aspects of personal identity in order for a person to join a group and achieve an adequate social identity, Brewer's (1991) optimal distinctiveness theory focuses more directly on the cognitive strategies that can be used to balance "standing outside of" and "belonging to" groups. Brewer proposed that both the need for inclusion (i.e., belonging to groups) and the need for distinctiveness (i.e., standing outside of groups as a distinct individual) can be satisfied by a person identifying with the ingroup (to arrive at a sense of inclusion) and making social comparisons between the ingroup and outgroup or outgroups (to arrive at a sense of distinctiveness). Thus, Brewer's theory focuses on the balance achieved through varying the strength of identification with an ingroup and the strength of differentiation between an ingroup and outgroups.

Extensions of the basic optimal distinctiveness theory argument suggest that the balancing of inclusion needs and distinctiveness needs can also be met in other ways. For example, instead of relying on intergroup social comparisons to achieve a sense of differentiation and distinctiveness, an individual could identify with a subgroup within the ingroup and compare the subgroup with other subgroups within the ingroup. Or, the individual could perceive the self as the most representative or the most distinct in the ingroup (the *primus inter pares*, "first among equals" effect; see Hornsey & Jetten, 2004; Pickett & Leonardelli, 2006).

The issue of inclusion versus exclusion is also central to the *common ingroup identity model* (Gaertner & Dovidio, 2000), which is influenced by a number of intergroup research traditions, including Sherif's (1966) concept of superordinate goals (see chap. 4, this volume) and Tajfel's minimal group studies (Tajfel et al., 1971). This model is also similar to self-categorization theory, in that it places the spotlight on the recategorization of the social world so that under certain conditions group members come to perceive themselves as belonging to subgroups encompassed by a superordinate group identity. For example, if the salience of a common ingroup identity increases (such as "We all support the same national football team"), a superordinate identity will come to dominate social relations without individuals abandoning their less inclusive group memberships (such as those based on ethnicity).

Barlow, Taylor, and Lambert (2000) argued, however, that a focus on subjective identification with a category could be misleading. Their findings demonstrate that in some cases ethnic minority members can feel that they belong to a common or superordinate group (such as "American") more than they feel majority group members view them as belonging. Conversely, in a study that assessed the mutual perceptions of both minority and majority groups in interaction, it was found that minority group members exaggerated the extent to which they were excluded by majority group members (Moghaddam, Taylor, Tchoryk-Pelletier, & Shepanek, 1994). Such intergroup perceptual biases highlight the delicacy and complexity of the task of developing common identities for minority and majority groups, while maintaining inclusion and differentiation during intergroup contact (following R. J. Brown & Hewstone, 2005).

Discussions of identity in the intergroup literature have included explicit proposals that humans have certain basic identity needs. This trend evolved particularly through the influence of social identity theory (Tajfel & Turner, 1979, 1986), which emerged out of Europe to become the most influential intergroup theory since the 1970s. Following the tradition established by Tajfel and his associates, discussions of identity in the intergroup literature have focused on social identity.

The two identity needs discussed most extensively in the intergroup literature are the proposed needs for a positive and distinct social identity. Little serious attention has been given to the question of the source of these assumed needs. Are they inherited? Are they in our genes? Are they fixed and unchanging? I argue that rather than being fixed and innate, identity needs are malleable, created by social demands, and best understood in the context of cultural evolution.

What is the evolutionary function of identity? Why should people have evolved to ask, and be concerned, about "what sort of persons" they are? The answer, I argue, is that group members who were more effective at gaining support from other group members had better survival chances. Strategies for gaining support from others include bullying and force as well as being pleasing and useful to others. If "Jane" is liked and valued by the rest of her group and "Joan" is not, the group is more likely to invest in Jane's future and make sacrifices to protect her rather than Joan. In a group of hunter–gatherers 20,000 years ago, it was first and foremost functional, just as it is today, for group members to be concerned with the question "What sort of person am I?" Far from being esoteric and existentialist, this question is practical and directly relevant to survival (related to this, evolutionary theorists have for some time acknowledged and discussed the functional value of altruism; e.g., Trivers, 1971).

Identity did not just serve individual survival functions, it also affected group survival. Socially created identity needs have served essential behavior-regulation and group-cohesion purposes. Groups that could teach their members to pay closer attention to evaluations and feedback from other group members would be better coordinated and more efficient.

In the contemporary world, children are taught to seek the approval and positive evaluation of others, first, at home (e.g., parents teaching children to be polite) and then in the formal education system, through which are applied enormous resources and formal authority to this task. This is exemplified by school examinations and the aspirations of students for higher grades and degrees (and the subsequent global inflation of grades and degrees; see Moghaddam, 1997, chaps. 3 and 5). By teaching children to aspire to be evaluated in certain ways (e.g., to want to see oneself as a "star" in school), society regulates behavior and achieves higher group cohesion. The preference that the child learns for positive evaluation from other group members, a preference clearly arising from social demands, is then interpreted by psychologists as a so-called need for a positive identity.

Just as the need for positive evaluation is functional, so is the need for distinctiveness. Children learn early in their development that they are not all able to be stars on the same criteria; their chances of achieving positive evaluations improve when they find a "vacant space" and show talent in a way that is novel in the group. Thus, they develop the ability to differentiate to maximize their chances of gaining positive attention and resources.

My analysis of the crucial role of differentiation follows directly from a line of thinking that begins with Darwin (1859/1993) and continues with Durkheim (1893/1964) and Lemaine (1974). Whereas the economist A. Smith (1776/1976) highlighted the role of specialization in increasing production, thinkers following the Darwinian tradition have emphasized the role of specialization in finding or creating vacant spaces toward improving survival chances. Of course, increasing production through specialization can also serve as a mechanism for improving survival chances, but it does not necessarily involve social creativity (this is demonstrated by research, discussed earlier in this chapter, by Lemaine and others; e.g., Lemaine et al., 1978).

IMPLICATIONS OF IDENTITY THEORIES FOR DEMOCRACY

Identity theories have profound implications for democracy, starting with the kind of socialization practices needed to develop psychological citizens capable of sustaining a thriving democratic society. As is clear from attempts to export democracy to countries such as Iraq following the American-led invasion in 2003, a mismatch between psychological citizens and democratic ideals can have disastrous consequences. What kind of a psychological citizen is required to make democracy work? In addressing this question, let us begin by clarifying that although democracy has a few core universal requirements, democracy can work in many different ways, depending on cultural conditions. There is no one ideal standard. For example, there are important differences across Western societies in how democracy works (as discussed earlier in chap. 1, this volume).

Consider when citizens ask, "What kind of a person am I?" To sustain democracy, citizens must answer that they see themselves engaged and identifying with the larger civic society and not just their family or ethnic group or religious group or some other faction of society. In social identity theory (Tajfel & Turner, 1979, 1986) terms, citizens must derive positiveness and distinctiveness in important ways from their membership in the larger society.

Self-categorization theory (J. C. Turner et al., 1987, 2006) and optimal distinctiveness theory (Brewer, 1991; Brewer & Gaertner, 2004) highlight flexibility in the ways in which the self is categorized and how identification takes place with various groups so that the person feels both a sense of belonging to groups and a sense of standing apart as a distinct individual. The challenge of socializing citizens to achieve a healthy balance is monumental and is only achieved to some degree by the major Western societies. For example, consider the fact that in the United States voter turnout steadily declined since the 19th century (Teixeira, 1992), and now, even in the most important elections, only about 50% of the voting-age population turn out to vote. A "high" voter turnout in important U.S. midterm elections, such as the one held in 2006, is about 40%.

The low voter turnout in the United States indicates a weak identification among large sections of the adult U.S. population with the democratic process, and it raises fundamentally important questions about the socialization of psychological citizens in the United States. Should voting be a duty rather than a right in democratic societies? If citizens do not consider it their duty to vote in elections, should they be obligated to vote by law (e.g., as in Australia)? I have discussed this question with Americans who often claim that making voting a duty would be "un-American," but jury participation and many other activities are interpreted as duties in the United States, why not voting? The immediate answer is, "Because Americans do not see themselves as that kind of people." However, such identities can and often do change.

Another intersection between identity theories and democracy concerns identity needs. At first glance, it may seem that the implications of identity theories for democracy are straightforward: People should enjoy equal rights to satisfy common identity needs. Thus, for example, minority group members have an equal right to achieve a positive and distinct identity. Presumably, the state has an obligation to implement policies in areas such as education, through which this democratic goal could be achieved. However, closer scrutiny suggests a more complex set of issues, particularly related to the basis of identity needs.

As discussed earlier in this chapter, identity needs arise through socialization processes. Children can be taught to satisfy identity needs by participating in an infinite variety of different tasks, from sports to academic subjects, to arts, to socializing, and so on. In contemporary societies, these different areas of activity represent very different success probabilities because of the numbers of people who can succeed in each area. For example, the number of professional basketball players in the world is far lower than the number of professional accountants, teachers, and nurses. This means that the probability of a person with average talent and motivation becoming a professional basketball player is far lower than the probability that he or she will become an accountant, teacher, or nurse. Unfortunately, in many cases ethnic minority members are socialized to identify with success stories associated with sports and entertainment rather than with middle-class professions such as nursing and teaching (associated with this are continuing inequalities in higher education; see Niemann & Maruyama, 2005).

The channeling of minority talent into nonacademic domains such as sports has had tremendous impact in all Western societies: In 2006, the champion U.S. National Basketball Association team, the French World Cup final team, and the UK track and field team were dominated by athletes of African descent. One argument is that this success in sports, as well as success in rap music and many other domains of entertainment, can help ethnic minorities achieve higher collective esteem. However, an alternative viewpoint is that such success is very limited because the number of professional athletes and musicians is miniscule.

This channeling of minority talent to sports and entertainment has been coupled with an "every child is a star" movement that has spread in the education system of North America and is now influencing countries in the European Union. By perpetuating the message that every child is a star, many hope that minority children in particular will enjoy higher self- and collective esteem (and thus achieve positive personal and social identity). However, for some time now it has been evident that minorities do not have low self-esteem (Crocker & Major, 1989) and that inflating self-esteem can lead to problematic behavior (see readings in Baumeister, 1999).

Clearly, the every child is a star movement has not resulted in improved academic performance for minorities in schools, where the achievement gap between ethnic minorities and the White majority is considerable. For example, among eighth graders in U.S. schools, about 70% of African Americans and Latinos (with a combined population of about 83 million) are below even a basic understanding of science and only about 7% have proficient or advanced understanding (Schemo, 2006). Among Whites, about 28% have below-adequate understanding and 38% have proficient or advanced understanding. Such group-based inequalities are not being overcome through positive psychology policies.

6

SUBJECTIVE JUSTICE: FROM EQUITY THEORY TO RELATIVE DEPRIVATION THEORY

See how I am going on. Dissatisfied and uncomfortable and—what would it signify to me, being coarse and common, if nobody had told me so?
—Charles Dickens (1860–1861/1963, p. 144)

Pip, the working-class central character in *Great Expectations*, became dissatisfied with his own living conditions and status when he was lured into the seductive, affluent world of an insane heiress and coaxed to fall in love with the lovely Stella. Pip gradually learned to see himself in comparison to an ideal self that he imagined he would have to achieve to win Stella. Pip's lament (as quoted above) highlights an assumption that is central to a variety of theories—including just-world theory, equity theory, and relative deprivation theory (Runciman, 1966)—that are foundationally concerned with justice and assume that subjective interpretations of the world rather than objectively defined material conditions shape thoughts, feelings, and actions. Pip would not have been so dissatisfied with his situation, and so eager for change, if the alluring Stella had not persuaded him to see himself as "coarse and common." The deprivation Pip felt was personal, and his motivation was to improve his individual situation. Part of the character development Dickens articulated involves Pip maturing to recognize and act in response to more than just his own personal feelings of deprivation.

107

When people feel deprived because of their group rather than their personal situation, they might collectively take action to try to improve the fortune of their group. This collective deprivation is highlighted in another Dickensian masterpiece *A Tale of Two Cities* (1859/1999), the story set at the time of the French revolution. When the masses in Paris finally rebelled against the French aristocracy, they were propelled by feelings of collective injustice and deprivation. The cornered aristocrat, Foulon, was confronted by the rage and fury of "the people" rather than individual discontents:

> Foulon, who told the starving people they might eat grass! . . . Give us the blood of Foulon, Give us the head of Foulon, Give us the heart of Foulon, Give us the body and soul of Foulon, Rend Foulon to pieces, and dig him into the ground, that grass may grow from him! (p. 203)

Such intense feelings of deprivation and perceptions of injustice are at the heart of social movements and intergroup conflicts.

Whereas materialist theories (discussed in chap. 4, this volume) indicate that consciousness and subjective experiences are shaped by material conditions, the justice-centered theories we consider in this chapter begin with the assumption that subjective interpretations of material conditions are the most important influences on behavior (I use the term *subjective* rather than *commonsense justice* because it better captures the idea that our behavior in the realm of justice is often irrational and not at all what we would expect from "commonsense"). There is a strong irrationalist theme in *subjective justice*, in the sense that at both the individual and the collective levels, people are not always accurate in their assessments of why they are experiencing a sense of justice or injustice. In addition, the relationship between subjective justice and actual material conditions is often shaped by factors of which, again, the person is not aware. Even when people become aware of why they feel dissatisfied, they might not be able to change their situation. For example, Pip was manipulated to change his comparison target, but it was not his choice.

Pip would have been happy with his life as a blacksmith's apprentice if he had continued to compare himself with other orphans and kept in mind his sister's constant reminders of how lucky he was to be alive: "If it warn't for me, you'd have been to the churchyard long ago, and stayed there" (Dickens, 1860–1861/1963, p. 16). However, Pip's infatuation with Stella changed his comparison targets and made it impossible for him to be happy with himself and his situation as it was. Similarly, in *A Tale of Two Cities*, Dickens (1859/1999) described how working French people came to collectively see their situation as unjust and unbearable, in part because they saw it as legitimate to compare their own situation with that of their "masters."

However, it could be argued that the French Revolution is an example of a rare event in the course of human history, that is, one in which people collectively rebel and bring down a social system they see as unjust. From this perspective, emphasis is placed on the norm for people to conform and obey rather than to rebel and overturn the social order. Workers put up with boring jobs and low wages while their bosses amass fortunes; citizens fail to vote against their "elected representatives," even though "their" representatives routinely fail to deliver on election promises; ethnic minorities continue to put up with lower quality educational and health services in their neighborhoods, even though when it comes to serving their country, they are put in the front lines to fight in bloody wars. Even when the injustices are highly visible, such as the restoration of apartheid schooling in America (Kozol, 2005), conformity prevails. Justice theories provide intriguing explanations for these trends.

THE JUSTICE MOTIVE: JUST-WORLD THEORY

One line of explanation for why people put up with injustices is that they remain blind to them; in essence, people interpret the world as just. Lerner (1980) proposed a "need" for people to believe in a just world. For example, in a seminal study, both the tendency to try to help a victim when it seemed help would be effective and the tendency to blame the victim if her suffering could not be ended were explained by reference to a need to see the world as just (Lerner & Simmons, 1966). An extensive, if unsystematic, collection of research literature has shown that people tend to adopt a variety of strategies, such as "blaming the victim," to interpret the misfortune of others in a way that maintains the view that the world is just (Furnham, 2003; Hafer & Bègue, 2005). Whether the victims suffer rape, robbery, a natural disaster, or some other misfortune, their plight tends to be interpreted as somehow being "their own fault."

The ideological and societal implications of this *justice motive* (Lerner, 1980) has been integrated into the formulations of a variety of theories, particularly system justification theory (Jost & Banaji, 1994; see also chap. 5, this volume). When disadvantaged group members are motivated to interpret the world as just, they are less likely to take action against, or even to recognize, group-based inequalities. Whereas system justification theory and other ideological discussions of intergroup relations (e.g., Billig, 1976) focus on false consciousness, Lerner (1980) and others have developed alternative explanations of perceived justice.

From among these alternatives (see the discussion "Is the desire for justice reducible to other motives?" in Hafer & Bègue, 2005, p. 156), I am particularly interested in Lerner's (1980) original formulation depicting the developing child as becoming socialized through a social contract. In psychology, Freud is the preeminent theorist to have given central place, implicitly at least, to the role of social contract. From a Freudian perspective,

> Each individual comes to work out a personal social contract with parents and other authorities representing the larger society. On the one hand, certain wishes, motives, and feelings are repressed by individuals, as they struggle to conform with the norms and values of their cultures. The cost of such repression is sometimes enormous, and so high that it cripples the individual and prevents healthy functioning. On the other hand, by conforming to the morality of their cultures, individuals gain acceptance and support from others; they become part of the human group. (Moghaddam, 2005a, p. 52)

Lerner's formulation of a social contract also involves the idea that the developing child will be motivated by a desire to become an accepted member of society and will conform to achieve this goal. However, in his emphasis on the role of perceived justice in the social contrast, Lerner is closer to Rawls (1971).

In Rawls's (1971) hypothetical society, the principles of justice are chosen in a "veil of ignorance," in the sense that individuals must decide these principles without knowing their own group memberships in terms of sex, race, class, and so on. In this situation, individuals are motivated to achieve fairness because they themselves may be the victim if there is unfairness. In Lerner's (1980) formulation, irrespective of group membership, individuals are motivated to see the world as just and one in which everyone "gets what they deserve," because they want to believe that their own investments will be rewarded with "more desirable outcomes" (Lerner, Miller, & Holmes, 1976, p. 135). Thus, although justice is central to both schemes, in Rawls's hypothetical scheme people actually choose fairness, whereas in Lerner's scheme people are prone to misinterpret unfairness as fair so as to maintain the belief that they themselves are being, or will be, justly rewarded for their investment.

An important part of Lerner's (1980) *just-world theory* is the impact of shifts from short-term to long-term perspectives. Individuals faced with clear unfairness today can still shift their focus to the long term and stick to the conviction that everything works out fairly in the long term. Of course, the "long term" can, and often does, include the afterlife.

Religious conviction can be associated with greater tolerance for unfairness in this world in the belief that "justice will be served" in the next world ("It is easier for a camel to go through the eye of a needle than for a rich man to enter the Kingdom of God," Matt. 19:23–24; New International Version). However, this tolerance for present unfairness can still involve blaming the victim. Experimental evidence supports the idea that the more individuals give priority to long-term outcomes, the more they blame victims of unfair treatment and, in this way, maintain a view of the world as just in the present (e.g., Hafer, Bègue, Choma, & Dempsey, 2005).

Lerner's just-world theory is in a long tradition of "balance" theories in psychology that were particularly influenced by Heider (1958), who perhaps whimsically saw a much longer tradition ("Buddha had already glimpsed a part of balance theory around 500 BC"; see the interview with Heider in Evans, 1980, p. 17). The most influential representative of the balance tradition in intergroup relations has been equity theory, which I turn to next.

EQUITY THEORY

Equity theory concerns what people think is fair and what they do when they perceive unfairness in relationships (Adams, 1963; Homans, 1961; Walster, Walster, & Berscheid, 1978). How do people react when they or others receive rewards seen as undeserved or when they fail to receive the rewards they believe are deserved? How do people react when they experience or see others experience undeserved suffering? Such questions are at the heart of intergroup relations and often arise in situations of intergroup conflict. Thus, equity theory is suitable for interpreting intergroup relations, even though its origins lie in assessments at interpersonal rather than intergroup levels.

The central assumptions of equity theory are that people strive for justice in their social relations and that they experience anxiety when they see themselves in unjust relationships. Thus, similar to Lerner's (1980) just-world theory, equity theory assumes that the justice motive (Lerner, 1980) has a fundamental influence on behavior. Also similar to just-world theory is equity theory's depiction of human behavior as in some ways rational and in other ways irrational. In just-world theory, individuals rationalize in ways that make the world appear to be just, but they are irrational in that they are seldom conscious of their own motives and misperceptions in deciding fairness. A similar process is postulated in equity theory, although there is even a greater variety of ways in which the rational process can be psychologically distorted.

According to equity theory, in our everyday lives we estimate our inputs and outcomes, as well as the inputs and outcomes of others with whom we interact. Psychological distortion can come about through the selection, exaggeration, and/or minimization of inputs and outcomes. For example, "Jane" works in an advertising agency managed by "Helen." In her assessment of how fairly she is treated, Jane assesses her inputs and those of her boss as well as their respective outcomes. In the work context, inputs typically include levels of qualifications and expertise as well as years of experience and intelligence, drive, commitment, social skills, and other personal characteristics. Outcomes include money, job benefits (e.g., health care, life insurance), flexible work arrangements, status, and job satisfaction.

In evaluating inputs and outcomes in her work situation, Jane could exaggerate the importance of her boss having to "bear the responsibility of leadership" and the burden of having to make decisions about the direction of the entire company. She could think, "When I go home, I don't have to think about important management decisions and spend sleepless nights worrying." At the same time, Jane could minimize the importance of her years of experience in the advertising agency by saying to herself, "I only know about one small part of the company. My skills aren't very valuable."

Such psychological distortions can help explain how even when Jane earns a meager salary and her boss enjoys a gigantic income with enormous bonuses, Jane still sees the situation as fair. As do other people, Jane arrives at notions of equity by computing the ratio of inputs and outcomes for the self as compared with the ratio of inputs and outcomes for others. Her reasoning could be as follows:

> What I put into the company is of relatively little value [let us give it a value of 2], and what I get out of the company is also low [her outcome is also 2]. But my boss puts in a huge amount, at least 1,000, and her outcome is also high: 1,000.

Thus, both Jane and her boss have an input–outcome ratio of 1.

Another way for Jane to psychologically distort her picture of fairness is in the selection of particular others as comparison targets; that is, she might decide it is not even legitimate for her to compare the ratio of her inputs and outcomes with that of her boss. Instead, she might feel she should compare her input–outcome ratio with that of her coworkers or with workers in other offices in the same business sector.

Imagine if Jane now joins a labor union representing the interests of workers in her business sector. The labor union has little resources or power and is a minority group relative to management, which counts as a majority group in this relationship. If both the labor union (i.e., the minority group) and the management (i.e., the majority group) perceive their relationship to be equitable, then neither will be motivated to bring about change. However, if one or both perceive the relationship to be inequitable, there will be differences between them in the priorities they give to different strategies to restore equity. Whereas the labor union will give priority to the actual restoration of equity through real changes in inputs and outcomes, such as increased pay and/or better working conditions for employees, management will give priority to the psychological restoration of equity by increasing the value of the worker flexibility program, enhancing the quality of the office atmosphere, and so on.

An important difference between labor and management in this context will be the comparison targets they select for assessing equity. The labor union will be motivated to make upward social comparisons to "comparable others" who have lower inputs and higher outcomes (e.g., similarly qualified employees in a related business sector who work in better conditions and enjoy higher pay). Management, conversely, will select comparable others who work longer hours and receive equal or even less pay. In the struggle for resources between minority and majority groups, there are few strategies as powerful and flexible as the selection of comparison targets. By comparing one's group situation with Group X, one can feel and appear justly treated; however, by comparing one's group situation with Group Y, one can feel and appear as unjustly treated.

The subtlety of equity theory is that both groups in the relationship will be motivated to avoid seeing the relationship as inequitable. Both the more and the less powerful "buy into" the fairness of the system, particularly the more powerful. Management, in particular, wants to believe that the management–employee relationship is fair and that no exploitation is going on. In this important sense, equity theory is similar to Marxist theory: Both reject the "conspiratorial" view that the majority group believes that the system is unfair and that the minority group is being exploited. The system is particularly seen to be fair by the top executives, who have amassed a fortune of hundreds of millions of dollars and who receive multimillion dollar severance packages at the same time that "their" company declares bankruptcy and thousands of employees lose their jobs and most of their pension money.

THE ROLE OF PROCEDURES

An assumption shared by the various justice theories is that humans are motivated to maximize their rewards. This implies that humans give highest priority to distributive justice (i.e., the fairness of resource allocation; also discussed briefly in chap. 4, this volume). Have I been given my fair share of rewards? This has been the assumed central question for people assessing justice. However, an alternative view is that independent of the rewards I receive, procedural justice (i.e., the process through which decisions are made; also discussed briefly in chap. 4, this volume) is actually a more important influence on my assessment of fairness (see Tyler & Degoey, 1995, for an example of empirical support for the role of procedural justice).

Procedural justice includes a wide range of issues, such as how people feel they have been treated, whether they think they have been listened to, and whether their viewpoints have been given respect and consideration. The flexibility of the equity formula—the relationship between inputs and outcomes for the self (or ingroup) and inputs and outcomes for others (or the outgroup)—allows for a wide range of factors to be included as "input" and "outcome" on both sides of the equation. Because of this flexibility, procedural justice issues can easily be incorporated into the equity formula. A central question that has both research and applied importance concerns the possibly independent role of procedural justice in perceptions of fairness.

Since the initial formulation of the role of procedural justice by Thibaut and Walker (1975), increasing research attention has been given to the procedures used to arrive at particular distribution outcomes (e.g., Lind, Kanfer,

& Earley, 1990). However, there are alternative interpretations of the role of procedural justice in relation to distributive justice. Thibaut and Walker's (1975) so-called *self-interest model* (this term is used following Lind & Tyler, 1988, pp. 222–230) proposes that procedural justice is instrumentally important to people because they believe that how decisions are made will influence how rewards are distributed. In other words, I am not interested in being treated politely and being listened to simply for the sake of politeness and voice but rather because I expect my being treated politely and listened to means that I will be better rewarded.

However, it has been noted (e.g., Lerner, 1980) that the concern people have with justice is not always, if ever, exclusively a concern with outcomes. Tyler and his associates (e.g., Tyler & Huo, 2002) have spearheaded research efforts to explore the vital role of procedures in subjective perceptions of justice. The empirical research has been guided by what Lind and Tyler (1988, pp. 230–240) termed a *group value model*, aptly named because the researchers placed "special emphasis on the effects of values associated with group membership" (p. 231). The group value model highlights the psychological benefits and satisfaction derived from being a member of a group, independent of the instrumental benefits. A number of research studies support the idea that the trustworthiness and neutrality of authorities (e.g., the police), as well as feedback from authorities about the social status of an individual, contribute to perceptions of justice beyond explanatory power of the self-interest model (Tyler & Huo, 2002).

An important theme in the group value model is that the "command and control" tactics of the police and other authorities do not fully explain why people obey the law. In an extensive survey study involving citizens with recent experience of interactions with the police in California, Tyler and Huo (2002) found that the most important influence on people's perceptions of fair treatment was whether they felt they had been treated with politeness and respect. Those who felt they had not been treated respectfully were less trusting of authorities. These findings have clear implications for how the authorities should behave. There is a definite limit to how far coercion will succeed, in part because there are not enough officers to police the entire society:

> People do not so much comply with the law as they accept and consent to it, deferring to the law and those legal authorities whom they view as acting in a procedurally fair and trustworthy manner because, they feel, it is the right thing to do. (Tyler & Huo, 2002, p. 212)

The group value model suggests that obeying the law arises through participation in collective life and "doing the right thing" most of the time.

The quality of procedural justice in society can be conceived as part of what the political scientist Robert Putnam (1993) termed *social capital* (i.e., characteristics of social organization, such as norms, social networks, and trust, that enable societies to improve coordinated action). The research of Inglehart (1997) and others (e.g., Tyler & Huo, 2002) suggests that trust in the procedures of decision making plays a particularly important role in sustaining democracy. When people have trust in decision-making procedures (e.g., political elections), they are more likely to accept the outcomes of such processes, even though the outcomes are not to their liking this time. Higher trust influences citizens to continue to participate in the belief that procedures might favor them in the future and that their candidate might win in upcoming elections.

Clearly, trust and other relational values profoundly influence perceptions of justice (Heuer, Penrod, Hafer, & Cohn, 2002) and, in a practical way, the willingness of people to obey the law (Tyler, 2001b) and have confidence in authorities (Tyler, 2001a). At the heart of relational values are feelings of how one is being treated relative to others.

RELATIVE DEPRIVATION THEORY

> All societies are inegalitarian. But what is the relation between the inequalities in a society and the feelings of acquiescence or resentment to which they give rise? (Runciman, 1966, p. 3)

Runciman (1966) began his seminal study of attitudes toward inequalities in mid–20th century England with this key question, highlighting the rift between actual material conditions and psychological experiences of inequalities (the observation of inequalities was raised by Runciman not on the basis of the assumption shared by social dominance theory that inequalities are "natural" but rather as part of a puzzle about people's acceptance of inequalities; Sidanius & Pratto, 1999; see also chap. 4, this volume). As we saw in our discussion of materialist theories (chap. 4, this volume), traditions going back to both Marx (1852/1979; Marx & Engels, 1848/1967) and Pareto (1935) assume that the advantaged group who enjoy the largest share of material resources help construct ideologies that justify group-based inequalities as well as their own "superior" position. The general tendency on the part of the disadvantaged group, according to materialist theories, is acquiescence rather than resentment. However, the materialist theories do accept that under certain conditions group-based inequalities do lead to resentment. *Relative deprivation theory* (Runciman, 1966) is proposed as playing a key role in determining one outcome or the other.

Like procedural justice, relative deprivation can influence the "feel good" factor: how people feel about their situation irrespective of the objective outcome. The economist Adam Smith (1776/1976) pointed out that what people think of as the "necessities" of life tend to change over time. For example, are leather shoes a necessity? They are considered so if one lives in a Western society, but the ancient Egyptians and many other groups who came after them lived without feeling deprived because they lacked leather shoes. In the United States, an automobile is considered a necessity, one that "even the poor need to have"; but in many non-Western societies, an automobile is still considered a luxury. By implication, our sense of deprivation is relative.

In an attempt to pinpoint more precisely the characteristics of relative deprivation, Runciman (1966) proposed that

> A is relatively deprived of X when (1) he does not have X, (2) he sees some other person or persons, which may include himself at some previous or expected time, as having X (whether or not this is or will be in fact the case), (3) he wants X, and (4) he sees it as feasible that he should have X. (p. 11)

This attempt to identify the preconditions for relative deprivation established a tradition that Crosby (1976) and others followed (see Walker & Smith, 2002).

The term *relative deprivation* had been used 2 decades earlier by American researchers to interpret research findings reflecting a puzzling mismatch between material conditions and psychological experiences (Stouffer, Suchman, De Vinney, Star, & Williams, 1949). Two counterintuitive and often-cited findings from the World War II study of *The American Soldier* (Stouffer et al., 1949) are that African American soldiers who camped in the southern (and still segregated) regions of the United States expressed more satisfaction than African American soldiers in northern camps, and members of the air force expressed less satisfaction than members of the military police, despite the rate of promotions being higher in the air force.

The explanation for this mismatch between psychological experiences and material conditions came through the concept of relative deprivation (applied in a post hoc manner; Stouffer, 1962). African American soldiers stationed in the southern regions of the United States felt relatively better-off compared with other African Americans in the South, but African American soldiers stationed in the North felt relatively worse-off compared with the African Americans earning higher wages in northern factories, where the war had resulted in a labor shortage. Members of the military police who were not promoted were less likely to feel deprived, because fewer of their colleagues got promotions. Thus, most people they compared themselves with were in the same situation. However, the members of the air force had higher expectations for promotions, and their expectations were often not met. Thus, even though the probability of promotions was higher in the air force, feelings of relative deprivation were also higher.

From the earliest research on relative deprivation, it was clear that the process of social comparisons and the choice of comparison targets in important ways influence feelings of fairness (see Folger & Kass, 2000; Gartrell,

2002; Suls & Wheeler, 2000). A central challenge for relative deprivation theorists, as well as those supporting related theories dealing with reference groups, social exchange, and procedural and distributive justice (see Pettigrew 1967, 2002), is to explain the choice of social comparison targets—who compares with whom? I can feel relatively better-off if I compare my situation with professors at universities with lower pay scales than mine, or I can feel relatively worse-off by comparing the pay of my group, university professors, with the pay of senior university administrators.

Relative Deprivation and Behavior

The terms *egoistic deprivation* and *fraternalistic deprivation* were introduced by Runciman (1966, p. 40) to distinguish between a person feeling "relatively deprived because of own position as member of a group" and a person feeling "relatively deprived because of group's position in society" (p. 38, Figure 2). The neglect of this vitally important distinction has given rise to misunderstandings about the relationship between relative deprivation and collective action. H. J. Smith and Ortiz (2002) correctly pointed out that the "most negative reviews of the RD (relative deprivation) literature have neglected the theoretical distinction between group RD and personal RD" (p. 91). There is evidence from a variety of studies suggesting that fraternal, or group, relative deprivation is associated with participation in, or at least support for, collective action (Dion, 1986; Tougas & Beaton, 2002). For example, in a landmark study, Guimond and Dubé-Simard (1983) demonstrated that fraternal deprivation, not egoistic deprivation, was associated with support for the Quebec nationalist movement in Canada.

In addition to being linked with a greater tendency to support collective action by the ingroup, there is some evidence suggesting that fraternal deprivation is associated with stronger prejudices against target outgroups. For example, Vanneman and Pettigrew (1972) showed that among their White sample in the United States, those who felt only personal (i.e., egoistic) deprivation expressed the lowest levels of racial prejudice. The collectively (i.e., fraternalistic) and the "doubly" deprived—those who reported high personal and collective deprivation—showed the highest levels of racial prejudice. Fraternal deprivation among Muslims in India was found to be the best predictor of negative attitudes toward Hindus (Tripathi & Srivastava, 1981). Presumably, feelings of collective deprivation are associated with experiences of more intense frustration, with various forms of aggression against outgroups as one possible outcome (for a related discussion, see N. Miller, Pederson, Earlywine, & Pollock, 2003).

The most intriguing questions around relative deprivation concern major social upheavals and revolutions. The puzzle is why such events seldom occur, and alternative explanations for this rarity are the focus of several major theories, such as system justification theory (Jost & Banaji, 1994; see also chap. 5, this volume) and social dominance theory (Sidanius & Pratto, 1999; see also chap. 4, this volume). From Tocqueville (1856/2000) to modern researchers (e.g., Davies, 1974; Hepworth & West, 1988), a variety of evidence, particularly from historical sources, has been cited in support of the view that "revolutions are apt to occur at times of rising prosperity" (Runciman, 1966, p. 24). Presumably, rising prosperity is associated with rising expectations, and it is when prosperity declines or stops growing and expectations remain unmet that people experience fraternal relative deprivation. The comparisons implied in this situation are not with other people but with the self as one would be if conditions were different.

Associated with this line of argument is the view that relative deprivation arises from "counterfactual thoughts" about how if the conditions had been fairer, one's outcomes could have been better (Folger, 1986). Although almost all of the evidence in support of counterfactual thinking has been derived through research conducted on individual behavior, there are important implications for collective behavior: "When it is easier to imagine how one's group's outcomes could have been better, group relative deprivation should occur" (Olson & Roese, 2002, p. 282). Part of the challenge facing those who seek to instigate rebellion and revolution is to fire the imagination of the disadvantaged, so that they find it easier to believe that under fairer conditions their collective lives would have been much better.

Whether we refer to the instigators of rebellion and revolution as "the vanguard of the revolution," as in the Marxist tradition; the "counterelite," according to Pareto's (1935) elite theory tradition; or simply as "rebels" or "troublemakers," they are more likely to come from the privileged "advantaged" class than from among the "downtrodden." The relative deprivation these "privileged rebels" feel is "on behalf of others" (Tougas & Beaton, 2002, p. 124), as in the case of men who support affirmative action for women (Veilleux & Tougas, 1989). This very important type of relative deprivation is closer to what Runciman (1966) saw as fraternal rather than egoistic because it is intended to mobilize collective rather than individual action. However, it is different from Runciman's original fraternalistic category because it involves outgroup members (e.g., men) attempting to mobilize collective action by an ingroup (e.g., women).

Note that the instigators of rebellion and revolution are attempting to influence us to behave counter to the justice motive (proposed by Lerner, 1980). The justice motive highlights how people manipulate their constructions to manufacture and maintain a view of the world as fair, for example, by blaming the victims of crime (Hafer & Bègue, 2005). Instigators of rebellion attempt to "break the spell" of this justice motive and move people to view the world as unfair rather than fair, to break through the dominant group ideology (in system justification terms), and to see existing social arrangements as illegitimate and unstable (in social identity theory terms; Tajfel & Turner, 1979).

Health Consequences of Relative Deprivation

From an objective perspective, most humans are better-off now compared with previous generations in history (Cox & Alm, 1999). Despite the improvements in the general standard of living as measured by objective criteria, group-based inequalities and the transmission of status across generations persist in modern societies, particularly in North America (Bowles, Gintis, & Groves, 2005). In the United States, those born in families with incomes in the lower 20% of society have only about a 1-in-20 chance of achieving the average salary enjoyed by the top 20% income group. Moreover, there is accumulating evidence to suggest that larger inequalities in society have detrimental consequences for individual well-being.

A variety of research studies suggest that it is the relative rather than the absolute wealth that shapes feelings of deprivation and well-being. For example, income rank in an organization, rather than absolute income level, influences satisfaction and well-being (G. D. A. Brown, Gardner, Oswald, & Qian, 2004). If "Joe" earns $40,000 a year and is in the top 20% of the top earners in an organization, he will feel better about his situation than if he earns $45,000 a year and is in the bottom 20% of wage earners in an organization. Similarly, people whose neighbors earn a comparatively much higher salary tend to be less satisfied (Luttmer, 2005). Also, an impressive body of research shows that greater status inequalities have a detrimental impact on the health of lower status groups (Marmot, 2004). People who enjoy higher status and wealth also enjoy better health: Being relatively deprived means lower life expectancy and worse health.

SOURCES OF SUBJECTIVE JUSTICE, UNIVERSALS, AND THE CYCLE OF RIGHTS AND DUTIES

Given the pivotal role of subjective feelings about how we are being treated, it is important to ask the following: What is the source of subjective justice? Theoretical responses to this question fall into two broad categories: (a) *positive law* (i.e., rights and duties are human constructions and reflect varying cultural conditions) and (b) *natural law* (i.e., rights and duties are derived from divine, natural sources and discovered by humans). I have argued in support of the positive law tradition (Moghaddam & Riley, 2005), adopting a cultural evolutionary view of rights and duties (Moghaddam, 2000).

Subjective justice is postulated as being rooted in *primitive social relations* (i.e., elementary behaviors that evolved as part of a repertoire of skills necessary for group survival; Moghaddam, 2002). Empathy and turn taking are examples of primitive social relations: Both of these evolved very early in human evolution and are essential for group life. Primitive social relations evolved from functional needs; they are "experiential" (following Dershowitz,

2004), in the sense that they arise out of practical experiences and needs. For example, turn taking is necessary to achieve cooperative living: People have to take turns listening, talking, and being listened to, to communicate effectively with others. Long after these skills have evolved and become part of routine, everyday practices in a group, they are interpreted according to cultural values as involving rights and/or duties, such as in the right to take a turn in cross-examining witnesses in a court of law, the right to have a turn at an intersection, and the right to have a turn speaking as a candidate in a political debate.

If a sense of fairness is rooted in early evolution, then we should find some evidence of this in animal behavior—and indeed, we do. First, there is growing evidence that animals experience empathy. For example, mice displayed behavior that can be interpreted as empathy when they observed cagemates, but not strangers, experiencing pain (Langford et al., 2006). Given the foundational role that empathy plays in subjective justice, this is an important finding. Animals high on empathy would be recognized as particularly valuable group members, at least among groups of animals that differentiate between others on the basis of who are good collaborators (Melis, Hare, & Tomasello, 2006). Among those animals that have primitive forms of culture (van Schaik et al., 2003), some aspects of empathic behavior might be learned and passed on to others.

Second, and more directly, a wide range of field and experimental evidence has been gathered in support of the argument that animals have a sense of fairness (Bekoff, 2005). Both humans and animals probably acquire a sense of fairness through participation in play. When the rules of play that regulate behavior in a group of animals break down, fairness is violated, and play also breaks down (see readings in Bekoff, Allen, & Burghardt, 2002). Brosnan and de Waal (2003) reported on an intriguing experimental study that demonstrates that monkeys have a sense of fairness. Monkeys became less cooperative when they witnessed other monkeys receive a more favorable reward (a grape rather than the less favorable cucumber) for the same effort as they had exerted or for no effort at all. The negative reactions of monkeys who witnessed unequal reward distribution suggests they were reacting to being treated unfairly.

The biologist Marc Hauser (2006) pushed this line of argument further, proposing that people are born with an innate moral grammar that is akin to the inbuilt neural network for language put forth by Chomsky (1965). The inbuilt moral grammar shapes the kinds of rules humans construct and explains why many moral rules are so similar across cultures (e.g., "Thou shalt not kill," "Thou shalt not steal," as found in most cultures). The inbuilt moral grammar also explains why so many people find it difficult to articulate the rules of fairness they apply in everyday life. An alternative view is that moral grammar is passed on through culture (Moghaddam & Riley, 2005), including primitive animal cultures.

The Cycle of Rights and Duties in Interpersonal Relations

So far I have argued that there are evolutionary roots to modern justice and that there are certain universals in justice. A "relativist" objection to this view at the intergroup level is that rights, duties, and other elements of justice are simply the norms established by the most powerful factions in each group (Louis & Taylor, 2005, present a strong defense of this relativist position). For example, in the Catholic Church women do not presently have the right to be ordained as priests, and in the United States gay men and lesbians do not have the right to be formally married. These rights are determined by certain powerful factions (e.g., religious conservatives). A shift in power relations, so that religious conservatives lose ground and are forced to shift their positions, could lead to women, gay men, and lesbians gaining additional rights (as they have done over the past century).

Although the relativist argument is sound with respect to most rights and duties being norms established through control of power, there are certain patterns of support for rights and duties that are essential and universal. For example, in relationships characterized by change and instability, minorities give priority to rights and majorities give priority to duties (Moghaddam & Riley, 2005). This assertion holds at both interpersonal and intergroup levels. This is not because such a pattern is somehow "inbuilt" in humans, but rather it is because this pattern of behavior best serves the interests of minority and majority individuals and groups. When and if it serves their interests, minorities and majorities will show a different pattern of behavior—but for the most part they do not need to, and minorities highlight rights while majorities highlight duties.

At the interpersonal level, consider the relationship between a child and her parents (a relationship characterized by change, with the child becoming an adult and the parents becoming senior citizens; see readings in Killen & Smetana, 2006, for broader discussions of moral development). As the child learns to use the rhetoric of justice, she continually gives priority to rights, as in "That's not fair, I should be allowed to go out and play!" and "I should have the right to stay at the party until 12 o'clock!" In contrast, her parents give priority to duties, "No you can't go out to play until you've finished your homework" and "You're responsible to get back home by 10 o'clock at the latest, and you have to clean your room before you can go out." The child, who has less power, continually pushes to gain greater rights, whereas her parents, who have greater power, give priority to duties being carried out, such as homework. However, the cycle of rights and duties swings around as the child becomes an adult and has her own child. Now, the new mother places emphasis on duties as she socializes her child, and she is faced with a child who makes demands, as she used to do, based on rights.

The Rights and Duties Intergroup Cycle

The same cycle of rights and duties is evident at the intergroup level, at least during times of change and instability (perceived instability is also identified by social identity theory as one of the key factors, together with perceived legitimacy, that influence the strategies adopted by minority group members; Tajfel & Turner, 1979; see also chap. 5, this volume). Minority groups adopt the narrative of rights and attempt to mobilize by highlighting violations of their rights and demands for expanded rights. This is clearly evident at times of group mobilization, revolt, and revolution. For example, during the minority movements of the 1960s, the marchers shouted slogans in support of "women's rights," "Black rights," "gay rights," and so on, rather than "women's duties," "Black duties," or "gay duties." Revolutionaries focus on violations of rights, whereas the majority groups in power give priority to the duty to obey the law (Moghaddam, 2004). However, in a condition in which a minority group achieves power and becomes the majority group, the new majority switches focus from rights to duties (this prediction is in line with elite theory; Pareto, 1935; see also chap. 4, this volume). The revolutionaries of the past now turn the spotlight from violations of rights and what the people should demand to the necessity of carrying out duties and what the people have a responsibility to do, particularly to obey the law and support the new sociopolitical order.

I was in Iran immediately after the revolution of 1978, and I witnessed firsthand this dramatic shift in emphasis from rights to duties on the part of the new ruling group. Whereas before the revolution the Shah had been chastised for violating the rights of the people to enjoy a good standard of living and economic progress, after the revolution the people were told by the ruling mullahs that "economics is for asses" and that it is only in heaven that one receives one's real rewards. In this world, one's duty is to obey the supreme spiritual leader.

Thus, irrespective of the particular labels (e.g., *democratic, Islamic, socialist*) that minority and majority groups give themselves or are given, the cycle of rights and duties is evident in all intergroup relations during times of change and instability. Those with less power highlight rights, whereas those enjoying greater power give priority to duties.

IMPLICATIONS OF JUSTICE THEORIES FOR DEMOCRACY

Arguments in support of the superiority of democracy over other political systems, such as dictatorship or hereditary monarchy, revolve around the issue of justice. Democracy is assumed to be a more just system of government and to lead to fairer social relations, including at the intergroup level (although controversy surrounds the question of how much we can further democratize societies; see Leet, 2003). Thus, justice theories are directly relevant to discussions of democracy and intergroup relations.

The distinction between procedural and distributive justice has implications of central importance for democracy. On the one hand, citizens need to feel they are adequately involved in the decision-making process; on the other hand, the outcome of this process must yield a distribution of resources that is seen to be fair. It is not enough to focus exclusively on procedural justice to the neglect of distributive justice; nor is it enough to focus exclusively on distributive justice to the neglect of procedural justice.

Of course, there are cultural variations with respect to what is perceived to be fair. For example, what distribution of resources is fair? In the Scandinavian countries, the income difference between the very top company executives and the regular employees (as well as the university presidents and the professors) is far less than in the United States. An argument in favor of larger income differences is that it motivates people to be more entrepreneurial, but there are also some negative consequences to larger group-based inequalities.

Although the media, educational, religious, and other systems can, and generally do, work to justify extreme inequalities in the United States (and elsewhere), the detrimental health consequences of relative deprivation is difficult to avoid (Marmot, 2004). People who are relatively deprived (i.e., are of low rank and status in a group) tend to have lower life expectancies and worse health. If democracy also involves equality of opportunity in terms of health and well-being, then the United States is among the countries that can be faulted for failing to provide this basic "right" for large segments of the population.

However, although the justice theories place the issue of fairness at the center of discussions about democracy and intergroup relations, by highlighting the subjective nature of justice (Feather, 1999), these theories also point to the manipulation of subjective experiences of justice by the elite who enjoy greater control of resources, including the media and educational institutions. People can be persuaded to feel that their inputs are lower and that their outcomes are higher than they are in actuality; they can also be persuaded that others' inputs are higher and that others' outcomes are lower than they are in actuality. Influenced by the justice motive (Lerner, 1980), people can distort the actual situation and perceive injustices as justified. In this way, powerlessness, group-based injustices, and poverty can appear legitimate in a society that espouses democracy but is characterized by huge inequalities.

However, justice theories provide some measure of support for the idea of a minimal universal basis for democracy. Particularly from an evolutionary perspective, there seem to be certain universals in justice: a minimum level of fairness has to exist in order for collective life to proceed and for a society to survive at all. Among humans, as well as particular groups of animals, some level of empathy and a sense of fairness enhance survival chances. This sense of fairness, I propose, evolves on the basis of primitive social relations such as turn taking.

The legal scholar Dershowitz (2004) argued that the practical experience of great wrongs—injustices—leads people to recognize the rights that must be entrenched and maintained. However, rights are always vulnerable, and minorities give priority to rights, particularly in times of change (Moghaddam & Riley, 2005). Majority groups are more likely to give priority to duties, especially the duty to obey current rules and support the status quo. From this perspective, democracy is strengthened by the continuing struggle to redefine rights and duties because new rights come from the wrongs experienced by people.

The evolutionary perspective on justice I have discussed, coupled with a "rights from wrongs" argument, leads to a more optimistic long-term viewpoint. The minimal rights and duties inherent in primitive social relations serve as a foundation for the establishment of an increasingly enlarged set of rights, gained through practical experiences of wrongs. Associated with these processes are the growth of institutions and relationships that strengthen different forms of proceduralism, such as in legal and political spheres, which can support democracy (see Habermas, 1984, 1987).

III

PSYCHOLOGICAL
FOUNDATIONS OF POLICIES

INTRODUCTION: PSYCHOLOGICAL FOUNDATIONS OF POLICIES

A new democratic wave is sweeping the world, from the streets of Georgia and Ukraine, to the unprecedented 2004 and 2005 elections in Palestine, Afghanistan, and Iraq, to the new prospects for democratic development in Lebanon and Egypt. In 2004, more than 1 billion people voted in national elections.

—Muñoz (2006, p. 1)

The 21st century is viewed by some thinkers as heralding a new democratic era, with globalization and modernization bringing about the "final" triumph of liberal democracy. Whereas Marx (1852/1979; Marx & Engels, 1848/1967) predicted an "inevitable" historical progression toward the "end of history"—from feudalism, to capitalism, to socialism, and finally, to the classless society—Fukuyama (1992) argued that the end of history would come much earlier along this road. Thus, we are "not ever going to get to socialism" (Fukuyama, 2006, p. 116); rather we will come to a standstill when liberal democracy and capitalism become global. Indeed, the general assumption has been that "capitalism and democracy go hand in hand" (Stephens, 1993, p. 409).

Among the factors assumed to be causing a new democratic wave, the most commonly cited is globalization. It has been generally assumed that the new economic, organizational, and cultural interconnectedness results in global attempts to control conflicts, an idea that goes back at least to the 19th-century *Manchester School* of economic thought, which emphasized the social and political benefits of free trade.

Thus, a number of contemporary thinkers have focused on the roles of the global political economy and interconnectedness through commerce in shaping democratization and new concerns with regard to controlling intergroup conflicts (Held, McGrew, Goldblatt, & Perraton, 1999). Presumably, in a world that is commercially interconnected, each nation—because of economic interdependence—is to a greater degree invested in the prevalence of peace in other nations. The European Union, for example, came into being in part in an attempt to bind the fate of European nations and to prevent further world wars.

Other researchers have highlighted the role of the mass media. The term *CNN effect* has been coined to describe the influence of satellite news on intergroup conflicts in other parts of the world: Because news travels around the world in a matter of minutes, images of suffering cause people in different parts of the world to demand an end to violence, even though they are merely witnesses to violence against others (Jacobson, 2000). The idea, then, is that a global conscience comes into effect, a kind of universal *superego*, through the global mass media, resulting in a global concern for human rights.

In the framework of Lorenz's (1976) analysis of aggression, the CNN effect involves the revival of inhibitory mechanisms, which ordinarily prevent aggressive behavior when an attacker and a target are in close contact. Such inhibitory mechanisms have been sidestepped by long-range weapons, which allow killing without an aggressor witnessing the consequence of aggression, and are again made effective because television and other media directly confront us with images of violence. Even if a military pilot only sees lights on a radar screen when he attacks live targets, we at home are affected by television images of deaths and injuries that result from such "surgical strikes." The CNN effect is integral to globalization.

Huntington (1991) was among the most influential theorists to argue for the role of globalization in democratization, although he insightfully rejected Fukuyama's (1992) proposal that globalization is part of a movement toward the end of history. Huntington (1996) noted,

> History ends at least once and occasionally more often in the history of every civilization. As the civilization's universal state emerges, its people become blinded by what Toynbee called "the mirage of immortality" and convinced that theirs is the final form of human society. (p. 302)

However, Huntington (1991) and others warned that globalization is also associated with major intergroup challenges.

Just as "the mirage of immortality" can mislead us to believe our way of life represents the end of history, we can be lulled into assuming that globalization will always lead to democratization and smoother intergroup relations. I have used the term *fractured globalization* (see chap. 1, this volume) to underline the uneven and sometimes contradictory nature of globalization processes, which involve, among other things, increased contact between people and cultures that never previously experienced contact. Although the result need not be the "clash of civilizations" articulated by Huntington (1996), contact between groups with no previous history of large-scale interaction is associated with many new challenges and raises critical research and policy questions.

What is the best strategy for managing diversity in an age of globalization, when groups with no previous history of contact suddenly find themselves in interaction? Should we attempt to wash away cultural and linguistic differences, adopting an *assimilationist policy* intended to maximize homogeneity in society? Or, in contrast, should we adopt a *multicultural policy* designed to support, celebrate, and highlight intergroup differences?

The relevance and importance of these questions become even more apparent when we consider the relationship between assimilation, multiculturalism, and democracy. In what common and different ways are assimilation and multiculturalism compatible with democracy? There are a variety of possible positions that could be adopted in this regard. For example, on the one hand, it could be argued that the more democratic path is for every group to exercise the right to retain their own way of life, their traditions and languages, and to "go their own way." From this perspective, the duty of democratic society is to create conditions in which every group can exercise free choice to go down a multicultural path of sustaining, increasing, and celebrating differences.

Alternatively, it could be argued that to achieve a meritocracy and provide everyone—including newly arrived minority group immigrants who are often culturally and linguistically very different from the mainstream—with equal opportunities, the best democratic strategy is the assimilation of minorities into the mainstream. The adoption of mainstream culture and language would be more compatible with democracy, according to this argument, because it would allow for greater equality of opportunity and participation by a larger segment of the total population.

The two chapters in Part III further explore the question of the compatibility of assimilation and multiculturalism with democracy. These discussions build on the earlier consideration (see chap. 2, this volume) of constraints on social categorization and the organization of groups in societies.

7

PSYCHOLOGICAL FOUNDATIONS
OF ASSIMILATION

I hear America singing, the varied carols I hear.
                                    —Walt Whitman (1855/1955, p. 38)

God's crucible, the great Melting Pot where all the races of Europe are
melting and re-forming.
                                    —Israel Zangwill (1909, p. 37)

The visions of America celebrated by the poet Walt Whitman (1819–1892) and the playwright Israel Zangwill (1864–1926) had foundational features in common: The New World provided the immigrant nation the opportunity to merge its "varied carols" and form what Ralph Waldo Emerson (1803–1882), the leading light of the American transcendentalist movement, described as "a new race, a new religion, a new state" (Sherman, 1921, p. xxxvi). This new race, the Americans, would turn their backs on the prejudices of the Old World. Hardened and reshaped by their experiences in the ever-moving frontier (F. J. Turner, 1920), Americans would assimilate, creating a society characterized by cohesion, commonality, and peace.

The classic model of assimilation is associated with the University of Chicago's School of Sociology (Park, 1950; Park & Burgess, 1921). Shared experiences, social interactions, and increased contact, as well as common challenges, lead people to develop shared cultural characteristics. The melting away of differences is facilitated by the demands of modern economies, which lead people to be geographically mobile and to interact with strangers outside their families, neighborhoods, and ethnic communities. The Chicago model reminds us of 21st-century discussions of globalization because of

131

the shared assumption that economic factors will gradually shape greater cultural homogeneity. Although the Chicago model evolved in the United States and globalization models are evolving in other parts of the world in the context of the emerging global village, common to all is the same assimilationist proposition that economic factors shape a shared culture.

The classic Chicago model of assimilation proposes that minority group immigrants gradually adopt the culture of the majority group. Typically, first-generation immigrants live in inner-city ethnic neighborhoods, eat ethnic food, speak the heritage language, and work in low-level jobs. Over subsequent generations, these immigrants gain in education and status, move from ethnic, typically inner-city neighborhoods to more affluent suburban areas, abandon the heritage language and ethnic lifestyle, and take on the language and lifestyle of the majority group. Because this process involves the minority group assimilating into majority culture, I have termed this *minority-assimilation* (Moghaddam, 1998, p. 499).

A second type of assimilation is one I have termed *melting-pot assimilation* (Moghaddam, 1998, p. 499), involving the emergence of a new culture through the merging of all the different groups, both minority and majority. This is more in line with the plot in Zangwill's (1909) play *The Melting Pot.* All ethnic groups are cooked in the stew and the result is a new race, The Americans.

Whereas in minority-assimilation the cultural direction of society is clear because it is based on majority culture, in melting-pot assimilation it remains less clear because the future direction of cultural change depends on the characteristics of new minority immigrant groups. Because each new group is assumed to "melt in the pot" and contribute to the "stew," the characteristics of the stew would change as new groups, differing in ethnicity, religion, language, and so on, arrive and add their unique contributions.

THE ROLE OF GOVERNMENT IN ASSIMILATION

Assimilation is often discussed in association with the free-market economy. In 21st-century discussions of globalization, an assumption is that laissez-faire global economic policies will lead to increased assimilation. However, state intervention, the opposite of free-market policies, has also been used to encourage assimilation. There are at least two sets of factors that have led governments in some parts of the world to intervene in support of assimilation.

The governments of some third world societies have encouraged assimilation as a way to end tribal, ethnic, regional, and other "factional" allegiances and to strengthen allegiance to the nation state and the central government. In such third world contexts, tribal, regional and other local allegiances are viewed as primitive, "backward," and damaging to national development. Central governments have prohibited the use of local languages in schools, government offices, and other public domains and have tried to stamp out tribal customs. This enmity of many third world authorities toward tribes and local traditions is particularly intense in the case of nomads:

> Nomads who shun a part in the cash economy, who wear traditional clothing or none at all, who lack formal education, are considered as hindering the nation's development, as shaming it before outsiders. Discouraging, even abolishing nomads becomes a patriotic urge. (Dyson-Hudson, 1971, p. 23)

Thus, assimilation is seen as a necessary means to achieving a cohesive and modern nation state.

At the other end of the ideological spectrum from free-market capitalism, a different ideological basis has been used by governments in communist societies to intervene to strengthen assimilation. According to Marxist ideology, divisions on the basis of tribe, ethnicity, religion, gender, and other such criteria strengthen false consciousness and lead people away from the only grouping that should matter: social class (Marx & Engels, 1848/1967). Only social class "should" matter because progress toward the communist ideal of a classless society is possible solely through people accurately perceiving their class membership and class interests vis-à-vis the members of other classes. Consequently, in communist societies the central governments have generally intervened to strengthen assimilation.

However, the tactics and goals of governments do not necessarily change with shifts in avowed ideology. For example, prior to the collapse of the former Soviet Union, the Soviet central authorities took strong military action to crush the Chechen independence movement. After the end of communism in 1990, the Russian government continued with equal ferocity the policy of military action against the Chechen independence movement, vowing to crush "terrorists in Chechnya" (Speckhard, Tarabrina, Krasnov, & Akhmedova, 2004). Of course, those involved in the Chechen independence movement see themselves as freedom fighters, not terrorists, a common difference of opinion between central governments and activists in independence movements (see Moghaddam, 2006b, pp. 9–10). Irrespective of whether in a particular social context assimilation takes place through government intervention or through laissez-faire market forces, or a combination of both, certain psychological assumptions underlie assimilation, and I turn to these next.

PSYCHOLOGICAL FOUNDATIONS OF ASSIMILATION POLICY

Underlying assimilation are four major psychological assumptions concerning contact and prejudice; similarity attraction; divisions, conflict, and democracy; and meritocracy.

Contact and Prejudice

Assimilation policy is first and foremost based on the proposition that bringing people of different groups into contact with one another will result in decreased intergroup prejudice, an assumption receiving considerable research attention in the 21st century (Dixon & Rosenbaum, 2004; Eller & Abrams, 2003; McClelland & Linnander, 2006). Gordon Allport's (1897–1967) 1954 classic text *The Nature of Prejudice* has served as the most important guide to research in this area (Dovidio, Glick, & Rudman, 2005), although the *contact hypothesis* was already well established before Allport (Dovidio, Gaertner, & Kawakami, 2003, pp. 6–7). Allport's most important contribution was that he proposed specific preconditions for the prejudice-reducing role of intergroup contact: (a) The groups should enjoy equal status in the context in which contact takes place, (b) the context should be cooperative rather than competitive, (c) the groups should have common goals in this context, and (d) contact should "enjoy the sanction of the community" in which it takes place (Allport, 1954, p. 454).

The fate of the contact hypothesis has been in some ways contradictory. On the one hand, the contact hypothesis has had a historically important impact on social policy in the United States and many other countries, particularly in the area of education and neighborhood services. The assumption underlying such policies has been that desegregation—for example, bringing together Whites and African Americans in schools in the United States and Catholics and Protestants in schools in Northern Ireland (see Hewstone, 2003)—would lead to more harmonious intergroup relations. On the other hand, for decades after Allport's (1954) attempt to stipulate the conditions in which contact must take place to lead to beneficial results, researchers struggled to provide consistent empirical support for such conditions (Hewstone & Brown, 1986a). Indeed, additional research added to the number of preconditions so that opportunity for personal acquaintances and intergroup friendships came also to be seen as important factors (Pettigrew, 1997; Wright, Aron, McLaughlin-Volpe, & Ropp, 1997).

Two major research developments have taken place since the 1990s that may help improve our scientific understanding of contact. First, a number of attempts have been made to reformulate the contact hypothesis and progress beyond Allport's (1954) proposal. Following Pettigrew (1998a), Dovidio et al. (2003) formulated a model in which the preconditions for contact are mediated by basic psychological processes (e.g., social representation, affect) or contextual factors (e.g., functional relations between the groups). However, the danger is that although this model is more integrative, it may further complicate rather than clarify our picture of contact. Other researchers, influenced by a social identity tradition (Tajfel & Turner, 1979; see also chap. 5, this volume), have focused more on categorization processes associated with contact (Gaertner et al., 1999).

Pettigrew's (1998a, 1998b) influence led to greater focus on a longitudinal process involving the members of different groups interacting as individuals, "decategorizing," getting to know about one another, and forming emotional ties. Meta-analytic research (discussed next) suggests that instead of continuing to perceive each other as individuals isolated and different from the group, we can use contact to help us reappraise what constitutes the ingroup, which would in turn lead to recategorization (i.e., superordinate-level categorization). This focus on cognitive and affective long-term changes implies that under the right preconditions (including the friendship precondition; Pettigrew, 1998a), contact will lead individuals to eventually reconceptualize the way they categorize the social world so that "us" and "them" become seen as "we." Such a shift has also been discussed under the title of the common ingroup identity model (Gaertner & Dovidio, 2000; see also chap. 5, this volume), and corresponds to the fourth stage of Sherif's (1966) realistic conflict model, when superordinate goals are introduced to transform intergroup relations from conflict to cooperation (see chap. 4, this volume).

A second research development is the outcome of extensive meta-analyses conducted by Pettigrew and Tropp (2000, 2006). These analyses present a far more positive picture of contact outcomes, although a closer examination also suggests that the impact of contact is somewhat different for majority and minority groups (Tropp & Pettigrew, 2005). Whereas 3 decades earlier Hewstone and Brown (1986b, p. 3) declared that "contact is not enough," Pettigrew and Tropp (2006) concluded that, in general, contact has a favorable influence on intergroup relations, independent of the preconditions identified by Allport (1954)—implying that contact (without preconditions) could be enough. When such preconditions are met, then the positive outcomes of contact are further enhanced. Moreover, the impact of preconditions should be examined as a combined, interrelated bundle rather than in isolation from one another. Also, Allport discussed the impact of contact on ethnic and racial groups, but meta-analytic studies suggest that positive contact effects generalize across different kinds of groups, including work groups.

However, the generally positive outcome of contact is particularly true for majority rather than minority groups (Tropp & Pettigrew, 2005). This may be because for minority group members, exposure to majority group members can remind them of their being a target of prejudice (Tropp, 2003) and, more broadly, of their unfulfilled demand for equal rights (Moghaddam, 2004). As long as they remain within the confines of their ingroup and avoid contact with the majority group, minority group members can find protection against the stigma of prejudice (Crocker, Major, & Steele, 1998).

Thus, increased contact is assumed to lead to more harmonious intergroup relations. This is probably in part because the more people are exposed to something, the more they grow to like it (Zajonc, 1968), a relationship politicians attempt to put into effect by exposing their faces and voices to the unfortunate electorate in the days, weeks, months, and even years before elections. However, a second reason for the positive impact of contact on intergroup relations may well be that groups in contact often influence one another and become more alike. Next, I consider the assumption that research on similarity attraction supports assimilation policy.

Similarity Attraction

One of the strongest claims to a universal in human social behavior revolves around similarity attraction: Considerable evidence has accumulated to suggest that people are more positively disposed toward others who are more similar to them (Byrne, 1971). In close relationships, friendship and love are positively associated with similarity (Berscheid & Reis, 1998). Of course, people are also influenced by information about dissimilarity (Singh & Ho, 2000). For example, how people dress can indicate their social and political values, and those whose dress indicates "deviance" and dissimilarity from the mainstream, such as pro-gay values, are offered less help in the British context (Gray, Russell, & Blockley, 1991).

In the context of immigrant-receiving societies, similarity attraction may be at work initially in the choice immigrants (both legal and illegal) make to move to an adopted land and in the choice the adopted land makes of accepting them. Presumably, immigrants assume that they are in important ways compatible with the adopted land (e.g., in terms of personal responsibility and drive), and in turn the adopted land accepts immigrants who are seen to be compatible (e.g., having certain needed work skills and personality characteristics).

Over time, compatibility increases as both the immigrants and the adopted society change to fit better together. Research suggests that this same process of *selection compatibility* is at work in business organizations, which often become fairly homogeneous with respect to personality attributes of managers (B. Schnieder, Smith, Taylor, & Fleener, 1998). Three factors seem to be at work: (a) Individuals make choices depending on the attractiveness of the organization; (b) organizations make choices depending on the attractiveness of individuals; and (c) once new employees arrive, the organization socializes them, and they become even more similar (and attractive) by conforming to local norms.

Most research on the role of similarity–dissimilarity in human relations has been conducted at the interpersonal level, but there is also evidence to suggest that people are more positively disposed toward ingroup rather than outgroup members (i.e., those who are similar rather than dissimilar to them in terms of group membership). One example is Whites showing a preference for other Whites over ethnic minorities. There is some research evidence, in line with the widely different reactions of White and Black Americans to the "not guilty" verdict of the O. J. Simpson "trial of the 20th century," that jurors are more lenient toward defendants of their own race (Hymes, Leinart, Rowe, & Rogers, 1993) and that White jurors are particularly harsh when the defendant is Black and the victim of the crime is White (Pfeifer & Ogloff, 1991).

Presumably, we find it easier to empathize with those who share our group characteristics; this may be why male jurors tend to be more lenient toward men accused of rape (G. J. Fischer, 1997). However, such trends are becoming more subtle. There is some evidence that in this age of "political correctness," Whites in Western societies are more likely to favor helping the members of their own race when their choice can be attributed to factors other than race (see studies in Dovidio & Gaertner, 1986).

I collaborated with two colleagues to try to directly test the relationship between similarity and attraction among different ethnic groups in a multicultural context (Osbeck, Moghaddam, & Perreault, 1977). Our samples were from Algerian, Indian, Jewish, Greek, English Canadian, and French Canadian populations living in Quebec, Canada. In this context, Algerians, Indians, Jews, and Greeks are minority groups; English Canadians are a minority group in Quebec but the majority in the larger national context of Canada, whereas French Canadians are the majority group in Quebec but a minority in the national Canadian context. We examined the association between (a) how similar the members of each of these six groups perceived outgroup members to be to their ingroup and (b) how willing they were to have contact with outgroup members. We found a consistent positive association between similarity and attraction: The more outgroup members were seen as similar, the more a person was willing to have close contact with them.

The similarity-attraction hypothesis raises important questions concerning multicultural policies that highlight and celebrate differences, and I return to this topic later in this chapter. For now, our focus remains on the proposition that assimilation leads to a more homogeneous society, one that is characterized by greater similarity. The similarity-attraction literature (e.g., Neimeyer & Mitchell, 1988) suggests that when the members of a society see themselves as more similar to each other, they will be more positively inclined toward each other, and society will be more cohesive and peaceful. A corresponding claim, to which I now turn, is that assimilation melts away intergroup differences, helps avoid intergroup conflict, and enables the growth of democracy.

Divisions, Conflict, and Democracy

Assimilation policy is supported by two related arguments that focus on the proposed negative impact of diversity, generally, and ethnic plurality, in particular. A first argument is based on the potentially divisive nature of ethnic differences: A society that has multiple ethnic groups is at risk for ethnic conflict. For example, a study of Blacks, Latinos, Asians, and Whites in Chicago paints a picture of surprisingly high intolerance and intergroup bias (W. J. Wilson & Taub, 2006). Perhaps most disappointing is the prejudice and discrimination shown by minorities against other minorities. Multilingual societies face additional burdens, such as when "Francophonie" became "a raging issue that led to social unrest, terrorism, threats of separation and a referendum that came within a hair's breadth of breaking up Canada" (Krauthammer, 2006, p. 112). In ethnically homogeneous societies—Japan is often mentioned as an example—there are no "natural" rifts that could form the basis of conflict. Thus, for instance, in societies such as Rwanda, the ferocity of internal conflict results from the presence of so-called natural ethnic divisions, in this case between the Tutsi and the Hutu.

This argument about the conflict-nurturing role of ethnic divisions is often associated with the claim, at times made explicit, that ethnic diversity makes it more difficult for democracy to develop (Lijphart, 1977; Welsh, 1993) and easier for authoritarianism to become established: "The functional view of why ethnic divisions contribute to the development of authoritarianism is that they undermine social integration and societal consensus" (Stephens, 1993, p. 439). This is obviously an important claim, particularly given the enormous investments made to "spread democracy" around the globe in the 21st century.

Those who argue that diversity hurts democracy point out that in ethnically diverse societies, there is a tendency for voters to show allegiance to ethnic group membership rather than to vote on political issues and principles (Karatnycky, 2002). This is accentuated by the elites of each ethnic group, who are motivated to maintain and extend their own personal status through mobilizing the ethnic ingroup and appealing to ethnic group loyalty (Horowitz, 1993). Rather than build up political alliances on the basis of issues that cut across ethnic and sectarian lines, the political leaders become motivated to build alliances using ethnic affiliations. Thus, the political message becomes, "Vote for me because you are a member of Ethnic Group X and I am also a member of Ethnic Group X and best represent your interests."

Some critics have argued persuasively that there does not exist strong empirical evidence supporting the thesis that diversity hurts democracy (Fish & Brooks, 2004). Irrespective of the outcome of scientific debates on this question, however, the argument that diversity hurts democracy is likely to remain popular. After all, this argument is very useful to third world dictators, as well as to their external supporters, who want to justify their continued ban on a multiparty system and political and social freedoms by proposing that because of the diversity present in their societies, democracy is not possible. Associated with the idea of democracy is meritocracy, and in the next section I consider arguments that suggest assimilation policy strengthens meritocracy.

Meritocracy

The United States, the preeminent immigrant-receiving society, is often described as a "land of opportunity," a *meritocracy* (i.e., a social system that allows individuals to advance and be rewarded according to personal merit). The assumption, which could be mistaken, is that it does not matter what family, ethnicity, religion, or social class one is born into because where one ends up in the social hierarchy depends solely on individual effort and talent.

One line of argument is that the achievement of a meritocracy in the United States is only feasible if everyone, including the children of immigrants, compete on a level playing field. The best way to achieve a level playing field, it is argued, is through an assimilation policy. Such a policy would result in everyone achieving a sufficient level of *cultural literacy* (i.e., what citizens need to know to actively participate and succeed in their respective countries; Hirsch, 1988). Becoming culturally literate would mean providing minority group children access to, and knowledge of, the mainstream culture and language. This would help eliminate barriers toward meritocracy. For example, admissions to university programs would really become merit based, because if important university admissions tests such as the SAT, GRE, MCAT, and LSAT are culturally biased to favor those familiar with majority culture and language (a charge often made by critics), then such potential biases would become irrelevant when everyone shares the same advantage.

An assimilation policy that aims to achieve a common level of cultural literacy in a population would have to be founded on a solid common core curriculum in schools. The expectation is that through a common educational experience, citizens would more broadly achieve a substantial level of shared knowledge, values, and worldview. This shared knowledge and worldview can be considered an aspect of what Putnam (2000) termed *social capital*, the cultural gel (norms, rules, etc.) that binds societies and enables them to be dynamic and thriving.

ASSESSING ASSIMILATION POLICY

The ideal world depicted by assimilation is one in which all individuals and groups merge and become more and more similar, resulting in a homogeneous, harmonious society, through either melting-pot assimilation, minority-assimilation, or a combination of both. But how feasible is this policy? I address this question by assessing the psychological assumptions underlying assimilation.

Contact and Prejudice

Walk into the cafeteria of almost any North American or Western European school or university at lunch time, and you will notice a persistent pattern: Students tend to congregate in groups that are organized according to ethnicity. The actual ethnic groups involved vary across countries and regions. For example, in the United States context, the most prominent groups are White, African American, and Latino. In the cafeterias of most U.S. schools, and you will see the members of these three groups sitting separately (of course, a positive aspect of this could be that minorities use the opportunity of sitting together to develop a stronger collective identity; see Tatum, 2003; chap. 5, this volume). In French Canada, Haitians, Southeast Asians, and other ethnic groups will often group together, separate from White French Canadians. In England, Pakistani and Indian students tend to congregate at lunch time, separate from White English students. In France, North Africans often sit separate from White French students. Of course, there will be a few individuals who sit with ethnic outgroup members, and there will also be multiethnic groups—but the general pattern tends to be one of congregation based on ethnicity. This seems to point to a shortcoming in the contact hypothesis (see the contrasting views of Hewstone & Brown, 1986a, and Pettigrew, 1998a).

Given that students are studying in the same school, sitting in classes together, playing on the same sports teams, sharing resources and activities, why is contact not leading students to abandon ethnic affiliations? Why do we find that most of them sit with their ethnic ingroups at lunch time? Of course, one response to these critical questions is the claim that the preconditions for contact, as set out by Allport (1954) and revised by others (e.g., Pettigrew, 1998a), have not been met. For example, the ethnic groups in question (e.g., Whites, African Americans, and Latinos) do not enjoy equal status. However, meta-analytical studies (e.g., Pettigrew & Tropp, 2006) suggest that contact alone is enough for a reduction in prejudice. In this connection, a second response to these questions is that contact does lead to reduced prejudice, but this does not necessarily change the affiliation patterns of students and others in ethnically diverse settings. This is because ethnicity has a powerful influence on behavior, reflected by the long-standing concept of *ethnocentrism* (i.e., a biased tendency to perceive the characteristics of one's own group as superior to those of outgroups; Levine & Campbell, 1972) and does not "melt away" through contact with ethnic outgroup members (Worchel, 1999).

Similarity Attraction

Imagine you are invited to a party and when you arrive the hostess tells you that one of the other guests looks and acts exactly like you; in fact, this other person could be your double. It seems that you and this other person are so alike that it will be difficult to tell you apart. How do you react? The probability is that you feel threatened. This prediction arises from social identity theory (Tajfel & Turner, 1979, 1986; see also chap. 5, this volume), which proposes that individuals are motivated to achieve a distinct and positive social identity. The idea is that we want not only to be positively evaluated but also to be seen as being in some important way(s) different (Grant, 1993).

When outgroup members are in important ways too similar to us, we might feel unable to differentiate, to put enough "distance," between "us" and "them." In such situations, similarity can lead to negative rather than positive intergroup relations, as suggested by some experimental evidence (Moghaddam & Stringer, 1988; Mummendey & Schreiber, 1983). A useful way to interpret perceived threat associated with outgroup similarity is in terms of Darwinian evolutionary theory (see Moghaddam, 2005a, chap. 19). Individuals and groups compete for resources to improve their chances of survival. In this competition, similar others can be a help, but they can also represent additional competition for scarce resources, including "vacant space" to achieve a positive and distinct identity. For example, if the members of my group are attempting to achieve a distinct identity on the criterion of creativity to be seen as the "creative group," I might feel particularly threatened when confronted by the members of another group who are also attempting to present themselves as the creative group. In such situations, groups attempt to differentiate rather than to focus on similarities, because similarity is threatening (see Lemaine, 1974; Lemaine, Kastersztein, & Personnaz, 1978).

Divisions, Conflict, and Democracy

The idea that we could manage society so that divisions, rifts, and differences would become minimized and homogeneity would become maximized is very appealing at one level. Surely, such a society would be peaceful because there would be a minimal influence of group-based distinctions and conflicts. Unfortunately, the assumption that such homogeneity would end intergroup bias and conflict is not supported by research evidence or real-world experiences.

First, consider the criteria according to which "homogeneity" would need to be achieved. Presumably, the members of different groups could melt away their differences in terms of values, norms, language, clothing style, food preferences, and other types of thought and action. Even if this were possible, how could groups melt away their physical differences, including skin color and body shape? Even the strongest supporters of assimilation have not suggested that physical differences between groups must be melted away. Consequently, there will always exist physical differences that could form the basis of intergroup bias and conflict. Given that physical differences play an enormously important role in social categorization and intergroup bias, the persistence of physical differences could overshadow homogeneity in other group characteristics.

Second, research using the minimal group paradigm (Tajfel, Flament, Billig, & Bundy, 1971; D. M. Taylor & Moghaddam, 1994, chap. 4; see also chap. 5, this volume) clearly demonstrates that even an apparently trivial intergroup difference can be used as a basis for intergroup bias. In hundreds of studies using the minimal group paradigm, participants were placed in a group on the basis of a "trivial" criterion for group formation, such as a dot-estimation task or a preference for a particular abstract painter or color. Even though participants did not know the identity of other group members, expect to interact with other group members in the future, or expect to receive any of the "rewards" they allocated to the ingroup or the outgroup, they nevertheless acted in a biased manner in favor of the ingroup. An implication of the findings of these studies is that people actively ascribe meaning to the characteristics of groups and socially construct the role and importance of intergroup differences. Experimental evidence shows that a criterion for group formation and intergroup difference that is trivial in one context can be reinterpreted as important and serve as a basis for intergroup bias in another context (Moghaddam & Stringer, 1986)..

Similarly, in the world outside the laboratory, the role and importance of criteria for intergroup differentiation and bias can change across contexts. Immigrants manifest this type of behavior when they move from their heritage land and settle in the adopted land: Criteria (e.g., local speech accent, clan or tribal affiliation) that used to play an important role in assigning group differences and status in the Old Country can suddenly become irrelevant in the New World in part because people in the New World do not recognize such differences. Thus, even what may appear to be a trivial intergroup difference can be reinterpreted as important. The implication is that no matter how homogeneous we shape society, differences between groups can still be manufactured and interpreted as important and serve as a basis for intergroup differentiation, discrimination, and even conflict. Given that physical differences (e.g., skin color) between ethnic groups will persist, such differences represent a huge resource for manufacturing a basis for intergroup conflict. Consequently, there are weaknesses in the idea that intergroup discrimination and conflict can be avoided through creating a homogeneous society.

Meritocracy

What about the idea that assimilation must be the preferred policy for managing cultural diversity because assimilation fits best with meritocracy? This is an intuitively appealing idea particularly because the avowed goal is to give every individual an equal opportunity to compete on a level playing field. The goal of equality of opportunity is compelling. However, we need to look more closely at the ways in which assimilation policy could influence equality of opportunity and the ways it could not.

Assimilation policy is intended to influence equality of opportunity by equipping ethnic minorities with the same cultural and linguistic tools as enjoyed by majority group members. However, assimilation is not intended to directly close gaps in income and material resources between the "haves" and the "have nots" in society. Thus, successful immigrants would be expected to assimilate and make their way up the status hierarchy, but the gap between social classes in society would not decrease. Consequently, the impact of economic inequalities on equality of opportunity would not be altered by assimilation.

This is a major shortcoming because equality of opportunity is seriously influenced by economic factors. For example, families with low incomes and low education levels are less likely to own a computer and to have Internet access in their homes (Calvert, Rideout, Woolard, Barr, & Strouse, 2005), and children from deprived families do relatively poorly in measures of physical and cognitive development (Bornstein & Bradley, 2003). As young adults, these children are not served well by the "outreach" programs of elite colleges (K. Fischer, 2006). Indeed, intervention programs in general have not done a good job of leveling the playing field, because economic inequalities continue to increase the advantages of the advantaged (Ceci & Papierno, 2005). Thus, although assimilation policy can influence cultural and linguistic spheres and in this way improve equality of opportunity for some minority individuals, such assimilation does not change the economic inequalities present in the larger society. Consequently, the inequality of opportunity that arises from economic disparities continues to detrimentally impact on the poorest sector of society.

IMPLICATIONS OF ASSIMILATION POLICY FOR DEMOCRACY

A central justification for assimilation policy is that it enhances equality of opportunity by helping to create a level playing field on which all individuals can compete on the basis of individual merit. Of course, equality of opportunity is not synonymous with democracy, but it is an integral component of democracy. Equality of opportunity is part of the American Dream idealized by actual and would-be immigrants to North America, where assimilation has been a dominant theme in cultural development.

Assimilation enables newcomers to more fully participate in community life as well as political and social activities at local and national levels. This is because assimilation leads to cultural literacy and language proficiency, tools that are essential for the psychological citizen to develop in a manner that allows for active participation in society. The influence of assimilation could help counter the "bowling alone" trend identified by Putnam (2000), whereby participation in community activities has decreased in the United States, and the widely discussed decline in political participation among U.S. citizens (Teixeira, 1992). Perhaps if assimilation took place more fully, newcomers would become more politically active.

However, assimilation and taking on the "American way of life" might lead to fuller participation only in the economic sphere and not the wider social and political spheres. This would be the case if newcomers interpret "becoming American" in a narrow way. After all, if the American middle class is neglecting the community and lowering their participation in political life, then why should newcomers not follow this model? Initially, at least, newcomers seem to give priority to economic participation and the ideal of equality of opportunity in the marketplace but consider assimilation in social and political spheres to be less palatable. In my own interviews with immigrants and refugees, I have been struck by how often they say the equivalent of,

> I came to America because it is the land of opportunity, and I want my children to become educated and to get good jobs, but I do not like American values or American foreign policy, and I do not want my children to become Americans in their family life.

The narrower economic interpretation of assimilation has both negative and positive implications for planned democracy (in which greater efforts are made to limit income disparities between the rich and the poor; see the discussion at the end of chap. 1, this volume). On the negative side, the increasing economic inequalities and the higher poverty rates among ethnic minorities in the United States, with a similar pattern emerging in the United Kingdom and most other countries of the European Union, suggest that the outcome of narrow economic assimilation will be the growth and solidification of an ethnic underclass in Western societies.

Signs of this trend are already clear. Travel to any major city in North America or Western Europe, and you will see ethnic minorities doing the grinding manual work that keeps airports, roads, buses, trains, hotels, hospitals, universities, restaurants, schools, nurseries, and homes running. At all the major universities, ethnic minorities make up almost all of the cleaning and maintenance staff and, proportionally, very few of the senior faculty and higher administration. Of course, some token figures are found higher up, but these tokens do not signal a success for assimilation.

On the positive side, an economic interpretation of assimilation at least suggests that cultural and linguistic heritages of ethnic minorities might be maintained. This would counter the minority-assimilation (Moghaddam, 1998) form of assimilation, whereby ethnic minorities melt away into the mainstream culture. Whereas supporters of minority-assimilation policy appeal to universalist arguments such as equality of opportunity, critics propose that this policy gives opportunities to the members of one culture only and suppresses all others, forcing them to change themselves in ways that run contrary to their original or root identity.

In essence, assimilation is criticized as extending the policy of colonialism, but in a new location. Whereas in previous centuries White Europeans would impose their values on third world people in their own third world societies, now they impose these values on third world people who have moved, or been forcibly transported at one time or another, to the West. Moreover, this alien culture and language is imposed under the guise of fairness and universal principles; however, critics contend that from the first it is "a particularism masquerading as the universal" (C. Taylor, 1992, p. 44)

Associated with criticisms leveled against assimilation policy is an important claim: that minorities have a right to maintain their cultures and languages. This right, too, is couched in universalist language, particularly the so-called universal right for people to develop their own identities in their own particular, distinct directions. Related to these claims that minorities have rights to develop and maintain their own cultures and identities is the claim that the government has a duty to create the conditions in which these rights can be fully exercised. Thus, we reach an interesting crossroad in the evolution of Western democracies, where both supporters and opponents of assimilation policy appeal to universalist principals and claim that the government has a duty to support certain (contradictory) policies for managing diversity in the name of democracy. In chapter 8, I show that supporters of multiculturalism policy also make universalist claims and demand government support "for the sake of democracy."

8

PSYCHOLOGICAL FOUNDATIONS
OF MULTICULTURALISM

For about a quarter of a century before and almost 2 centuries after the birth of Christ, the Roman empire experienced *Pax Romana*, a period of peace and relative comfort during which diverse cultural and linguistic groups co-existed within the empire under a fairly uniform legal umbrella. Although Rome was the center of the identity that dominated the empire, this identity was in important ways dynamic and influenced by multiple peripheral forces and minority groups (Laurence & Berry, 1998). People in different parts of the Roman empire had multiple identities, seeing themselves (not necessarily in the same ways) as Roman but also as having local ties and local identities (Huskinson, 1999). There are other examples of cultural diversity in regions and empires of the ancient world, such as in the Near East (Goedicke & Roberts, 1975), where trade, communications, and travel were often the norm rather than the exception (see Rudmin, 2003, pp. 9–11).

Given this feature of the ancient world, are we justified in treating cultural diversity in the 21st century as, in some respects, new and special? I believe we are justified. First, we are justified because the unprecedented scope, depth, and speed of globalization in the 21st century has brought about a new level of interconnectedness, contact, and mixing among culturally diverse groups. Second, we are justified because of the explicit policies adopted by some central governments to go beyond simply "tolerating" diversity and, instead, intervene directly to support and strengthen diversity.

Not only is the movement of people, goods, services, and cultural phenomena generally taking place across national borders to a much higher degree than ever before; some central governments are adopting policies to strengthen diversity within their borders. Such direct government intervention in support of minority cultures and languages is new and warrants special attention. Thus, my argument is that cultural diversity in the modern world is in some important respects new and different from traditional "pluralistic" societies or empires, such as ancient Rome.

The focus of this chapter is multiculturalism as a policy for managing cultural diversity. The literature on multiculturalism has mushroomed since the 1960s (Buenker & Ratner, 2005; Kymlicka & He, 2005; Máiz & Requejo, 2005; Parekh, 2006), and there is considerable variation in the meaning ascribed to this term. In much of the literature, as well as in mass media and everyday discussions, the term *multiculturalism* is often mentioned in relation to any society in which there is cultural diversity. For example, cities that have large ethnic minority populations (e.g., Los Angeles: Latinos; London: South Asians; Paris: North Africans; Berlin: Turks; Toronto: Italians) tend to be referred to as "multicultural." Or, to take another example, schools in which there are students from different cultural backgrounds are often referred to as being multicultural schools.

Beyond this merely descriptive approach, some discussions of multiculturalism attempt to move toward a particular goal in terms of a preferred type or level of diversity. For example, an index of cultural diversity is now routinely used as part of assessment in higher education. In many educational institutions, achieving a "culturally diverse" student and faculty body has become an explicitly stated goal, in a similar way that achieving a balance between the numbers of male and female students continues to be a much discussed challenge. Just as having "too few" female students (and now male students) in higher education is seen to be problematic, having too few minority group members is seen as undesirable and even unjust.

Multiculturalism as an avowed goal, an ideal adopted by society, has been approached in two main ways. The first, which I have termed *laissez-faire multiculturalism*, involves the government authorities and the majority group adopting a "hands off" approach and allowing market forces to determine the critical mix in society. As far as economic conditions allow, minority groups enjoy the freedom to retain their cultures and languages. In such a situation, there is no governmental attempt to assimilate minorities and to force immigrant children to "melt into" the mainstream.

The result of laissez-faire multiculturalism could be that a mixture of individualistic and collective strategies are adopted by immigrants, with some of them attempting to individually assimilate and achieve social mobility in the new land and others adopting a more group-based strategy (Moghaddam, Taylor, & Lalonde, 1987). Discriminatory barriers may prevent many minority group members from individually progressing up the social hierarchy in the adopted land, but as a collective, the newcomers might be able to gain power in a particular sector of the economy. The result may be the emergence of *ethnic economic enclaves* (documented for some time now; e.g., see Logan, Zhang, & Alba, 2002; K. L. Wilson & Martin, 1982), geoeconomic sectors in which the ethnic minority are economically and politically prominent (e.g., Cuban ethnic enclaves in Miami, South Asian ethnic enclaves in East London). Where there is laissez-faire multiculturalism, ethnic economic enclaves would emerge in large part through market forces.

An alternative type of multiculturalism is *planned multiculturalism*, in which the government authorities and the majority group directly intervene to support and strengthen cultural and linguistic diversity. The Canadian government was the first among Western democracies to officially adopt, in 1972, a policy of planned multiculturalism at the federal level (Fleras & Elliot, 1992). This was soon followed by Australia adopting a similar multicultural policy in 1978 (however, Australia retained one official language, English, whereas Canada established two official languages, English and French), with a number of reforms leading to *A New Agenda for Multicultural Australia* (see http://www.immi.gov.au/media/publications/multicultural/agenda/index.htm), as announced by Prime Minister John Howard in 1999. Australia's 21st-century multiculturalism policy follows the Canadian model of being interventionist (Australian Government, 2004), as does the New Zealand biculturalism policy: The federal government funds programs that directly support minority cultures.

The rise in multicultural consciousness in immigrant-receiving countries, including the United States, has come about in large part because of changing demographics and the transformed profile of immigrant populations, from Western Europeans to Asians and Africans, from a largely White-only population to a mostly non-White population (an excellent overview of immigrant America is provided by Portes & Rumbart, 2006). For example, whereas in 1850 about 97% of the foreign-born population of the United States, by far the largest immigrant-receiving country, was of European origin, in 1970, 1990, and 2003 the percentages declined to 67%, 26%, and 13.7%, respectively (see National Research Council, 1997, Table 2.2; U.S. Census, 2004, Figure 1). The level of the foreign-born population in the United States with Latin American origins went from about 1% in 1850 to 19% in 1970, to 43% in 1990, and to 53.3% in 2003. Asians experienced a similar, although less spectacular, increase, moving from less than 1% of the foreign-born population of the United States before 1900 to 3% in 1950, 9% in 1970, and 25% after 1990.

The collective political mobilization of native people has also influenced the changes in policy toward cultural diversity: Up until the 1960s it was not unusual for native children in Australia, Canada, and the United States to be separated from their native parents and placed in White foster families as a means of assimilating them more quickly and effectively. In the post–1960s era, native people around the world have been more politically active in support of their collective rights, and this has helped to bolster multicultural policies.

PSYCHOLOGICAL ASSUMPTIONS UNDERLYING MULTICULTURALISM POLICY

The policy of multiculturalism, particularly as developed by Canada, has a number of foundational psychological assumptions. The pioneering role and international status of Canada in multiculturalism has meant that these assumptions have gained importance in various other contexts in which multiculturalism has gained influence. We can identify these assumptions by returning to the origins of Canadian multiculturalism, particularly the flamboyant leadership of Pierre Elliot Trudeau (1919–2000). The psychological assumptions underlying Canadian multiculturalism are clearly identifiable in a statement made to the Canadian House of Commons in October 8, 1971, by then Prime Minister Trudeau, as discussed in the sections that follow.

The Cultural Free-Market Assumption

The starting psychological assumption, the *cultural free-market assumption*, underlying multiculturalism policy is that in the cultural marketplace, "there is no official culture, nor does any ethnic group take precedence over any other" (Trudeau, 1971/1992, p. 281). A kind of free market is envisaged, in which the role of the government is to allow individuals freedom to choose their cultural identities: "The individual's freedom would be hampered if he were locked for life within a particular cultural compartment by the accident of birth or language" (p. 281). However, note that in this cultural free market, an egalitarian situation is also envisaged, in which one ethnic group does not take precedence over others.

The Heritage Culture–Retention Assumption

The second psychological assumption underlying multiculturalism policy is that given "unhampered" choice, ethnic minorities will be positively motivated to retain their *heritage cultures*, meaning the cultures passed down to them from their parents. This is not simply because such cultures have been inherited but because some groups have a "collective will to exist" (Trudeau, 1971/1992, p. 281). Trudeau stated that "adherence to one's ethnic group is influenced not so much by one's origin or mother tongue as by one's sense of belonging to the group" (p. 281). Presumably, minority group members will feel a sense of belonging to their groups and will be motivated to continue their minority cultures. I shall refer to this as the *heritage culture–retention assumption*.

Note that the heritage culture–retention assumption contradicts the assimilationist assumption that minority group members are motivated to melt into the mainstream of the adopted land. The assimilationist assumption proposes that newcomers want to "become" American, Canadian, Australian, New Zealander, and so on, rather than retain their heritage identity (e.g., as Chinese, Indian, Pakistani). Note that in the European context, assimilation implies immigrants being positively motivated to become English, French, German, Swedish, and so on, as well as to adopt a superordinate European identity on top of a "new" national identity.

The Multiculturalism Hypothesis: The Original and Variations

> National unity, if it is to mean anything in the deeply personal sense, must be founded on confidence in one's own individual identity; out of this can grow respect for others and a willingness to share ideas, attitudes, and assumptions. (Trudeau, 1971/1992, p. 281)

This is how Canadian Prime Minister Trudeau introduced what later became interpreted by Canadian researchers as the *multiculturalism hypothesis* (see Berry, 1984; Berry, Kalin, & Taylor, 1977; Lambert & Taylor, 1990). I was fortunate to be collaborating with Wallace Lambert and Donald Taylor at McGill University (Montreal, Quebec, Canada) in the late 1980s, and they generously included me in a meeting with Pierre Elliott Trudeau, during which our small group discussed his historic statement on multiculturalism and our ongoing research on assumptions underlying the policy. Trudeau came unescorted to the meeting at the McGill psychology department; he lived close by, and I often saw him walking along the streets of Montreal (imagine an American president walking in city streets without an armed escort!). He was a very astute person, but it was clear that he had not predicted the ways in which the assumptions in his statement would be scrutinized and tested by academic researchers.

What did academic researchers find when they tested the multiculturalism hypothesis? The answer to this question depends on how we interpret multiculturalism. Although multiculturalism as federal government policy originated in Canada, the "ethnic revival" associated with multiculturalism was clearly recognized more broadly in the United States (Glazer & Moynihan, 1970; Hirschman, 1983), and the task of interpreting multiculturalism soon took on a life of its own on the wider world stage. Perhaps inevitably, there emerged different interpretations of a "multiculturalism hypothesis," often with no reference to the original Canadian government policy. Thus, it is useful to begin with the original interpretation of the multiculturalism hypothesis and then consider additional variations.

Ingroup Confidence and Outgroup Acceptance

Perhaps the most straightforward interpretation of Trudeau's (1971/1992) statement (as quoted in the previous section) is that confidence in one's own personal identity will lead one to be open and accepting toward others. Given one's own personal identity is in large part based on one's ethnic ingroup, and given that the term *others* includes outgroups, presumably those who feel secure in their own ethnic group identity will be more accepting and open toward outgroup members. This interpretation seems to match the original intent of Canadian government policy, which aimed to support and strengthen ethnic groups, that is, "the small and weak groups no less than the strong and highly organized" (p. 282).

Ingroup Affiliation and Outgroup Bias

An alternative version of the multiculturalism hypothesis proposes that there is no association between the strength and direction of ingroup association and the strength and direction of outgroup bias. In particular, people who strongly identify with their ingroup do not necessarily show negative bias against outgroups. This optimistic view is in line with Allport's (1954) argument that negative attitudes toward outgroups are not necessary to achieve solidarity with the ingroup. Brewer (1999) summed up this modern optimism in this way: "Ingroup love is not a precursor of outgroup hate" (p. 442). He added the caution that "the very factors that make ingroup attachment and allegiance important to individuals also provide a fertile ground for antagonism and distrust of those outside the ingroup boundary" (p. 442).

The optimism of the multiculturalism hypothesis is in sharp contrast to a tradition established in the seminal work of Freud (1953–1964; see also chap. 3, this volume) and Sumner (1906), in which it was assumed that positive ingroup relations are associated with hostility toward outgroups. Indeed, ethnocentrism is seen to be universal and associated with outgroup derogation (LeVine & Campbell, 1972). It is interesting to note that some researchers (e.g., Negy, Shreve, Jensen, & Uddin, 2003) have assumed that social identity theory (Tajfel & Turner, 1979, 1986; see chap. 5) proposes that the more strongly individuals identify with the ingroup, the more negatively biased they will be toward outgroups (this interpretation is controversial, a topic we return to later in the chapter).

Minority and Majority Endorsement of Multiculturalism and Intergroup Attitudes

A third interpretation of the multiculturalism hypothesis is that the implications of minority group behavior toward cultural diversity is different than the implications of majority group behavior, and the government should adopt different policies toward minority and majority groups. When minority groups endorse assimilation rather than multiculturalism, they are supporting their own "melting away." When majority groups endorse assimilation, they are more likely to be endorsing their own survival. When minority groups endorse multiculturalism, they are supporting their own survival, but when majority groups endorse multiculturalism, they are supporting the survival of minority outgroups. The Canadian policy focuses on support for minority groups, the assumption being that the most powerful group (English Canadians) does not need support to feel confident and be open and accepting toward others.

TESTING ASSUMPTIONS UNDERLYING MULTICULTURALISM

In the sections that follow, I reflect on some empirical evidence that can be used to critically assess a number of the assumptions underlying multiculturalism policy.

The Cultural Free-Market Assumption

What did Prime Minister Trudeau mean when he said that in multicultural Canada no culture takes "precedence over any other" (1971/1992, p. 281)? Obviously, he was not implying that all cultural groups have equal power and compete in a free-market situation. If this were the case, there would be no need to introduce federal government legislation to support smaller groups to maintain their heritage cultures because they could maintain their cultures without outside help. Rather than referring to the relative power of each culture, the cultural free-market assumption refers to the relative merit of each culture. The claim is that in the competition between cultures, the government takes the position that all cultures have equal merit, that there is no "official culture," and that the Canadian government will not give advantage to one culture over another.

A major shortcoming of this leveling approach is its relativism; it assumes that all cultural values are equal as long as they meet the legal requirements of the country. For example, in the domain of arts and literature, are all cultures equal? Surely not. Even if we consider variations within a single cultural group, this assumption is suspect: For example, in English drama, Elizabethan drama reached heights unrivaled by drama in other major eras.

There are certain highs and lows in cultural achievements, both historically (i.e., across time, within cultures) and cross-culturally (i.e., across cultures, at any one time). To state only that there are cultural "differences" is to avoid the responsibility of making judgments. If you assess my plays as different from that of Shakespeare's but refuse to take the further step of making a judgment on the quality of my plays as compared with his, you are denying me the opportunity to recognize the difference between my drama and the greatest drama and a chance to learn how to do better. In essence, you are violating my rights but are doing so in an apparently neutral way.

The Heritage Culture–Retention Assumption

What about the assumption that different groups are positively motivated toward cultural diversity and the retention of their own cultural heritages, in particular? Early in the history of official multiculturalism policy in Canada, research showed there to be general support for the retention of heritage cultures (Berry et al., 1977) as well as heritage languages (O'Bryan, Reitz, & Kuplowski, 1975). In the context of the United States, evidence has shown fairly positive attitudes toward heritage-culture retention among some minority groups (Lambert & Taylor, 1990; Negy et al., 2003), but the picture becomes more ambiguous and complex when we also consider trends in Europe (Arends-Tóth & Van de Vijver, 2003; Verkuyten, 2005; Zagefka & Brown, 2002). Indeed, there has for some time been evidence of groups being ambivalent toward heritage-culture retention (Moghaddam & Taylor, 1987).

Why are minority group attitudes toward heritage-culture retention at least sometimes ambivalent? Part of the explanation is that minority groups experience discrimination, and they come to believe that if they retain their heritage cultures they could become "more visible" and, therefore, easier targets of negative biases and actions. This interpretation was suggested by a study showing that the longer women from India live in Canada, the more they feel themselves to be outsiders (Moghaddam & Taylor, 1987). In Western Europe, discrimination continues to be a major problem for immigrants (Pettigrew, 1998b). If I am a minority group member experiencing discrimination, my culture could have both disadvantages and advantages: It could attract more negative attention and make me more vulnerable, or I could withdraw and gain protection by living inside the boundaries of my group (there is a well-established tradition of considering this kind of protection; see Crocker & Major, 1989). Thus, the assumption that all groups are positively motivated toward heritage-culture retention is questionable, particularly in the case of minority groups.

The Multiculturalism Hypothesis: The Original and Variations

As suggested earlier in this chapter, a major shortcoming of the multiculturalism hypothesis is that there is no generally accepted definition of the hypothesis. There are now many multiculturalism hypotheses.

Ingroup Confidence Leads to Outgroup Acceptance

Lambert, Memegis, and Taylor (1986) stayed close to the original statement made by Trudeau (1971/1992) and interpreted the multiculturalism hypothesis as proposing that feelings of pride and security in the heritage group will lead to acceptance toward others. Verkuyten (2005) agreed with this interpretation: "The multiculturalism hypothesis suggests a relationship of mediation in that multiculturalism is assumed to lead to a more positive and strong identity, which in turn would result in a more accepting attitude toward other groups" (p. 123). This interpretation of multiculturalism matches a rational view of humans. It suggests that a rational being who feels confidence and pride in the ingroup would have no (rational) reason to be biased against outgroups. Presumably, bias against outgroups arises from feelings of insecurity, and groups who feel secure and have pride in themselves will not be biased.

However, history seems to cast doubt on this assumption: Did the Nazis not have pride in themselves; did they not feel secure in their own heritage culture? Surely, the Nazis had enormous pride and were overconfident in their own superiority, right? But clearly, the Nazis were not accepting toward outgroups! There are numerous other examples we could cite, including religious fundamentalists intent on annihilating the followers of other faiths—clearly, there are many examples of groups who seem to feel secure and have pride in themselves but who are not accepting toward others. Indeed, if we march through historical examples of groups who have been notoriously intolerant toward outgroups, it would seem that ingroup pride and confidence is one of their most striking characteristics.

However, in defense of an interpretation of multiculturalism that assumes pride and confidence would lead to acceptance of others, it could be claimed that a deeper, irrationalist understanding of security and pride is needed. From this viewpoint, it could be argued that the Nazis', religious fundamentalists', and other groups' intent on annihilating their "enemies" only appears on the surface to feel secure. In practice, they have deep feelings of insecurity and exaggerated self-esteem and collective esteem (see related discussions in Baumeister, 1999). They attack outgroups because of their insecurities; thus, the nurturing of genuine feelings of pride and security in the heritage group will lead to acceptance toward others.

Ingroup Affiliation Does Not Result In Bias Against Outgroups

Love for the ingroup does not mean hate for the outgroup: We noted that this optimistic interpretation of multiculturalism, in line with Allport (1954), is contradicted by a long tradition of thinkers, including Freud (1953–1964; see also chap. 3). More recently, social identity theory (Tajfel & Turner, 1979, 1986; see also chap. 5, this volume) was interpreted as predicting that the more strongly individuals identify with the ingroup, the more negatively biased they will be against outgroups, but this interpretation is controversial (J. C. Turner & Reynolds, 2004, have rejected this interpretation of social identity theory, made by Hinkle & Brown, 1990, among others).

Perhaps part of the controversy involving pessimistic and optimistic interpretations of a link between ingroup identification and outgroup bias is explained by the different behavioral patterns of majority and minority groups in this area. For example, Negy et al. (2003) found that among Whites and Latinos, but not among African Americans, the more individuals identified with the ethnic ingroup, the higher they were on ethnocentrism (i.e., favoring the ingroup and showing negative attitudes toward outgroups). In a study of native Dutch and Turkish participants living in Holland, Verkuyten (2005) found that majority group members who endorsed multiculturalism were less likely to identify with their ethnic ingroup and to show negative outgroup bias. In contrast, the more majority group members endorsed assimilation, the more they identified with their ethnic ingroup and showed negative outgroup bias. The pattern was the reverse for minority group members: The more minority group members endorsed multiculturalism, the more likely they were to identify with their ethnic ingroup and to show negative outgroup bias. In contrast, the more minority group members endorsed assimilation, the less they identified with their ethnic ingroup and showed negative outgroup bias.

In summary, the optimism assertion that "ingroup love is not a precursor of outgroup hate" (Brewer, 1999, p. 442) might be valid in some contexts, but it has major shortcomings in other contexts, depending on the majority–minority status of the group(s) involved.

Minority and Majority Endorsement of Multiculturalism and Intergroup Attitudes

In Canada and other countries where multiculturalism is official government policy, the main goal of such policy is the maintenance of heritage cultures (and sometimes languages), with a focus on minority rather than majority groups. For example, in Canada multiculturalism is designed to support the heritage cultures of Greek, Haitian, Chinese, and other ethnic minorities, and not the English majority. This strategy is presumably intended to enhance a sense of security and pride among ethnic minorities and, in this way, increase positive attitudes toward and acceptance of outgroups.

However, are not the most problematic sources of discrimination in Canada and other societies majority rather than minority groups? Indeed, it is English and French Canadians who enjoy the greater power and can (and sometimes do) discriminate against outgroups. If Haitian Canadians or some other minority group attempt to discriminate against outgroups, their actions are not likely to have serious consequences (for majority group targets, at least), simply because Haitians and other such minorities do not have any real power in Canada. However, when English and French Canadians discriminate against outgroups, the consequences of their actions are far more likely to be serious (for minority group targets, at least), because they have political and economic clout. They can, and do, monopolize in key areas such as jobs and housing.

Of course, it could be claimed that because majority groups enjoy greater power and status, there is less need to help them achieve a sense of security and pride. However, if this were the case, and if a sense of security and pride were supposed to lead to acceptance of others, then it would stand to reason that outgroup tolerance would be higher among majority group members. Therefore, this assumption is highly questionable. Although higher education correlates with greater tolerance toward others, majority groups as a whole are not necessarily more tolerant toward outgroups than are minority groups.

MULTICULTURALISM IN THE EUROPEAN UNION

The challenges of selecting an appropriate and effective policy for managing cultural and linguistic diversity are brought into sharp focus by examining the history and current state of the European Union. The beginnings of the European Union can be traced back at least to discussions that followed World War I (1914–1918), the so-called Great War that was to "end all wars," when Europeans were considering different political possibilities for preventing future war. Unfortunately, no tangible progress was made until after World War II (1939–1945), when in 1957 six countries (i.e., France, West Germany, Italy, Holland, Belgium, and Luxemburg) signed the Treaty of Rome (see http://www.hri.org/docs/Rome57/) to found the European Economic Community (EEC), building on a trade agreement reached in 1951 regarding coal and steel (see Dinan, 2004, for a detailed history of the European Union). The United Kingdom, Denmark, and Ireland joined the EEC in 1973, and the gradual expansion culminated in the establishment of the European Union in 1992 through the Maastricht Treaty (see http://www.eurotreaties.com/maastrichtext.html) and the absorption of most East European states to form a union of 25 EU members in 2004.

The European Union now has common policies in trade, agriculture, defense and security, and to some degree, foreign policy. There is also a common EU policy on human rights, guaranteed by the European Convention for the Protection of Human Rights and Fundamental Freedoms (see http://www.echr.coe.int/NR/rdonlyres/D5CC24A7-DC13-4318-B457-5C9014916D7A/0/EnglishAnglais.pdf). This is important and relevant to multiculturalism because minority groups are protected against discrimination and guaranteed freedom of expression, which could help them retain heritage cultures and languages. A further strengthening of basic rights and political links between EU members will be achieved if the EU Constitutional Treaty (see http://www.unizar.es/euroconstitucion/Home.htm) is ratified; such ratification, however, has been blocked by popular votes in several EU countries.

Although the ratification of the EU Constitutional Treaty is proving to be a challenge, perhaps the greatest challenge facing the European Union concerns European identity: What kind of a person is a European? The European Union is dedicated to the principle of unity in diversity, meaning that it will, on the one hand, promote the diversity of its cultures and, on the other hand, bring to the forefront "the common cultural heritage" of Europe (Article 151 TEC; see http://europa.eu.int/eur-lex/en/treaties/dat/C_2002325EN.003301.html). However, what is the common cultural heritage of Europe? Some have supported the claim made by Pope Benedict XVI in March 2006 that common Christian values and roots are what best identify Europe. By giving priority to a common Christian heritage, the boundaries of Europe could also be defined; so far, the borders of Europe have been left undefined in formal EU declarations.

However, the attempt to use a common Christian heritage to define Europe faces strong opposition, first, by those who endorse a secular rather than a religious vision of the European Union and, second, by those who would like the European Union to eventually include Turkey—an Islamic society (during his trip to Turkey in 2006, Pope Benedict XVI reversed course and endorsed the idea of Turkey joining the European Union). A third objection to defining European identity in religious terms arises from defenders of religious minorities, the millions of Muslims, Jews, and other non-Christians who now live in the European Union. These objections have meant that there is no reference to Christianity or God, or any acknowledgments of Europe's religious inheritance, in the EU Constitutional Treaty that reached agreement in 2004 (but has yet to reach final ratification).

If "Christian values" do not serve as an effective basis for European identity, another possibility is political and social values and institutions. Such values and institutions are already used, as reflected in the so-called Copenhagen Criteria (see the discussion on challenges facing EU expansion; Ingham & Ingham, 2002), which indicate that to qualify for EU membership a new applicant country must have stable democratic institutions, a market economy, and effective administrative structures. These criteria have been applied and can be said to be effective in the sense that they have prevented certain applicant countries from joining the European Union; for example, Turkey's application has so far not met these criteria.

However, is the sharing of civic values and institutions, as well as a political system within an economic free-trade zone, a sufficient foundation for the development of common culture and shared collective identity? This civic approach seems to ignore deep historical divisions and cultural gulfs; will this neglect not become a basis for fragmentation and balkanization? Besides, cultural differences are already preventing the ratification of the EU Constitution, and intense debates and divisions on issues such as stem cell research are widening, suggesting that it will not be possible for Europeans to ignore cultural divisions, including differences in moral and religious orientations.

In relation to civic values, it could be argued that the most important characteristic common to European societies is the "social net" they provide their citizens in the form of unemployment and retirement benefits, government health and education services, and support for the family (e.g., through daycare services as well as maternal and paternal leave). In practice, the left-leaning governments of Europe support the family through actual policies, whereas the right-leaning U.S. administrations pay lip service to "family values" but fail to provide adequate financial support for working families. European societies, including the United Kingdom, have much stronger employee protection laws than does the United States (one reason academics in Europe do not need tenure is that they already enjoy protection from arbitrary firing in the same way that all employees are protected).

Because the European Union is so new, its search for an effective shared identity—the "glue" that will hold the 25 (and increasing) diverse nation states together—exemplifies the challenge of achieving unity in diversity; however, in some respects, the same challenge continues to confront the United States, Canada, Australia, and other historically immigrant-receiving societies. One reason why traditional immigrant-receiving societies are facing a renewed challenge is because prior to the 1960s, immigrants to these countries primarily came from Western Europe. The new waves of tens of millions of immigrants from outside Western Europe are culturally far more different from the mainstream of their host societies.

Reflecting Back From North American Experiences

In assessing the challenge faced by the European Union in absorbing millions of immigrants from outside the Western tradition, it is instructive to look across to North American, where a similar challenge has been undertaken. By 2008, the number of Latinos in the United States will be about 45 million, although this is a rough estimate because the number of Latinos illegally in the United States is estimated to be anything from 11 to 15 million. Parts of California, Florida, Texas, and Arizona already serve as Latino economic enclaves, meaning that the local economy is dominated by Latinos. In these Latino economic enclaves, those who are not functional in Spanish find it difficult to find work, and this has led to some friction between Latinos and African Americans, who sometimes feel pushed out of their "traditional" job areas in some parts of Florida, California, and other states. Rather than remaining confined to small ethnic neighborhoods (e.g., Chinatown), Latinos are becoming a more prominent national presence. Government services, particularly in education and health, have come under intense pressure to adapt to meet the needs of Spanish-speaking clientele.

The "Latino threat" has resulted in a backlash in the English-speaking majority, both White and African American. A highly visible indication of this is the so-called English-only movement, the avowed goal of which is to declare English the national language of the United States. The English-only movement has been politicized (e.g., see Crawford, 2007), and even in the classroom there is considerable controversy about the merits of teaching English only versus using a bilingual or multilingual strategy to teach both immigrant and mainstream children (Stritikus & Suarez-Orozco, 2002). The politicization of the debate over whether there should be a national language is unfortunate because it has detracted from our ability to consider both pros and cons.

Do nations need national languages? Is it wrong to establish a national language in the United States? If one considers long-term prospects, a strong case can be made for establishing English as the national language of the United States. The Egyptians, the Chinese, the Greeks, the Romans, the British—unless we suffer the illusion of immortality, we must accept that the United States will follow these former world powers and sooner or later experience a decline. The question is not whether but when the decline will occur. What will be the basis of the U.S. decline? One clear possibility is internal divisions and fragmentation. Even more powerful than the historic North–South split in the United States, divisions on the basis of language are possible and must be considered.

When the United States does experience a decline, the tensions over language differences could indeed heighten, much like to the north, where Canada faces a continuing threat of fragmentation based on language groups: the French and the English. Areas such as Texas, New Mexico, California, and Florida may well return to a different, Spanish destiny, separate from English-speaking America. The establishment of English as the national language would delay or lessen this possibility.

Europe began with multiple languages, but it is moving toward unilingualism, at least in business and education and particularly among the elite. Proficiency in English is now a necessary qualification for educational and career advancement in Europe. This trend is placing increasing pressure on minority languages. This complex issue is best considered in relation to social class.

Social Class, Bilingualism, and Language Policies

On the international stage, English is achieving monopoly status in business, higher education, and research. International business meetings and research conferences are invariably conducted in English, and sometimes local languages are also used. Associated with this trend is the growth of an international elite group of corporate and educational leaders who are immersed in the English language and who have developed a worldview that is different from the rest of the populations in their societies.

This trend reflects the growth of *dual perceptions* (i.e., different perceptions of social reality that have evolved in elite and nonelite sectors of societies; after Moghaddam & Taylor, 1985). In each nation state around the world, there now exists an elite group who maintains international communications in English and who shares a common worldview with elites in other countries.

Within nation states, on the issue of unilingualism versus multilingualism, it is necessary to distinguish between national policy and private practices. Irrespective of whether there is a national language in countries such as the United States, children born into the middle and upper classes are far more likely to receive training in English and one, or more, other language(s). In Canada, the "other" language is French, whereas in the United States, it is Spanish or Mandarin Chinese. Immersion (bilingual) education is being practiced in affluent neighborhoods, supported by language education provided by private tutors and nannies who speak Spanish, Chinese, or some other minority language as their mother tongue.

The quality of language education received by children is being determined by the same factor that determines the quality of all other education: social class. As Golden (2006) and others have demonstrated, the children whose families can afford the rapidly increasing cost of higher quality education are far more likely to end up entering elite institutions. Only about 3% of 1st-year students at the most selective U.S. universities come from the bottom 25% income group, whereas 75% come from the top 25% income group. Having arrived at the elite universities with better second-language proficiency, the selected students gain additional advantages by benefiting from the more in-depth language training provided by elite universities through study abroad and other such programs. Latinos could potentially use bilingualism as an asset, but like other minorities who are concentrated in lower economic strata, Latinos find that their educational opportunities are correspondingly low (for the latest information about Latinos in education, see the numerous reports available from Hispanics Across America [http://www.haamerica.org/] as well as the Pew Hispanic Center [http://pewhispanic.org/], who's Web site is also accessible from that of The Pew Charitable Trusts: http://www.pewtrust.com; for an example of research highlighting Latino adaptive style in the new land, see Varela, Steele, & Benson, 2007).

THE IMPLICATIONS OF MULTICULTURALISM FOR DEMOCRACY

As economic and technological forces push globalization forward and bring the global village closer to reality, multiculturalism has emerged as a serious alternative to assimilation as a policy for managing diversity. This alternative is viewed by some, particularly minority group members, as morally superior and more in line with democratic values.

The term *multiculturalism* implies that in the global context and within an individual society (a) different minority and majority cultures should be given equal value, (b) there should be a sharing of cultures across groups, and (c) intergroup differences should be celebrated and sustained. Multiculturalism is based on the assumption that groups have a democratic right to develop in different cultural directions and that authorities have the corresponding duty to bring about conditions in which this collective right can be exercised. Associated with this idea is the assumption that individuals and groups have a right to enjoy positive self- and collective-esteem, respectively. In some circles, high self- and collective-esteem have come to be seen as essential as any other democratic right, such as the right to vote. Denial of esteem rights is seen as leading to other problems, such as inabilities to be open and accepting toward others and even being aggressive toward others.

To more fully illuminate the implications of multiculturalism for democracy, one can begin by distinguishing between actual and symbolic differences between groups. At both national and global levels, in many ways, actual intercultural differences have decreased through globalization and the spread of consumer goods and services. The mass media, computers, cars, and consumer products generally have created greater similarities in lifestyles across societies so that even places such as the United States and China now have a great deal in common. At the national level, regional and local differences are decreasing through the same macroeconomic and technological forces. In practice, then, the world is becoming culturally more similar.

This decrease in actual intercultural differences globally and nationally has been associated with an opposing trend: the rise of symbolic differences. The members of different groups, who actually live lives that are very similar to one another, are now constructing intergroup differences, rediscovering or manufacturing "traditions," and adopting cultural carriers that symbolize their collective "differentness" (Moghaddam, 2002). Examples of this include the numerous African cultural practices and products, such as those associated with the annual Kwanzaa celebrations held December 26 through January 1, which continue to be rediscovered and adopted as carriers by African Americans.

As suggested by the findings of the minimal group paradigm studies (Tajfel et al., 1971; see also chap. 5, this volume), even minor differences can serve as a basis for intergroup differentiation and distinctiveness: It is not the objective meaning of an intergroup difference but the meaning ascribed to a difference that shapes intergroup relations. If Group A and Group B are actually very similar in lifestyle but are seen by group members to be very different, then it is perceptions of differences that can shape their intergroup relations. Moreover, when groups perceive it as a collective right to manufacture and celebrate differences, democratic societies are faced with the challenge of setting limits on the ways in which, and the extremes to which, groups can search for and construct "differentness." In addition to highlighting the rights of groups to manufacture and celebrate differences, there is also a need to give importance to the duties of groups to maintain certain core values. Of course, core values can only be agreed on when groups accept limits to relativism.

The acceptance of group-based diversity as a right confronts democracies with formidable challenges related to relativism: On what basis does a government support or limit diversity? Consider, for example, the now annual "Christmas wars" in North America and the accusation that certain groups are trying to "steal Christmas" (see O'Reilly, 2006, for a right-wing version of the ongoing "culture wars"). A "Christmas incident" at Seattle–Tacoma International Airport in Seattle, Washington, reported in *The New York Times* under the title "A lawsuit threat is gone and Christmas trees return" (Yardley, 2006), exemplifies the dilemma faced by authorities. Airport authorities removed Christmas trees after a Jewish Orthodox educational group threatened a lawsuit unless a menorah was also put on display. The authorities felt that if they added a menorah they would have to add symbols from other religions. An official summed up the dilemma in this way: "If you are going to add one, then where do you stop?" (p. A24).

An implication of multiculturalism is that democracy would be richer if more and more symbols and more and more groups were added (as discussed in chap. 1, this volume, an argument found in the domains of both cultural diversity and biological diversity is that greater diversity is better), but it would be a fundamental challenge to set limits on diversity on the basis of justice principles. This challenge is highlighted by the plight of Western authorities confronted by non-Western values and practices. For example, consider the following two events that have influenced Islamic–Western relations over the last few decades: (a) the fatwa (which still stands) issued by Iran's supreme leader Ayatollah Khomeini against the Indian British author Salman Rushdie for writing the "blasphemous" novel *Satanic Verses* and (b) the killing of the Dutch filmmaker Theo van Gogh by a Dutch Moroccan Muslim for the "crime" of insulting Islam through his art. Clearly, policies based on a relativist philosophy are inadequate for dealing with such terrible events. Rather, what is required is a set of principles that are applied universally. It is in this relation that, once again, it is useful to turn to the distinction between distributive and procedural justice.

Using the research of Tyler and others on procedural justice (e.g., Tyler & Degoey, 1995; Tyler & Huo, 2002; see also chap. 6, this volume) as a point of departure, I propose that the best hope for constructively managing diversity in multicultural contexts is to involve as many groups as possible in the procedures of decision making. Such involvement will itself influence the sense of justice experienced by the groups involved, independent of the outcomes of the decision-making process. Involvement in procedures will also increase the likelihood that the members of different groups will come to recognize "common principles" as fair.

Assessments of the experiences of minorities, such as Muslims in Europe (e.g., Buruma, 2006; White, 1997), suggest that minorities remain in large part disengaged from procedures of decision making. In such a situation, minorities may continue to feel "separate and unequal" and disengaged even when authorities allocate more resources to them, for example, through affirmative action. A greater investment in strengthening procedural justice will not end controversies about affirmative action and other programs designed to alter resource distribution (e.g., consider the different approaches of Sowell, 2004, and Niemann & Maruyama, 2005, on the issue of affirmative action); however, by involving more groups in procedures, outcomes will also become fairer, both in practice and in how they are perceived.

REFERENCES

Abrams, D. (1994). Political distinctiveness: An identity optimizing approach. *European Journal of Social Psychology, 24,* 357–365.

Abrams, D., & Hogg, M. A. (Eds.). (1999). *Social identity and social cognition.* Oxford, England: Blackwell.

Adams, J. S. (1963). Toward an understanding of inequity. *Journal of Abnormal and Social Psychology, 67,* 422–436.

Adorno, T. W., Frenkel-Brunswik, E., Levinson, D. J., & Sanford, B. W. (1950). *The authoritarian personality.* New York: Harper & Row.

Ahn, W. K., Goldstone, R. L., Love, B. C., Markman, A. B., & Wolff, P. (Eds.). (2005). *Categorization inside and outside the laboratory: Essays in honor of Douglas L. Medin.* Washington, DC: American Psychological Association.

Akhtar, S. (Ed.). (2006). *Freud along the Ganges: Psychoanalytic reflections on the people and culture of India.* New York: Other Press.

Allen, W. E., & Chagnon, N. A. (2004). The tragedy of the commons revisited. In Y. T. Lee, C. McCauley, F. M. Moghaddam, & S. Worchel (Eds.), *The psychology of ethnic and cultural conflict* (pp. 23–47). Westport, CT: Praeger Publishers.

Allport, G. W. (1954). *The nature of prejudice.* Cambridge, MA: Addison-Wesley.

Altemeyer, B. (1988). *Enemies of freedom: Understanding right-wing authoritarianism.* San Francisco: Jossey-Bass.

Altemeyer, B. (1994). Reducing prejudice in right-wing authoritarians. In M. P. Zanna & J. M. Olson (Eds.), *The psychology of prejudice: The Ontario Symposium* (Vol. 7, pp. 131–148). Hillsdale, NJ: Erlbaum.

Arends-Tóth, J., & Van de Vijver, F. J. R. (2003). Multiculturalism and acculturation: Views of Dutch and Turkish-Dutch. *European Journal of Social Psychology, 33,* 249–266.

Argyle, M. (1994). *The social psychology of social class.* New York: Routledge.

Ashmore, R. D., & Jussim, L. (Eds.). (1997). *Self and identity: Fundamental issues.* New York: Oxford University Press.

Australian Government, Department of Immigration and Multicultural Affairs. (2004). *A diverse Australia: The current policy.* Retrieved October 5, 2007, from http://www.immi.gov.au/living-in-australia/a-diverse-australia/government-policy/australians-together/current-policy/index.htm

Barlow, K. M., Taylor, D. M., & Lambert, W. E. (2000). Ethnicity in America and feeling "American." *The Journal of Psychology, 134,* 581–600.

Baskin, Y. (2002). *A plague of rats and rubber vines.* Washington, DC: Island Press.

Baumeister, R. F. (Ed.). (1999). *Self in social psychology.* New York: Psychology Press.

Baumeister, R. F., & Leary, M. R. (1995). The need to belong: Desire for interpersonal attachments as a fundamental human motivation. *Psychological Bulletin, 117,* 497–529.

Beeghley, L. (1996). *The structure of social stratification in the United States* (2nd ed.). Boston: Bacon & Allyn.

Bekoff, M. (2005). *Wild justice and fair play: Cooperation, forgiveness, and morality in animals.* Chicago: University of Chicago Press.

Bekoff, M., Allen, C., & Burghardt, G. M. (Eds.). (2002). *The cognitive animal.* Cambridge, MA: MIT Press.

Berkowitz, L. (Ed.). (1969). *Roots of aggression.* New York: Atherton Press.

Berry, J. W. (1984). Multiculturalism policy in Canada: A social psychological analysis. *Canadian Journal of Behavioral Science, 16,* 353–370.

Berry, J. W., Kalin, R., & Taylor, D. M. (1977). *Multiculturalism and ethnic attitudes in Canada.* Ottawa, Ontario, Canada: Supply and Services Canada.

Berscheid, E., & Reis, H. T. (1998). Attraction and close relationships. In D. T. Gilbert, S. T. Fiske, & G. Lindzey (Eds.), *The handbook of social psychology* (Vol. 2, 4th ed., pp. 193–281). New York: McGraw-Hill.

Billig, M. G. (1976). *Social psychology and intergroup relations.* London: Academic Press.

Boaz, D. (1997). *Libertarianism: A primer.* New York: Free Press.

Bornstein, M. H., & Bradley, R. H. (2003). *Socioeconomic status, parenting, and child development.* Mahwah, NJ: Erlbaum.

Bowles, S., Gintis, H., & Groves, M. O. (Eds.). (2005). *Unequal chances: Family background and economic success.* Princeton, NJ: Princeton University Press.

Brauer, M., Judd, C. M., & Gliner, M. D. (1995). The effects of repeated expressions on attitude polarization during group discussions. *Journal of Personality and Social Psychology, 68,* 1014–1029.

Breakwell, G. (1986). *Coping with threatened identities.* London: Methuen.

Breslin, S., Hughes, C., Phillips, N., & Rosamond, B. (Eds.). (2001). *New regionalism(s) in the global political economy: Theories and cases.* London: Routledge.

Brewer, M. B. (1991). The social self: On being the same and different at the same time. *Personality and Social Psychology Bulletin, 17,* 475–482.

Brewer, M. B. (1999). The psychology of prejudice: Ingroup love or outgroup hate? *Journal of Social Issues, 55,* 429–444.

Brewer, M. B. (2000). Reducing prejudice through cross-categorization: Effects of multiple social identities. In S. Oskamp (Ed.), *Reducing prejudice and discrimination* (pp. 165–183). Mahwah, NJ: Erlbaum.

Brewer, M. B., & Gaertner, S. L. (2004). Toward reduction of prejudice: Intergroup contact and social categorization. In M. B. Brewer & M. Hewstone (Eds.), *Self and social identity* (pp. 298–318). Oxford, England: Blackwell.

Brewer, M. B., & Gardner, W. (1996). Who is this "we"? Levels of collective identity and self representations. *Journal of Personality and Social Psychology, 71,* 83–93.

Brewer, M. B., & Miller, N. (1996). *Intergroup relations.* Pacific Grove, CA: Brooks/Cole.

Brewer, M. B., & Roccas, S. (2001). Individual values, social identity, and optimal distinctiveness. In C. Sedikides & M. B. Brewer (Eds.), *Individual self, relational self, collective self* (pp. 219–237). Philadelphia: Psychology Press.

Brosnan, S. F., & de Waal, F. B. M. (2003). Monkeys reject unequal pay. *Nature, 425,* 297–299.

Brown, G. D. A., Gardner, J., Oswald, A., & Qian, J. (2004). *Does wage rank affect employees' wellbeing?* Retrieved October 5, 2007, from http://www.warwick.ac.uk/staff/G.D.A.Brown/RFTWagesSept04.pdf

Brown, R. J. (2000). Social identity theory: Past achievements, current problems and future challenges. *European Journal of Social Psychology, 30,* 745–778.

Brown, R. J., & Hewstone, M. (2005). An integrative theory of intergroup contact. In M. P. Zanna (Ed.), *Advances in experimental social psychology* (Vol. 37, pp. 255–343). San Diego, CA: Academic Press.

Buenker, J. D., & Ratner, L. A. (Eds.). (2005). *Multiculturalism in the United States: A comparative guide to acculturation and ethnicity.* Westport, CT: Greenwood Press.

Buruma, I. (2006). *Murder in Amsterdam: The death of Theo van Gogh and the limits of tolerance.* New York: Oxford University Press.

Byrne, D. (1971). *The attraction paradigm.* New York: Academic Press.

Calvert, S. L., Rideout, V. J., Woolard, J. L., Barr, R., & Strouse, G. A. (2005). Age, ethnicity, and socioeconomic patterns in early computer use: A national survey. *American Behavioral Scientist, 48,* 590–607.

Campbell, D. T. (1956). Enhancement of contrast as a composite habit. *Journal of Abnormal and Social Psychology, 56,* 350–355.

Cawelti, J. G. (1965). *Apostles of the self-made man: Changing concepts of success in America.* Chicago: The University of Chicago Press.

Ceci, S. J., & Papierno, P. B. (2005). The rhetoric and reality of gap closing: When the "have-nots" gain but the "haves" gain even more. *American Psychologist, 60,* 149–160.

Chagnon, N. A. (1997). *Yanomamo* (5th ed.). New York: Harcourt Brace.

Chaucer, G. (1977). *The Canterbury tales* (N. Coghill, Trans.). London: Penguin Classics.

Chirot, D., & Seligman, M. E. P. (Eds.). (2001). *Ethnopolitical warfare: Causes, consequences, and possible solutions.* Washington, DC: American Psychological Association.

Chomsky, N. (1965). *Aspects of the theory of syntax.* Cambridge, MA: MIT Press.

Cohen, R. (2007, September 17). The nordic option. *The New York Times,* p. A23.

Cox, W. M., & Alm, R. (1999). *Myths of rich & poor: Why we're better off than we think.* New York: Basic Books.

Crawford, J. (2007). *Language policy web site & emporium.* Retrieved September 23, 2006, from http://ourworld.compuserve.com/homepages/JWCRAWFORD/home.htm

Crocker, J., & Major, B. (1989). Social stigma and self-esteem: The self-protective properties of stigma. *Psychological Review, 96,* 608–630.

Crocker, J., Major, B., & Steele, C. M. (1998). Social stigma. In D. T. Gilbert, S. T. Fiske, & G. Lindzey (Eds.), *Handbook of social psychology* (4th ed., pp. 504–553). Boston: McGraw-Hill.

Crosby, F. (1976). A model of egotistical relative deprivation. *Psychological Review, 83*, 85–113.

Crystal, D. (2000). *Language death*. Cambridge, England: Cambridge University Press.

Darwin, C. (1993). *The origin of species by natural selection or the preservation of favored races in the struggle for life*. New York: Modern Library. (Original work published 1859)

Davies, J. C. (1974). The J-curve and power struggle theories of collective violence. *American Sociological Review, 39*, 607–619.

Dawkins, R. (1989). *The selfish gene* (2nd ed.). Oxford, England: Oxford University Press.

Dehaene, S., Izard, V., Pica, P., & Spelke, E. (2006, January 20). Core knowledge of geometry in an Amazonian Indigene group. *Science, 311*, 381–384.

Dershowitz, A. (2004). *Rights from wrongs: A secular theory of the origins of rights*. New York: Basic Books.

Devine, F. (1997). *Social class in America and Britain*. Edinburgh, England: University of Edinburgh Press.

Diab, L. N. (1970). A study of intragroup and intergroup relations among experimentally produced groups. *Genetic Psychology Monographs, 82*, 49–82.

Dickens, C. (1963). *Great expectations*. New York: Signet Classic. (Original work published 1860–1861)

Dickens, C. (1994). *Martin Chuzzlewit*. Hertfordshire, England: Wordsworth Classics. (Original work published 1843–1844)

Dickens, C. (1999). *A tale of two cities*. New York: AMSCO. (Original work published 1859)

Dinan, D. (2004). *Europe recast: A history of the European Union*. Boulder, CO: Rienner.

Dion, K. L. (1986). Responses to perceived discrimination and relative deprivation. In J. M. Olson, C. P. Herman, & M. P. Zanna (Eds.), *Relative deprivation and social comparison: The Ontario Symposium* (Vol. 4, pp. 159–180). Hillsdale, NJ: Erlbaum.

Dixon, J. C., & Rosenbaum, M. S. (2004). Nice to know you? Testing contact, cultural, and group threat theories of anti-Black and anti-Latino stereotypes. *Social Science Quarterly, 85*, 257–280.

Dollard, J., Bood, L., Miller, N., Mowrer, O., & Sears, R. (1939). *Frustration and aggression*. New Haven, CT: Yale University Press.

Dovidio, J. F., & Gaertner, S. L. (Eds.). (1986). *Prejudice, discrimination, and racism*. Orlando, FL: Academic Press.

Dovidio, J. F., Gaertner, S. L., & Kawakami, K. (2003). Intergroup contact: The past, present, and the future. *Group Processes & Intergroup Relations, 6*, 5–21.

Dovidio, J. F., Glick, P., & Rudman, L. (Eds.). (2005). *On the nature of prejudice: Fifty years after Allport*. Malden, MA: Blackwell.

du Gay, P., Evans, J., & Redman, P. (Eds.). (2000). *Identity: A reader*. Thousand Oaks, CA: Sage.

Durkheim, E. (1964). *The division of labor in society.* New York: Macmillan. (Original work published 1893)

Dyson-Hudson, N. (1971). Nomadic people find freedom and identity in the life they follow. In R. L. Breeden (Ed.), *Nomads of the world* (pp. 8–25). Washington, DC: National Geographic Society.

Ehrenreich, B. (2002). *Nickel and dimed: On (not) getting by in America.* New York: Holt.

Ehrlich, P. R. (2000). *Human natures: Genes, cultures, and the human prospect.* Washington, DC: Island Press.

Eibl-Eibesfeldt, I. (1989). *Human ethology.* New York: Gruyter.

Eimas, P. D., & Quinn, P. C. (1994). Studies in the formation of perceptually based basic-level categories in young infants. *Child Development, 65,* 903–917.

Ellemers, N., Spears, R., & Doosje, B. (Eds.). (1999). *Social identity: Context, commitment, content.* Oxford, England: Blackwell.

Eller, A., & Abrams, D. (2003). "Cringos" in Mexico: Cross-sectional and longitudinal effects of language school-promoted contact on intergroup bias. *Group Processes & Intergroup Relations, 6,* 55–75.

Ellis, W. D. (1959). *Source book of Gestalt psychology.* New York: Harcourt, Brace.

Elton, G. (1994). *The English.* Oxford, England: Blackwell.

Evans, R. I. (1980). *The making of social psychology: Discussions with creative contributors.* New York: Gardner Press.

Farrell, M., Hettne, M., & Van Langenhove, L. (Eds.). (2005). *Global politics of regionalism.* Pluto Press.

Feather, N. T. (1999). *Values, achievement, and justice: Studies in the psychology of deservedness.* New York: Kluwer Academic/Plenum Publishers.

Festinger, L. (1954). A theory of social comparison processes. *Human relations, 7,* 117–140.

Festinger, L. (1957). *A theory of cognitive dissonance.* Stanford, CA: Stanford University Press.

Figes, O., & Kolonitskii, B. E. (1999). *Interpreting the Russian revolution: The language and symbols of 1917.* New Haven, CT: Yale University Press.

Finkel, N., & Moghaddam, F. M. (Eds.). (2005). *The psychology of rights and duties: Empirical contributions and normative commentaries.* Washington, DC: American Psychological Association

Fischer, G. J. (1997). Gender effects on individual verdicts and on mock jury verdicts in a simulated acquaintance rape trial. *Sex Roles, 36,* 491–501.

Fischer, K. (2006, May 12). Elite colleges lag in serving the needy. *The Chronicle of Higher Education,* pp. A1, A12, A14–A16.

Fish, M. S., & Brooks, R. S. (2004). Does diversity hurt democracy? *Journal of Democracy, 15,* 154–166.

Fisher, R. A. (1999). *The genetical theory of natural selection: A complete variorum edition.* Oxford, England: Clarenden. (Original work published 1930)

Fitzgerald, F. S. (1925). *The great Gatsby*. New York: Scribner.

Fleras, A., & Elliot, J. L. (1992). *Multiculturalism in Canada: The challenge of diversity*. Scarborough, Ontario, Canada: Nelson Canada.

Folger, R. (1986). A referent cognitions theory of relative deprivation. In J. M. Olson, C. P. Herman, & M. P. Zanna (Eds.), *Relative deprivation and social comparison: The Ontario Symposium* (Vol. 4, pp. 33–55). Hillsdale, NJ: Erlbaum

Folger, R., & Kass, E. E. (2000). Social comparison and fairness: A counterfactual simulations perspective. In J. Suls & L. Wheeler (Eds.), *Handbook of social comparison: Theory and research* (pp. 423–441). New York: Plenum Press.

Frank, R. (2007). *Richistan: A journey through the American wealth boom and the lives of the new rich*. New York: Crown.

Frank, R., & Cook, P. (1995). *The winner-takes-all society*. New York: Simon & Schuster.

Frank, T. (2005). *What's the matter with Kansas? How conservatives won the heart of America*. New York: Owl Books.

Freud, S. (1953–1964). *The standard edition of the complete psychological works of Sigmund Freud* (J. Strachey, Ed. & Trans., Vols. 1–24). London: Hogarth Press. (Original work published 1886–1939)

Freud, S. (1955). Group psychology and the analysis of the ego. In J. Strachey (Ed. & Trans.), *The standard edition of the complete psychological works of Sigmund Freud* (Vol. 18, pp. 67–143). London: Hogarth Press. (Original work published 1921)

Freud, S. (1957). Thoughts for the times on war and death. In J. Strachey (Ed. & Trans.), *The standard edition of the complete psychological works of Sigmund Freud* (Vol. 14, pp. 271–302). London: Hogarth Press. (Original work published 1915)

Freud, S. (1960). Jokes and their relation to the unconscious. In J. Strachey (Ed. & Trans.), *The standard edition of the complete psychological works of Sigmund Freud* (Vol. 8, pp. 9–236). London: Hogarth Press. (Original work published 1905)

Freud, S. (1961). Civilization and its discontents. In J. Strachey (Ed. & Trans.), *The standard edition of the complete psychological works of Sigmund Freud* (Vol. 21, pp. 64–145). London: Hogarth Press. (Original work published 1930)

Fukuyama, F. (1992). *The end of history and the last man*. New York: Free Press.

Fukuyama, F. (2006). Democracy and "the end of history" revisited. In H. Muñoz (Ed.), *Democracy rising: Assessing the global challenges* (pp. 115–120). Boulder, CO: Rienner.

Furnham, A. (2003). Belief in a just world: Research progress over the past decade. *Personality and Individual Differences, 34*, 795–817.

Gaertner, S. L., & Brown, R. J. (Eds.). (2002). *Intergroup processes*. Oxford, England: Blackwell.

Gaertner, S. L., & Dovidio, J. F. (2000). *Reducing intergroup bias: The common ingroup identity model*. Philadelphia: Psychology Press.

Gaertner, S. L., & Dovidio, J. F. (2005). Understanding and addressing contemporary racism: From aversive racism to the common ingroup identity model. *Journal of Social Issues, 61*, 615–639.

Gaertner, S. L., Dovidio, J. F., Rust, M. C., Nier, J. A., Banker, B. S., Ward, C. M., et al. (1999). Reducing intergroup bias: Elements of intergroup cooperation. *Journal of Personality and Social Psychology, 76,* 388–402.

Gamble, A., & Payne, A. (Eds.). (1996). *Regionalism and world order.* Basingstoke, England: Macmillan.

Gartrell, C. D. (2002). The embeddedness of social comparison. In I. Walker & H. J. Smith (Eds.), *Relative deprivation: Specification, development, and integration* (pp. 164–184). Cambridge, England: Cambridge University Press.

Gazzaniga, M. S. (1992). *Nature's mind: The biological roots of thinking, emotions, sexuality, language, and intelligence.* New York: Basic Books.

Geertz, C. (1958, Winter). Ethos, worldview, and the analysis of sacred symbols. *The Antioch Review,* 421–437.

Gibson, J. J. (1979). *The ecological approach to visual perception.* Boston: Houghton Mifflin.

Giddens, A., & Held, D. (Eds.). (1982). *Classes, power, and conflict: Classical and contemporary debates.* Berkeley: University of California Press.

Gladney, D. C. (2007). Cultural identity in China: The rising politics of ethnic difference. In G. Spindler & J. E. Stockard (Eds.), *Globalization and change in fifteen cultures* (pp. 53–72). Belmont, CA: Thompson.

Glazer, N., & Moynihan, D. P. (1970). *Beyond the melting pot* (2nd ed.). Cambridge, MA: MIT Press.

Goedicke, H., & Roberts, J. J. M. (Eds.). (1975). *Unity and diversity: Essays in the history, literature, and religion of ancient Near East.* Baltimore: Johns Hopkins University Press.

Golden, D. (2006). *The price of admission: How America's ruling class buys its way into elite colleges—and who gets left outside the gate.* New York: Crown.

Gorke, M. (2003). *The death of our planet's species: A challenge to ecology and ethics.* Washington, DC: Island Press.

Grant, P. R. (1993). Reactions to intergroup similarity: Examination of the similarity-differentiation and similarity-attraction hypotheses. *Canadian Journal of Behavioural Science, 25,* 28–44.

Gray, C., Russell, P., & Blockley, S. (1991). The effects upon helping behaviour of wearing pro-gay identification. *British Journal of Social Psychology, 30,* 171–178.

Greenberg, J., Solomon, S., Pyszczynski, T., Rosenblatt, A., Burling, J., Lyon, D., et al. (1992). Assessing the terror management analysis of self-esteem: Converging evidence of an anxiety-buffering function. *Journal of Personality and Social Psychology, 63,* 913–922.

Greenhouse, S. (2006, August 31). Three polls find workers sensing deep pessimism. *The New York Times,* p. A17.

Greenwald, A. G., & Banaji, M. R. (1995). Implicit social cognition: Attitudes, self-esteem, and stereotypes. *Psychological Review, 102,* 4–27.

Guimond, S., Dambrun, M., Michinov, N., & Duarte, S. (2003). Does social dominance generate prejudice? Integrating individual and contextual determinants of intergroup cognitions. *Journal of Personality and Social Psychology, 84,* 697–721.

Guimond, S., & Dubé-Simard, L. (1983). Relative deprivation theory and the Quebec nationalist movement: The cognition–emotion distinction and the person–group deprivation issue. *Journal of Personality and Social Psychology, 44,* 526–535.

Habermas, J. (1984). *The theory of communicative action* (Vol. 1). Boston: Beacon.

Habermas, J. (1987). *The theory of communicative action* (Vol. 2). Boston: Beacon.

Hafer, C. L. (2000). Do innocent victims threaten the belief in a just world? Evidence from a modified Stroop task. *Journal of Personality and Social Psychology, 79,* 165–173.

Hafer, C. L., & Bègue, L. (2005). Experimental research on just-world theory: Problems, developments, and future challenges. *Psychological Bulletin, 131,* 128–167.

Hafer, C. L., Bègue, L., Choma, B. L., & Dempsey, J. L. (2005). Belief in a just world and commitment to long-term deserved outcomes. *Social Justice Research, 18,* 429–444.

Hamilton, A., Madison, J., & Jay, J. (1996). *The federalist papers* (B. F. Wright, Ed.). New York: Barnes & Noble. (Original work published 1787–1788)

Harmon-Jones, E., & Mills, J. (Eds.). (1999). *Cognitive dissonance: Progress on a pivotal theory in social psychology.* Washington, DC: American Psychological Association.

Harré, R. (1984). *Personal being: A theory of individual psychology.* Cambridge, MA: Harvard University Press.

Hart, C. W. M., Pilling, A. R., & Goodale, J. C. (2001). *The Tiwi of North Australia* (3rd ed.). Belmont, CA: Wadsworth.

Hauser, M. D. (2006). *Moral minds.* New York: HarperCollins.

Heider, F. (1958). *The psychology of interpersonal relations.* New York: Wiley.

Heine, S. J. (2005). Where is the evidence for pancultural self-enhancement? A reply to Sedikides, Gaertner, and Togushi (2003). *Journal of Personality and Social Psychology, 89,* 531–538.

Held, D. A., McGrew, D., Goldblatt, D., & Perraton, J. (1999). *Global transformations: Politics, economics, and culture.* Cambridge, England: Polity Press.

Helfrich, H. (Ed.). (2003). *Time and mind II: Information processing perspectives.* Cambridge, MA: Hogrefe & Huber.

Hepworth, J. T., & West, S. G. (1988). Lynchings and the economy: A time-series reanalysis of Hovland and Sears (1940). *Journal of Personality and Social Psychology, 55,* 239–247.

Heuer, L., Penrod, S., Hafer, C. L., & Cohn, I. (2002). The role of resource and relational concerns for procedural justice. *Personalty and Social Psychology Bulletin, 28,* 1468–1482.

Hewstone, M. (2003). Intergroup contact: Panacea for prejudice? *The Psychologist, 16,* 352–355.

Hewstone, M., & Brown, R. J. (1986a). *Contact and conflict in intergroup encounters.* Oxford, England: Blackwell.

Hewstone, M., & Brown, R. J. (1986b). Contact is not enough: An intergroup perspective on the contact hypothesis. In M. Hewstone & R. J. Brown (Eds.), *Contact and conflict in intergroup encounters* (pp. 3–44). Oxford, England: Blackwell.

Heyerdahl, T. (1989). *Easter Island: The mystery solved.* New York: Random House.

Hinkle, S., & Brown, R. J. (1990). Intergroup comparisons and social identity: Some links and lacunae. In D. Abrams & M. A. Hogg (Eds.), *Social identity theory: Constructive and critical advances* (pp. 48–70). London: Harvester Wheatsheaf.

Hirsch, E. D., Jr. (1988). *Cultural literacy: What every American needs to know.* New York: Vintage Books.

Hirschman, A. O. (1983). America's melting pot reconsidered. *Annual Review of Sociology, 9,* 393–423.

Hogg, M. A., & Abrams, D. (Ed.). (2001). *Intergroup relations: Essential readings.* London: Psychology Press.

Homans, G. C. (1961). *Social behavior: Its elementary forms.* New York: Harcourt, Brace & World.

hooks, b. (2000). *Where we stand: Class matters.* New York: Routledge.

Hoover, K. (Ed.). (2004). *The future of identity: Centennial reflections on the legacy of Erik Erikson.* New York: Lexington Books.

Hornsey, M. J., & Jetten, J. (2004). The individual within the group: Balancing the need to belong and the need to be different. *Personality and Social Psychology Review, 8,* 248–264.

Horowitz, D. L. (1993). Democracy in divided societies. *Journal of Democracy, 4,* 18–38.

Huddy, L. (2004). Contrasting theoretical approaches to intergroup relations. *Political Psychology, 25,* 947–967.

Huntington, S. (1991). *The third wave: Democratization in the late 20th century.* Norman: University of Oklahoma Press.

Huntington, S. (1996). *The clash of civilizations and the remaking of world order.* New York: Touchstone.

Huskinson, J. (Ed.). (1999). *Experiencing Rome: Culture, identity, and power in the Roman Empire.* London: Routledge.

Hymes, R. W., Leinart, M., Rowe, S., & Rogers, W. (1993). Acquaintance rape: The effect of race of defendant and race of victim on White juror decisions. *Journal of Social Psychology, 133,* 627–634.

Ibarra, P. (Ed.). (2003). *Social movements and democracy.* New York: Palgrave/MacMillan.

Ingham, H., & Ingham, M. (Eds.). (2002). *EU expansion to the East: Prospects and problems.* Cheltenham, England: E. Elgar.

Inglehart, R. (1997). *Modernization and post-modernization: Cultural, economic, and political change in 43 societies.* Princeton, NJ: Princeton University Press.

Israel, J., & Tajfel, H. (Eds.). (1972). *The context of social psychology*. London: Academic Press.

Jackson, R. L. (2006). *Scripting the Black masculine body: Identity, discourse, and racial politics in popular media*. Albany: State University of New York.

Jacobson, P. V. (2000). Focus on the CNN effect misses the point: The real media impact on conflict management is invisible and indirect. *Journal of Peace Research, 37*, 131–143.

Janis, I. L. (1989). *Crucial decisions: Leadership in policymaking and crisis management*. New York: Free Press.

Jost, J. T. (2006). The end of the end of ideology. *American Psychologist, 61*, 651–670.

Jost, J. T., & Banaji, M. R. (1994). The role of stereotyping in system justification and the production of false consciousness. *British Journal of Social Psychology, 33*, 1–27.

Jost, J. T., Banaji, M. R., & Nosek, B. A. (2004). A decade of system justification theory: Accumulated evidence for conscious and unconscious bolstering of the status quo. *Political Psychology, 25*, 881–919.

Josh, J. T., Blount, F., Pfeffer, J., & Hunyady, G. (2003). Fair market ideology: Its cognitive–motivational underpinnings. *Research in Organizational Behavior, 25*, 53–91.

Jost, J. T., & Burgess, D. (2000). Attitudinal ambivalence and the conflict between group and system justification motives in low status groups. *Personality and Social Psychology Bulletin, 26*, 293–305.

Jost, J. T., & Hunyady, O. (2002). The psychology of system justification and the palliative function of ideology. *European Review of Social Psychology, 13*, 111–153.

Jost, J. T., & Kay, A. C. (2005). Exposure to benevolent sexism and complementary gender stereotypes: Consequences for specific and diffuse forms of system justification. *Journal of Personality and Social Psychology, 88*, 498–509.

Jost, J. T., Pelham, B. W., & Carvallo, M. (2002). Non-conscious forms of system justification: Cognitive, affective, and behavioral preferences for higher status groups. *Journal of Experimental Social Psychology, 38*, 586–602.

Jost, J. T., Pelham, B. W., Sheldon, O., & Sullivan, B. N. (2003). Social inequality and the reduction of ideological dissonance on behalf of the system: Evidence of enhanced system justification among the disadvantaged. *European Journal of Social Psychology, 33*, 13–36.

Jost, J. T., & Thompson, E. P. (2000). Group-based dominance and opposition to equality as independent predictors of self-esteem, ethnocentrism, and social policy attitudes among African Americans and European Americans. *Journal of Experimental Social Psychology, 36*, 209–232.

Jowitt, K. (2001). Ethnicity: Nice, nasty, and nihilistic. In D. Chirot & M. E. P. Seligman (Eds.), *Ethnopolitical warfare: Causes, consequences, and possible solutions* (pp. 27–48). Washington, DC: American Psychological Association.

Joyce, P. (Ed.). (1995). *Class*. Oxford, England: Oxford University Press.

Kant, I. (1996). *Critique of pure reason* (W. S. Pluhar, Trans.). Indianapolis, IN: Hackett. (Original work published 1787)

Karatnycky, A. (2002). The 2001 Freedom House Survey: Muslim countries and the democracy gap. *Journal of Democracy, 13,* 99–112.

Katz, B. (Ed.). (2005). *Reflections on regionalism.* Washington, DC: Brookings Institution Press.

Kay, A. C., Jimenez, M. C., & Jost, J. T. (2002). Sour grapes, sweet lemons, and the anticipatory rationalization of the status quo. *Personality and Social Psychology Bulletin, 28,* 1300–1312.

Kay, A. C., & Jost, J. T. (2003). Complimentary justice: Effects of "poor but happy" and "poor but honest" stereotype exemplars on system justification and implicit activation of the justice motive. *Journal of Personality and Social Psychology, 85,* 823–837.

Kay, A. C., Jost, J. T., & Young, S. (2005). Victim derogation and victim enhancement as alternative routes to system justification. *Psychological Science, 16,* 240–246.

Kelly, G. (1955). *The psychology of personal constructs.* New York: Norton.

Killen, M., & Smetana, J. G. (Eds.). (2006). *Handbook of moral development.* Mahwah, NJ: Erlbaum.

Kozol, J. (2005). *The shame of a nation: The restoration of apartheid schooling in America.* New York: Crown.

Krauthammer, C. (2006, June 12). In plain English: Let's make it official. *Time,* 112.

Krugman, P. (2006, February 27). Graduates versus oligarchs. *The New York Times,* p. 23.

Kymlicka, W., & He, B. (Eds.). (2005). *Multiculturalism in Asia.* New York: Oxford University Press.

Lalonde, R. N., & Silverman, R. A. (1994). Behavioral preferences in response to social injustice: The effects of group permeability and social identity salience. *Journal of Personality and Social Psychology, 66,* 78–85.

Lambert, W. E., Memegis, L., & Taylor, D. M. (1986). Greek Canadians' attitudes toward own group and other Canadian ethnic groups: A test of the multiculturalism hypothesis. *Canadian Journal of Behavioral Science, 18,* 35–51.

Lambert, W. E., & Taylor, D. M. (1990). *Coping with cultural and racial diversity in urban America.* New York: Praeger Publishers.

Landau, B. (1998). Object shape, object function, and object name. *Journal of Memory and Language, 38,* 1–27.

Langford, D. J., Crager, S. E., Shehzad, Z., Smith, S. B., Sotocinal, S. G., Levenstadt, J. S., et al. (2006, June 30). Social modulation of pain as evidence for empathy in mice. *Science, 312,* 1967–1970.

Laurence, R., & Berry, J. (Eds.). (1998). *Cultural identity in the Roman Empire.* London: Routledge.

Leet, M. (2003). Democracy and the individual: Deliberative and existential negotiations. *Philosophy & Social Criticism, 29,* 681–702.

Lemaine, G. (1974). Social differentiation and social originality. *European Journal of Social Psychology, 4,* 17–52.

Lemaine, G., Kastersztein, J., & Personnaz, B. (1978). Social differentiation. In H. Tajfel (Ed.), *Differentiation between social groups* (pp. 269–300). London: Academic Press.

Lerner, M. J. (1980). *The belief in a just world: A fundamental delusion.* New York: Plenum Press.

Lerner, M. J., Miller, D. T., & Holmes, J. G. (1976). Deserving and the emergence of forms of justice. In L. Berkowitz & E. Walster (Eds.), *Advances in experimental social psychology* (pp. 133–162). New York: Academic Press.

Lerner, M. J., & Simmons, C. H. (1966). Observer's reactions to the "innocent victim": Compassion or rejection? *Journal of Personality and Social Psychology, 4,* 203–210.

Levin, S. (2004). Perceived group differences and the effects of gender, ethnicity, and religion on social dominance orientations. *Political Psychology, 25,* 31–48.

LeVine, R. A., & Campbell, D. T. (1972). *Ethnocentrism: Theories of conflict, ethnic attitudes, and group behavior.* New York: Wiley.

Lijphart, A. (1977). *Democracy in plural societies.* New Haven, CT: Yale University Press.

Lind, E. A., Kanfer, R., & Earley, P. C. (1990). Voice, control, and procedural justice: Instrumental and noninstrumental concerns in fairness judgments. *Journal of Personality and Social Psychology, 59,* 952–959.

Lind, E. A., & Tyler, T. R. (1988). *The social psychology of procedural justice.* New York: Plenum Press.

Lindsey, D. T., & Brown, A. M. (2002). Color naming and the phototoxic effects of sunlight on the eye. *Psychological Science, 13,* 506–512.

Lipset, S. M. (1996). *American exceptionalism: A double-edged sword.* New York: Norton.

Lofland, J. (1996). *Social movement organizations: Guide to research on insurgent realities.* Edison, NJ: Aldine Transaction.

Logan, J. R., Zhang, W., & Alba, R. D. (2002). Immigrant enclaves and ethnic communities in New York and Los Angeles. *American Sociological Review, 67,* 299–322.

Lorenz, K. (1976). *On aggression.* New York: Bantam Books.

Louis, W. R., & Taylor, D. M. (2005). Rights and duties as group norms: Implications of intergroup research for the study of rights and responsibilities. In N. Finkel & F. M. Moghaddam (Eds.), *The psychology of rights and duties: Empirical contributions and normative commentaries* (pp. 105–134). Washington, DC: American Psychological Association.

Luttmer, E. F. P. (2005). Neighbors as negatives: Relative earnings and well-being. *Quarterly Journal of Economics, 120,* 963–1002.

Máiz, R., & Requejo, F. (Eds.). (2005). *Democracy, nationalism, and multiculturalism.* London, New York: Frank Cass.

Mann, C. C. (2005). *1491: New revelations of the Americas before Columbus*. New York: Knopf.

Maquet, J. J. (1961). *The premise of inequality in Ruanda: A study of political relations in a central African community*. London: Oxford University Press.

Marmot, M. G. (2004). *The status syndrome: How social standing affects our health and longevity*. New York: Times Books/Henry Holt.

Marx, K. (1976). *Capital* (Vol. 1, I. B. Fowkes, Trans.). Harmondsworth, England: Penguin. (Original work published 1867)

Marx, K. (1979). The eighteenth brumaire of Louis Bonaparte. In *Collected works of Karl Marx and Frederick Engels* (Vol. 11, pp. 99–197). London: Lawrence and Wishart. (Original work published 1852)

Marx, K., & Engels, F. (1967). *Communist manifesto*. New York: Pantheon. (Original work published 1848)

McAdam, D. (1999). *Political process and the development of Black insurgency, 1930–1970*. Chicago: University of Chicago Press.

McCarthy, T. D., & Wolfson, M. (1996). Resource mobilization by local social movement organizations: Agency, strategy, and organization in the movement against drunk driving. *American Sociological Review, 61*, 1070–1088.

McCarthy, T. D., & Zald, M. N. (1977). Resource mobilization and social movements: A partial theory. *American Journal of Sociology, 82*, 1212–1241.

McClelland, K., & Linnander, E. (2006). The role of contact and information in racial attitude change among White college students. *Sociological Inquiry, 76*, 81–115.

McGarty, C. (1999). *Categorization in social psychology*. Thousand Oaks, CA: Sage.

McGuire, W. J., & McGuire, C. V. (1981). The spontaneous self-concept as affected by personal distinctiveness. In A. Norem-Hebeisen, M. D. Lynch, & K. Gergen (Eds.), *The self-concept: Advances in theory and research* (pp. 147–171). New York: Ballinger.

McMurrer, D. P., & Sawhill, I. V. (1998). *Getting ahead: Economic and social mobility in America*. Washington, DC: Urban Institute Press.

Meisel, J. H. (Ed.). (1965). *Pareto & Mosca*. Englewood Cliffs, NJ: Prentice Hall.

Melis, A. P., Hare, B., & Tomasello, M. (2006, March 3). Chimpanzees recruit the best collaborators. *Science, 311*, 1297–1300.

Merchant, K. (2003, August 20). Service industries go global. *Financial Times*, p. 15.

Milgram, S. (1974). *Obedience to authority: An experimental view*. New York: Harper & Row.

Miller, G. A., Galanter, E., & Pribram, K. (1960). *Plans and the structure of behavior*. New York: Holt, Rinehart & Winston.

Miller, N., Pederson, W. C., Earlywine, M., & Pollock, V. E. (2003). A theoretical model of triggered displaced aggression. *Personality and Social Psychology Review, 7*, 75–97.

Moghaddam, F. M. (1997). *The specialized society: The plight of the individual in an age of individualism*. New York: Praeger Publishers.

Moghaddam, F. M. (1998). *Social psychology: Exploring universals in social behavior.* New York: Freeman.

Moghaddam, F. M. (2000). Toward a cultural theory of human rights. *Theory & Psychology, 10,* 291–312.

Moghaddam, F. M. (2002). *The individual and society: A cultural integration.* New York: Worth.

Moghaddam, F. M. (2003). Interobjectivity and culture. *Culture & Psychology, 9,* 221–232.

Moghaddam, F. M. (2004). The cycle of rights and duties in intergroup relations. *New Review of Social Psychology, 3,* 125–130.

Moghaddam, F. M. (2005a). *Great ideas in psychology: A cultural and historical introduction.* Oxford, England: Oneworld.

Moghaddam, F. M. (2005b). The staircase to terrorism: A psychological exploration. *American Psychologist, 60,* 161–169.

Moghaddam, F. M. (2006a). Catastrophic evolution, culture, and diversity management policy. *Culture & Psychology, 12,* 415–434.

Moghaddam, F. M. (2006b). *From the terrorist's point of view: What they experience and why they come to destroy.* Westport, CT: Praeger Publishers.

Moghaddam, F. M. (2006c). Interobjectivity: The collective roots of individual consciousness and social identity. In T. Postmes & J. Jetten (Eds.), *Individuality and the group: Advances in social identity* (pp. 155–174). London: Sage.

Moghaddam, F. M. (2007). Freud, das ich und die literatur [Freud, the ego and literature]. In *Die welt auf der couch* (pp. 19–25). Vienna, Austria: Bundesministeriums Für Europäische Und Internationale Angelegenheiten.

Moghaddam, F. M., & Crystal, D. (1997). Revolutions, Samurai, and reductons: Change and continuity in Iran and Japan. *Journal of Political Psychology, 18,* 355–384.

Moghaddam, F. M., & Riley, C. J. (2005). Toward a cultural theory of rights and duties in human development. In N. Finkel & F. M. Moghaddam (Eds.), *The psychology of rights and duties: Empirical contributions and normative commentaries* (pp. 75–104). Washington, DC: American Psychological Association.

Moghaddam, F. M., & Stringer, P. (1986). "Trivial" and "important" criteria for social categorization in the minimal group paradigm. *Journal of Social Psychology, 126,* 345–354.

Moghaddam, F. M., & Stringer, P. (1988). Outgroup similarity and intergroup bias. *Journal of Social Psychology, 128,* 105–115.

Moghaddam, F. M., & Taylor, D. M. (1985). Psychology in the developing world: An evaluation through the concepts of "dual perception" and "parallel growth." *American Psychologist, 40,* 1144–1146.

Moghaddam, F. M., & Taylor, D. M. (1987). The meaning of multiculturalism for visible minority immigrant women. *Canadian Journal of Behavioural Science, 19,* 121–136.

Moghaddam, F. M., Taylor, D. M., & Lalonde, R. N. (1987). Individualistic and collective mobility integration strategies among Iranians in Canada. *International Journal of Psychology, 22*, 310–313.

Moghaddam, F. M., Taylor, D. M., Tchoryk-Pelletier, P., & Shepanek, M. (1994). The warped looking-glass: How minorities perceive themselves, believe they are perceived, and are actually perceived by majority group members in Quebec, Canada. *Canadian Ethnic Studies, 26*, 112–123.

Mummendey, A., & Schreiber, H. J. (1983). Better or just different? Positive social identity by discrimination against, or by differentiation from, outgroups. *European Journal of Social Psychology, 13*, 301–313.

Muñoz, H. (2006). Introduction: The growing community of democracies. In H. Muñoz (Ed.), *Democracy rising: Assessing the global challenges* (pp. 1–8). Boulder, CO: Rienner.

Murithi, T. (2005). *The African Union: Pan-Africanism, peacebuilding, and development.* Burlington, VT: Ashgate Publishing.

Murphy, W. F. (2007). *Constitutional democracy: Creating and maintaining a just political order.* Baltimore: Johns Hopkins University Press.

Myers, D. (2003). *Intuition.* New Haven, CT: Yale University Press.

Myers, N., & Kent, J. (2004). *The new consumers.* Washington, DC: Island Press.

National Research Council. (1997). *The new Americans: Economic, demographic, and fiscal effects of immigration.* Washington, DC: National Academy Press.

Negy, C., Shreve, T. L., Jensen, B. J., & Uddin, N. (2003). Ethnic identity, self-esteem, and ethnocentrism: A study of social identity versus multicultural theory of development. *Cultural Diversity and Ethnic Minority Psychology, 9*, 333–344.

Neimeyer, R. A., & Mitchell, K. A. (1988). Similarity and attraction: A longitudinal study. *Journal of Social and Personality Relationships, 5*, 131–148.

Niemann, Y. F., & Maruyama, G. (2005). Inequalities in higher education. *Journal of Social Issues, 61*, 407–426.

Nisbett, R. E., & Ross, L. (1980). *Human inferences: Strategies and shortcomings of social judgment.* Englewood Cliffs, NJ: Prentice-Hall.

Nisbett, R. E., & Wilson, T. D. (1977). Telling more than we know: Verbal reports on mental processes. *Psychological Review, 84*, 231–259.

Oakes, P. J., & Turner, J. C. (1990). Is limited information processing capacity the cause of social stereotyping? In W. Stroebe & M. Hewstone (Eds.), *European Review of Social Psychology* (Vol. 1, pp. 111–135). Chichester, England: Wiley.

O'Bryan, K. G., Reitz, J. G., & Kuplowski, O. (1975). *Non-official languages: A study in Canadian multiculturalism.* Ottawa, Ontario, Canada: Minister for Multiculturalism, Government of Canada.

Ohmae, K. (1990). *The borderless world: Power and strategy in the interlinked world economy.* London: Harper Business.

Olson, J. M., & Hafer, C. L. (2001). Tolerance of personal deprivation. In J. T. Jost & B. Major (Eds.), *The psychology of legitimacy: Emerging perspectives on ideology, justice, and intergroup relations* (pp. 157–175). New York: Cambridge University Press.

Olson, J. M., & Roese, N. J. (2002). Relative deprivation and counterfactual thinking. In I. Walker & H. J. Smith (Eds.), *Relative deprivation: Specification, development, and integration* (pp. 265–287). Cambridge, England: Cambridge University Press.

O'Reilly, B. (2006). *Culture warrior*. New York: Broadway.

Osbeck, L., Moghaddam, F. M., & Perreault, S. (1977). Similarity and attraction among majority and minority groups in a multicultural context. *International Journal of Intercultural Relations, 21,* 113–123.

Oyserman, D., Coon, H. M., & Kemmelmeier, M. (2002). Rethinking individualism and collectivism: Evaluation of theoretical assumptions and meta-analysis. *Psychological Bulletin, 128,* 3–72.

Palmer, J. A., & Palmer, L. K. (2002). *Evolutionary psychology: The ultimate origins of behavior*. Boston: Allyn & Bacon.

Panter-Brick, C., Layton, R. H., & Rowley-Conwy, P. (Eds.). (2001). *Hunter–gatherers: An interdisciplinary perspective*. New York: Cambridge University Press.

Parekh, B. (2006). *Rethinking multiculturalism*. New York: Palgrave/Macmillan.

Pareto, V. (1935).*The mind and society: A treatise on general sociology* (Vols. 1–4). New York: Dover.

Park, R. E. (1950). *Race and culture*. Glencoe, IL: Free Press.

Park, R. E., & Burgess, E. W. (1921). *Introduction to the science of society*. Chicago: University of Chicago Press.

Pettigrew, T. F. (1967). Social evaluation theory. In D. Levine (Ed.), *Nebraska Symposium on Motivation* (Vol. 15, pp. 241–315). Lincoln: University of Nebraska Press.

Pettigrew, T. F. (1997). Generalized intergroup contact effects on prejudice. *Personality and Social Psychology Bulletin, 23,* 173–185.

Pettigrew, T. F. (1998a). Intergroup contact theory. *Annual Review of Psychology, 49,* 65–85.

Pettigrew, T. F. (1998b). Reactions toward the new minorities of Western Europe. *Annual Review of Sociology, 24,* 77–103.

Pettigrew, T. F. (2002). Summing up: Relative deprivation as a key social psychological concept. In I. Walker & H. J. Smith (Eds.), *Relative deprivation: Specification, development, and integration* (pp. 351–373). Cambridge, England: Cambridge University Press.

Pettigrew, T. F., & Tropp, L. R. (2000). Does intergroup contact reduce prejudice? Recent meta-analytic findings. In S. Oskamp (Ed.), *Reducing prejudice and discrimination: Social psychological perspectives* (pp. 93–114). Mahwah, NJ: Erlbaum.

Pettigrew, T. F., & Tropp, L. R. (2006). A meta-analytic test of intergroup contact theory. *Journal of Personality and Social Psychology, 90,* 751–783.

Pfeifer, J. E., & Ogloff, J. R. (1991). Ambiguity and guilt determination: A modern racist perspective. *Journal of Applied Social Psychology, 21,* 1713–1725.

Pickett, C. L., & Leonardelli, G. J. (2006). Using collective identities for assimilation and differentiation. In T. Postmes & J. Jetten (Eds.), *Individuality and the group: Advances in social identity* (pp. 56–73). London: Sage.

Pippa, N., & Ingelhart, R. (2005). *Sacred and secular: Religion and politics worldwide.* New York: Cambridge University Press.

Plato. (1987). *The republic* (D. Lee, Trans.). Harmondsworth, England: Penguin.

Popper, K. R. (1966). *The open society and its enemies* (5th ed.). London: Routledge & Kegan Paul.

Portes, A., & Rumbart, R. G. (2006). *Immigrant America: A portait* (3rd ed.). Berkeley: University of California Press.

Postmes, T., & Jetten, J. (Eds.). (2006). *Individuality and the group: Advances in social identity.* London: Sage.

Pratto, F., Sidanius, J., Stallworth, L. M., & Malle, B. F. (1994). Social dominance orientation: A personality variable predicting social and political attitudes. *Journal of Personality and Social Psychology, 67,* 741–763.

Putnam, R. (1993). *Making democracy work: Civic traditions in modern Italy.* Princeton, NJ: Princeton University Press.

Putnam, R. (2000). *Bowling alone: The collapse and revival of American community.* New York: Simon & Schuster.

Pyszczynski, T., Solomon, S., & Greenberg, J. (2004). *In the wake of 9/11: The psychology of terror.* Washington, DC: American Psychological Association.

Rabbie, J. M., & Horwitz, M. (1969). Arousal of ingroup–outgroup bias by a chance or win loss. *Journal of Personality and Social Psychology, 13,* 269–277.

Rand, A. (1971). *The fountainhead.* New York: Signet. (Original work published 1943)

Rattner, S. (2003, June 16). Inured to inequality. *The Washington Post,* p. A23.

Rawls, J. (1971). *A theory of justice.* Cambridge, MA: Harvard University Press.

Reader, J. (1998). *Africa: Biography of a continent.* New York: Knopf.

Reicher, S., & Haslam, S. A. (2006). On the agency of individuals and groups: Lessons from the BBC prison study. In T. Postmes & J. Jetten (Eds.), *Individuality and the group: Advances in social identity* (pp. 237–257). London: Sage.

Roberts, A. (2006). What kind of democracy is emerging in Eastern Europe? *Post-Soviet Affairs, 22,* 37–64.

Rosamond, B. (2000). *Theories of European integration.* Basingstoke, England: Palgrave/Macmillan.

Rosch, E. (1978). Principles of categorization. In E. Rosch & B. B. Lloyd (Eds.), *Cognition and categorization* (pp. 27–48). Hillsdale, NJ: Erlbaum.

Rosch, E., & Lloyd, B. B. (Eds.). (1978). *Cognition and categorization.* Hillsdale, NJ: Erlbaum.

Rothbart, M., Davis-Stitt, C., & Hill, J. (1997). Effects of arbitrarily placed category boundaries on similarity judgments. *Journal of Experimental Social Psychology, 33,* 122–145.

Rubin, M., & Hewstone, M. (2004). Social identity, system justification and social dominance: Commentary on Reicher, Jost et al., and Sidanius et al. *Political Psychology, 25*, 823–844.

Rudmin, F. W. (2003). Critical history of the acculturation psychology of assimilation, separation, integration, and marginalization. *Review of General Psychology, 7*, 3–37.

Runciman, W. G. (1966). *Relative deprivation and social justice*. Harmondsworth, England: Penguin.

Ryan, L. (1981). *The Aboriginal Tasmanians*. St. Lucia, Australia: University of Queensland Press.

Sandbrook, R., Edelman, M., Heller, P., & Teichman, J. (2006). *Social democracy in the global periphery*. New York: Cambridge University Press.

Saville-Troike, M. (2006). *Introducing second language acquisition*. Cambridge, England: Cambridge University Press.

Schaller, M., Simpson, J. A., & Kenrick, D. T. (Eds.). (2006). *Evolution and social psychology*. London: Psychology Press.

Schama, S. (1989). *Citizens: A chronicle of the French Revolution*. New York: Vintage Books.

Schemo, D. J. (2006, November 16). Most students in big cities lag behind in basic science. *The New York Times*, p. A20.

Schmitt, M. T., Branscombe, N. R., & Kappen, D. (2003). Attitudes toward group-based inequality: Social dominance or social identity? *British Journal of Social Psychology, 42*, 161–186.

Schneider, B., Smith, D. B., Taylor, S., & Fleener, J. (1998). Personality and organizations: A test of the homogeneity of personality hypothesis. *Journal of Applied Psychology, 83*, 462–470.

Schneider, D. J. (2004). *The psychology of stereotyping*. New York: Guildford Press.

Sedikides, C., Gaertner, S. L., & Vevea, J. J. (2005). Pancultural self-enhancement reloaded: A meta-analytic reply to Heine (2005). *Journal of Personality and Social Psychology, 89*, 539–551.

Sen, A. (1999). *Development as freedom*. New York: Knopf.

Sen, A. (2006). *Identity and violence: The illusion of destiny*. New York: Norton.

Shain, B. A. (1994). *The myth of American individualism: The Protestant origins of American political thought*. Princeton, NJ: Princeton University Press.

Shapiro, I. (2003). *The state of democratic theory*. Princeton, NJ: Princeton University Press.

Sharansky, N., & Dermer, R. (2004). *The case for democracy: The power of freedom to overcome tyranny and terror*. New York: PublicAffairs.

Sherman, S. P. (1921). Introductory note. In *Essays and poems of Emerson* (pp. vii–xlv). New York: Harcourt, Brace.

Sherif, M. (1951). A preliminary experimental study of intergroup relations. In J. H. Rohrer & M. Sherif (Eds.), *Social psychology at the crossroads* (pp. 388–424). New York: Harper and Brothers.

Sherif, M. (1966). *Group conflict and cooperation: Their social psychology*. London: Routledge & Kegan Paul.

Sherif, M., Harvey, O. J., White, B. J., Hood, W. R., & Sherif, C. W. (1961). *Intergroup conflict and cooperation: The Robber's Cave experiment*. Norman: University of Oklahoma.

Sherif, M., & Sherif, C. W. (1953). *Groups in harmony and tension*. New York: Harper and Brothers.

Sherif, M., & Sherif, C. W. (1969). *Social psychology*. New York: Harper & Row.

Sherif, M., White, B. J., & Harvey, O. J. (1955). Status in experimentally produced groups. *American Journal of Sociology, 60*, 370–379.

Shikibu, M. (2000). *The tale of Genji* (E. G. Seidensticker, Trans.). New York: Knopf.

Sidanius, J., Levin, S., Liu, J. H., & Pratto, F. (2000). Social dominance orientation and the political psychology of gender: An extension and cross-cultural replication. *European Journal of Social Psychology, 30*, 41–67.

Sidanius, J., Liu, J., Pratto, F., & Shaw, J. (1994). Social dominance orientation, hierarchy attenuators and hierarchy enhancers: Social dominance theory and the criminal justice system. *Journal of Applied Social Psychology, 24*, 338–366.

Sidanius, J., & Pratto, F. (1999). *Social dominance: An intergroup theory of social dominance and oppression*. Cambridge, England: Cambridge University Press.

Sidanius, J., Pratto, F., van Laar, C., & Levin, S. (2004). Social dominance theory: Its agenda and method. *Political Psychology, 25*, 845–880.

Singh, R., & Ho, S. Y. (2000). Attitudes and attraction: A new test of the attraction, repulsion and similarity–dissimilarity asymmetry hypotheses. *British Journal of Social Psychology, 39*, 197–211.

Smallwood, S. (2003, December 12). American women surpass men in earning doctorates. *Chronicle of Higher Education*, p. A10.

Smith, A. (1976). *An inquiry into the nature and causes of the wealth of nations* (Vols. 1–2; R. H. Campbell & A. S. Skinner, Eds.). London: Clarendon Press. (Original work published 1776)

Smith, E. R., & Zárate, M. A. (1990). Exemplar and prototype use in social categorization. *Social Cognition, 8*, 243–262.

Smith, H. J., & Ortiz, D. J. (2002). Is it just me? The different consequences of personal and group relative deprivations. In I. Walker & H. J. Smith (Eds.), *Relative deprivation: Specification, development and integration* (pp. 91–118). Cambridge, England: Cambridge University Press.

Sowell, T. (2004). *Affirmative action around the world: An empirical study*. New Haven, CT: Yale University Press.

Speckhard, A., Tarabrina, N., Krasnov, V., & Akhmedova, K. (2004). Observations of suicide terrorists in action: The Chechen terrorist takeover of a Moscow theater. *Terrorism and Political Violence, 16*, 305–327.

Spindler, G., & Stockard, J. E. (Eds.). (2007). *Globalization and change in fifteen cultures*. Belmont, CA: Thomson.

Spini, D., & Doise, W. (2005). Universal rights and duties as normative social representations. In N. Finkel & F. M. Moghaddam (Eds.), *The psychology of rights and duties: Empirical contributions and normative commentaries* (pp. 21–48). Washington, DC: American Psychological Association.

Steele, C. M. (1997). A threat in the air: How stereotypes threaten intellectual identity and performance. *American Psychologist, 52,* 613–629.

Stephens, J. D. (1993). Capitalist development and democracy: Empirical research on the social origins of democracy. In D. Copp, J. Hampton, & J. E. Roemer (Eds.), *The idea of democracy* (pp. 409–446). New York: Cambridge University Press.

Sterling-Folker, J. (Ed.). (2006). *Making sense of international relations theory.* Boulder, CO: Reinner.

Stevenson, R. L. (1998). Foreign children. In *The book of 1,000 poems* (p. 410). New York: Wings Books.

Stone, J. (2007). *When she was White: The true story of a family divided by race.* New York: Miramax.

Stouffer, S. A. (1962). *Social research to test ideas.* New York: Free Press.

Stouffer, S. A., Suchman, E. A., De Vinney, L. C., Star, S. A., & Williams, R. M. (1949). *The American Soldier: Adjustments during army life* (Vol. 1). Princeton, NJ: Princeton University Press.

Stritikus, T., & Suarez-Orozco, M. M. (Eds.). (2002). *Immigrant children and the politics of English-only: View from the classroom.* New York: LFB Scholarly Publishing.

Sullivan, J. L., & Transue, J. E. (1999). The psychological underpinnings of democracy: A selective review of research on political tolerance, interpersonal trust, and social capital. *Annual Review of Psychology, 50,* 625–650.

Suls, J. M., & Wheeler, L. (Eds.). (2000). *Handbook of social comparison: Theory and research.* New York: Plenum Press.

Sumner, W. G. (1906). *Folkways.* Boston: Ginn.

Tajfel, H. (1959). Quantitative judgement in social perception. *British Journal of Psychology, 50,* 16–29.

Tajfel, H. (1970). Experiments in intergroup discrimination. *Scientific American, 223,* 96–102.

Tajfel, H. (1978a). Introduction. In H. Tajfel (Ed.), *Differentiation between social groups* (pp. 1–23). London: Academic Press

Tajfel, H. (1978b). Social categorization, social identity, and social comparison. In H. Tajfel (Ed.), *Differentiation between social groups* (pp. 61–76). London: Academic Press.

Tajfel, H., Flament, C., Billig, M. G., & Bundy, R. F. (1971). Social categorization and intergroup behaviour. *European Journal of Social Psychology, 1,* 149–177.

Tajfel, H., & Turner, J. C. (1979). An integrative theory of intergroup conflict. In W. G. Austin & S. Worchel (Eds.), *The social psychology of intergroup relations* (pp. 33–47). Monterey, CA: Brooks/Cole.

Tajfel, H., & Turner, J. C. (1986). The social identity theory of intergroup behavior. In S. Worchel & W. G. Austin (Eds.), *Psychology of intergroup relations* (pp. 7–24). Chicago: Nelson-Hall.

Tajfel, H., & Wilkes, A. L. (1963). Classification and quantitative judgement. *British Journal of Psychology, 54*, 101–113.

Tarrow, S. G. (1998). *Power in movement: Social movements and contentious politics.* Cambridge, England: Cambridge University Press.

Tatum, B. D. (2003). *Why are all the Black kids sitting together in the cafeteria? A psychologist explains the development of racial identity.* New York: Basic Books.

Taylor, C. (1992). The politics of recognition. In A. Guttmann (Ed.), *Multiculturalism and "the politics of recognition"* (pp. 25–73). Princeton, NJ: Princeton University Press.

Taylor, D. M. (2002). *The quest for identity.* Westport, CT: Praeger Publishers.

Taylor, D. M., & McKirnan, D. J. (1984). A five-stage model of intergroup relations. *British Journal of Social Psychology, 23*, 291–300.

Taylor, D. M., & Moghaddam, F. M. (1994). *Theories of intergroup relations: International social psychological perspectives.* Westport, CT: Praeger Publishers.

Taylor, D. M., Moghaddam, F. M., & Bellerose, J. (1989). Social comparison in an intergroup context. *Journal of Social Psychology, 129*, 499–515.

Teixeira, R. A. (1992). *The disappearing American voter.* Washington, DC: Brookings Institution Press.

Tesser, A., Felson, R. B., & Suls, J. M. (Eds.). (2000). *Psychological perspectives on self and identity.* Washington, DC: American Psychological Association.

Thibaut, J., & Walker, L. (1975). *Procedural justice: A psychological analysis.* Hillsdale, NJ: Erlbaum.

Thoreau, H. D. (2003). Walden *and* Civil Disobedience. New York: Barnes and Noble Classics. (Original work published 1849)

Tilly, C. (2003). When do (and don't) social movements promote democratization? In P. Ibarra (Ed.), *Social movements and democracy* (pp. 21–45). New York: Palgrave/MacMillan.

Tilly, R., & Welfens, P. J. J. (Eds.). (2000). *Economic globalization, international organizations and crisis management: Contemporary and historical perspectives on growth, impact, and evolution of major organizations in an interdependent world.* Berlin, Germany: Springer Publishing Company.

Tocqueville, A. de (2000). *Democracy in America* (J. P. Mayer, Ed., & G. Lawrence, Trans.). New York: Perennial Classics. (Original work published 1856)

Tolstoy, L. (1957). *War and peace* (Vols. 1–2; R. Edmonds, Trans). Harmondsworth, England: Penguin. (Original work published 1869)

Tougas, F., & Beaton, A. M. (2002). Personal and group relative deprivation: Connecting the "I" to the "we." In I. Walker & H. J. Smith (Eds.), *Relative deprivation: Specification, development, and integration* (pp. 119–135). Cambridge, England: Cambridge University Press.

Tripathi, R. C., & Srivastava, R. (1981). Relative deprivation and intergroup attitudes. *European Journal of Social Psychology, 11*, 313–318.

Trivers, R. (1971). The evolution of reciprocal altruism. *Quarterly Review of Biology, 46*, 35–56.

Tropp, L. R. (2003). The psychological impact of prejudice: Implications of intergroup contact. *Group Processes and Intergroup Relations, 6*, 131–149.

Tropp, L. R., & Pettigrew, T. F. (2005). Relationships between intergroup contact and prejudice among minority and majority status groups. *Psychological Science, 16*, 951–957.

Trudeau, P. E. (1992). Statement by the Prime Minister in the House of Commons, October 8, 1971. In *Multiculturalism in Canada: The challenge of diversity* (pp. 281–283). Scarborough, Ontario, Canada: Nelson Canada. (Original work published 1971)

Turner, F. J. (1920). *The frontier in American life*. New York: Holt.

Turner, J. C. (1982). Toward a cognitive redefinition of the social group. In H. Tajfel (Ed.), *Social identity and intergroup relations* (pp. 15–40). Cambridge, England: Cambridge University Press.

Turner, J. C., Hogg, M. A., Oakes, P. J., Reicher, S. D., & Wetherell, M. S. (1987). *Rediscovering the social group: A self-categorization theory*. Oxford, England: Blackwell.

Turner, J. C., & Oakes, P. J. (1989). Self-categorization theory and social influence. In P. B. Paulus (Ed.), *The psychology of group influence* (2nd ed., pp. 233–275). Hillsdale, NJ: Erlbaum.

Turner, J. C., & Onorato, R. (1999). Social identity, personality, and the self-concept: A self-categorization perspective. In T. R. Tyler, R. Kramer, & O. John (Eds.), *The psychology of the social self* (pp. 11–46). Mahwah, NJ: Erlbaum.

Turner, J. C., & Reynolds, K. L. (2003). Why social dominance theory has been falsified. *British Journal of Social Psychology, 42*, 199–206.

Turner, J. C., & Reynolds, K. J. (2004). The social identity perspective in intergroup relations: Theories, themes, and controversies. In M. B. Brewer & M. Hewstone (Eds.), *Self and social identity* (pp. 259–277). Oxford, England: Blackwell.

Turner, J. C., Reynolds, K. J., Haslam, S. A., & Veenstra, K. E. (2006). Reconceptualizing personality: Producing individuality by defining the personal self. In T. Postmes & J. Jetten (Eds.), *Individuality and the group: Advances in social identity* (pp. 11–36). London: Sage.

Tyler, T. R. (2001a). Public trust and confidence in legal authorities. *Behavioral Sciences and the Law, 19*, 215–235

Tyler, T. R. (2001b). Trust and law abidingness: A proactive model of social regulation. *Boston University Law Review, 81*, 361–406.

Tyler, T. R., & Degoey, P. (1995). Collective restraint in a social dilemma situation: The influence of procedural justice and community identification on the empowerment and legitimacy of authority. *Journal of Personality and Social Psychology, 69*, 482–497.

Tyler, T. R., & Huo, Y. J. (2002). *Trust in the law*. New York: Russell Sage Foundation.

United Nations. (2005). *Resource mobilization and the creation of an enabling environment for poverty eradication in the least developed countries*. New York: Author.

U.S. Census. (2004). *The foreign-born population in the United States: 2003*. Retrieved October 5, 2007, from http://www.census.gov/prod/2004pubs/p20-551.pdf

Van den Berghe, P. (1987). *The ethnic phenomenon*. New York: Praeger Publishers.

van Schaik, C. P., Ancrenaz, M., Borgen, G., Galdikas, B., Knott, C. D., Singleton, I., et al. (2003, January 3). Orangutan cultures and the evolution of material culture. *Science, 299*, 102–105.

Vanneman, R. D., & Pettigrew, T. F. (1972). Race and relative deprivation in the urban United States. *Race, 13*, 461–486.

Varela, R. E., Steele, R. G., & Benson, E. R. (2007). The contribution of ethnic minority status to adaptive style: A comparison of Mexican, Mexican American, and European American children. *Journal of Cross-Cultural Psychology, 38*, 26–33.

Veblen, T. (1953). *The theory of the leisure class*. New York: Mentor. (Original work published 1899)

Veilleux, F., & Tougas, F. (1989). Male acceptance of affirmative action programs for women: The result of altruistic or egoistical motives? *International Journal of Psychology, 24*, 485–496.

Verkuyten, M. (2005). Ethnic group identification and group evaluation among minority and majority groups: Testing the multiculturalism hypothesis. *Journal of Personality and Social Psychology, 88*, 121–138.

Wade, R. (2004). Is globalization reducing poverty and inequality? *World Development, 32*, 567–589.

Walker, I., & Smith, H. J. (Eds.). (2002). *Relative deprivation: Specification, development, and integration*. Cambridge, England: Cambridge University Press.

Walster, E., Walster, G. E., & Berscheid, E. (1978). *Equity: Theory and research*. Boston: Allyn & Bacon.

Walters, L., & Cunningham, P. A. (Eds.). (2005). *Twentieth century American fashion*. New York: Oxford University Press.

Walzer, M. (1997). *On toleration*. New Haven, CT: Yale University Press.

Waxman, S. (2007, May 29). "Pirates" haul so far estimated at $401 million. *The New York Times*, pp. B1, B8.

Weber, C. (2005). *International relations theory: A critical introduction*. London: Routledge.

Weber, E. J. (1991). *My France: Politics, culture, myth*. Cambridge, MA: Belknap Press of Harvard University Press.

Welsh, D. (1993). Domestic politics and ethnic conflict. In M. E. Brown (Ed.), *Ethnic conflict and international security* (pp. 43–60). Princeton, NJ: Princeton University Press.

White, J. B. (1997). Turks in the new Germany. *American Anthropologist, 99,* 754–769.

Whitman, W. (1955). *Leaves of grass.* New York: Signet/New American Library. (Original work published 1855)

Wilson, E. O. (1975). *Sociobiology: The new synthesis.* Cambridge, MA: Harvard University Press.

Wilson, K. L., & Martin, A. W. (1982). Ethnic enclaves: A comparison of the Cuban and Black economies in Miami. *American Journal of Sociology, 88,* 135–160.

Wilson, W. J., & Taub, R. P. (2006). *There goes the neighborhood: Racial, ethnic, and class tensions in four Chicago neighborhoods and their meaning for America.* New York: Knopf.

Worchel, S. (1999). *Written in blood.* New York: Worth.

Worchel, S., & Austin, W. G. (Eds.). (1986). *The psychology of intergroup relations* (2nd ed.). Monterey, CA: Brooks/Cole.

Worchel, S., Morales, J. F., Páez, D., & Deschamps, J. C. (Eds.). (1998). *Social identity: International perspectives.* London: Sage.

Wright, S. C., Aron, A., McLaughkin-Volpe, T., & Ropp, S. A. (1997). The extended contact effect: Knowledge of cross-group friendships and prejudice. *Journal of Personality and Social Psychology, 73,* 73–90.

Wright, S. C., & Taylor, D. M. (1998). Responding to tokenism: Individual action in the face of collective injustice. *European Journal of Social Psychology, 28,* 647–667.

Wright, S. C., Taylor, D. M., & Moghaddam, F. M. (1990). Responding to membership in a disadvantaged group: From acceptance to collective protest. *Journal of Personality and Social Psychology, 58,* 994–1003.

Yardley, W. (2006, December 13). A lawsuit threat is gone and Christmas trees return. *The New York Times,* p. A24.

Young, I. M. (1989). Polity and group differences: A critique of the ideal of universal citizenship. *Ethics, 99,* 250–274.

Zagefka, H., & Brown, R. J. (2002). The relationship between acculturation strategies, relative fit and intergroup relations: Immigrant-majority group relations in Germany. *European Journal of Social Psychology, 32,* 171–188.

Zajonc, R. B. (1968). Attitudinal effects of mere exposure. *Journal of Personality and Social Psychology, 9*(2, Pt. 2), 1–27.

Zandy, J. (Ed.). (2001). *What we hold in common: An introduction to working-class studies.* New York: Feminist Press at the City University of New York.

Zangwill, I. (1909). *The melting pot: Drama in four acts.* New York: Macmillan.

Zimbardo, P. (2007). *The Lucifer effect: Understanding how good people turn evil.* New York: Random House.

AUTHOR INDEX

SUBJECT INDEX

self-protective mechanisms of, 61
and social construction, 99
"Culture wars," 163
Cycle of rights and duties, 121–122

Darwin, Charles, 84, 103, 141
Dawkins, R., 51
Defense mechanisms, 53
Democracy, 47
    and assimilation, 143–145
        vs. multiculturalism, 129
    contextualized, 21, 25
    core features and variations of, 21–24
        electoral systems, 22
    and "end of history" (Fukuyama), 127
    and diversity, 24, 138–139
    and globalization, 20–21, 127, 128
    and globalization of values, 9
    and identity theories, 104–106
    and intergroup conflict, xiv
    and irrationalist perspective, 62
    and justice theories, 122–124
        and decision-making procedures,
        115
    in justification for war, 50
    and materialist theories, 86–88
    and multiculturalism, 129, 161–164
    as multigroup societies, 96
    planned, 144
        vs. free-market, 22
    psychological costs of, x
    worldwide spread of, 9–10, 11, 28
Denmark, and cartoons depicting
    Mohammed, xiii
Deprivation
    relative, 115–119
    and resource mobilization theory, 71,
    73
Derogation, of outgroups, 59–60
Dershowitz, Alan, 124
Dickens, Charles, 29, 108
    quoted, 107
Differentiation. See Fragmentation
Direct challenge strategy, 98
Disciplinary boundaries, 17
Displacement, of aggression, 55–56, 57, 63
Distinctiveness
    need for, 103
    and optimal distinctiveness theory, 101
Distributive justice, 86, 113
    vs. procedural justice, 123, 163
Diversity, biological (decline of), 14–15

Diversity, cultural
    in ancient world, 147
    change in policy toward, 149–150
    construction of, 32–37
    decline of, 14–15
    and democracy, 24, 138
    and globalization or globalism, xi, 147–
    148
    government management of, 23, 129,
    148, 163
        failure of, xiii
    and multiculturalism, 148, 161 (see also
        at Multiculturalism)
    and social capital, 24
Dollard, John, 56
Dual perceptions, 161
Durkheim, Émile, 103
Duties
    and intergroup relations, 20
        and minorities vs. majorities, 16, 77,
        121–122, 124
    and minority cultures, 24
    voting as, 104

Easter Island, 34–35
Eastern Europe, 8, 9, 157
Economic markets, 28
Education
    and cultural literacy, 139
    and tolerance, 157
Egoistic deprivation, 117
Ego justification, 79
Eibl-Eibesfeldt, I., 34
Electronic communications, 57–58
Elite(s)
    of English speakers, 161
    hierarchy among, 33
Elite theory
    of Pareto, 67, 69–70, 74
    of Plato, 70
Elton, Geoffrey, 27–28
Emerson, Ralph Waldo, 131
Empathy
    in animals, 120
    and survival, 123–124
    in primitive social relations, 119–120
"End of history," Fukuyama on, 127
    vs. Huntington, 128
England
    and sense of nationhood (Elton), 27–
    28
    See also United Kingdom

English language, predominance of, 3–4, 14, 160
English-only movement, 160
Equality
    for America, 41
    and myth of Western frontier, 38
    See also Inequalities
Equal opportunity
    and assimilation, 142–143
    and U.S. health care, 123
Equity theory, 111–113
Estate tax (inheritance tax), 87
Ethnic economic enclaves, 149
    for Latinos in U.S., 159
Ethnicity, in mobilization, 92
Ethnic minorities
    and common ingroup identity model, 102
    as identifying with sports and entertainment stars, 105
    and justice theories, 109
    and social comparisons, 96
    as underclass, 144
    See also Minority(ies)
Ethnic revival, 4
Ethnocentrism, 140, 156
    and minimal group paradigm, 94
    and terror management, 64
EU Constitutional Treaty, 158
European Convention for the Protection of Human Rights and Fundamental Freedoms, 157
European Economic Community (EEC), 157
European Journal of Social Psychology, 3–4
European Union, 157
    backlash against integration in, 11
    and change of allegiance, 13
    and economic independence, 128
    ethnic minorities in, 144
    expansion of, 8, 157
    France as part of and analogous to, 3
    and language, 14
    multiculturalism in, 157–161
    and nationalist sentiments, 4
"Every child is a star" movement, 105–106
Evolution
    catastrophic, 14–15
    collaboration in, 40
    and large-group identification, 12
    and runaway selection, 35–36
Evolutionary psychology
    and gender differences, 75

and hierarchy, 74
and identity needs, 100, 102–103
and intergroup relations, 84–85
and justice, 124
as materialist theory, 65
and source of subjective justice, 119–120
and threat of outgroup similarity, 141
Expectations, and fraternal relative deprivation, 118

Fairness
    sense of, 120
        in animals, 120
        and obedience to law, 114
    and social comparisons, 116–117
False consciousness, 39, 62, 67, 68, 78, 79, 83, 133
Fascism
    and Pareto, 66
    potentiality for (F-Scale), 57
Fashion carriers, 36–37
Federalist Papers (Hamilton, Madison, and Jay), 63
"Feel good" factor, 115
Feminist movement (women's movement), 72–73, 92
Festinger, Leon, 53
Five-stage model, 81–82, 82–83, 98
    and democracy, 88
"Foreign Children" (Stevenson), 60
Fountainhead, The (Rand), 38
Fractured globalization, 12–14, 128
Fragmentation
    and multiculturalism, 15
    in Near East, 7–8
    of Soviet Union, 8
    in Western world, 10–11
France
    development of identification with, 13
    and nationalism, 3–4
    North Africans in, xiii, 4, 11
Frank, T., 78
Fraternalistic deprivation, 117–118
Free-market democracy, 22
Free-market economics, 28
    and assimilation, 132
French Revolution, 12, 108
    in *Tale of Two Cities*, 108
Freud, Sigmund, 17, 50, 52–58
    and aggression toward outgroup, 55, 57, 66, 152, 155

under Roman Empire, 147
See also at Social identity
Identity motivation, 94–95
Identity needs, 92, 102–103
    and cultural systems, 100
    and democracy, 105
    evolutionary function of, 100, 102–103
    and group membership, 95
    as socially created, 103, 105
Identity theory(ies), 4–5, 19, 48
    and democracy, 104–106
Ideological constraints, on categorization, 37–43
Ideology(ies)
    and class, 39–40
    discrimination justified by, 77–78
    inequalities justified by, 51, 69, 79, 80, 115
        through individualistic strategies, 98
    and irrationality, 51
Immigrants, xiii–xiv
    in American exceptionalism, 42
    and assimilation, 132 (*see also* Assimilation)
    conversion of, 59
    and intergroup differentiation, 142
    and multiculturalism, 149
    as seeking economic advancement only, 144
    and similarity attraction, 136
    in United States, 59
        changing profile of, 149
        Latino, xiii, 58, 159, 161
    in Western Europe or European Union, 11
        discrimination against, 154
        as ethnic underclass, 144
        North Africans in France, xiii, 4, 11
        Turks in Germany, xiii, 11
        See also Ethnic minorities; Minority(ies)
Immortality, mirage or illusion of, 128, 160
Income, relative vs. absolute, 119
India, Muslim feelings of deprivation in, 117
Individual, self-contained, 37–39
Inequalities
    and assimilation, 143
    continuity and universality of, 87
    and democracy, 22
    detrimental consequences of, 119
    and education, 105, 106

ideologies as justifying, 51, 69, 79, 80, 115
    through individualistic strategies, 98
    and Marx, 50, 67, 68
    and Pareto's theory, 66, 67, 69, 78
    question of inevitability of, 18
    social Darwinists on, 84
    and social dominance theory, 71, 74–75, 76, 77–78, 82–83
    social systems as justifying, 123
    and system justification theory, 71, 78, 82–83
    in U.S., 41–43
    See also Hierarchies
Ingroup love and outgroup hate, 55, 57, 66, 152, 155, 156
Ingroup members, 4
Inheritance tax, 87
Inhibitory mechanisms, 128
Integration, in Western world, 8–10
Intelligent design, 59
Intergroup competition, in Sherif's study, 84
Intergroup conflict. *See* Conflict, intergroup
Intergroup differences, 4, 142
    actual vs. perceived, 162–163
    actual vs. symbolic, 162
    assimilation as melting, 137 (*see also* Assimilation)
    carriers of, 95
    and context, 142
    and multiculturalism, 15, 162 (*see also* Multiculturalism)
    and narcissism of minor differences, 50
    powerful as controlling, 95
    Sherif's study on, 83–84
Intergroup prejudice, and contact, 134–136
Intergroup relations
    and categorization, 29, 43
    challenges in, 16
    collective vs. individual explanations of, 93
    cycle of rights and duties in, 121–122
    and evolutionary theory, 84–85
    and identity, 19
    ingroup love and outgroup hate, 55, 57, 66, 152, 155, 156
    managing of, 6
    and minority cultures, 16, 24 (*see also* Assimilation; Multiculturalism)
    need to improve, 24
    and rights or duties, 20, 121–122, 124
    theories of, 17–19, 47

identity theory, 19, 49, 104–106 (*see also at* Identity)

irrationalist, 18, 48, 50–64 (*see also* Irrationalist perspective)

justice theories, 19, 48, 108–109 (*see also* Justice theories)

materialist, 18–19, 48, 51, 65–66 (*see also* Materialist theories)

Internet, 17

Internet use, and socioeconomic differences, 143

Interobjectivity, 99

Intersubjectivity, 99

Iran

elections in, 11

and Khomeini fatwa against Rushdie, 163

as monogroup society, 95–96

religiously inspired government of, 24

revolution and warfare in, 7, 12

and rights vs. duties, 122

Iraq

under Saddam Hussein, 7

U.S. invasion of

and aggressive sentiments toward citizens, 63–64

and globalization, xiii

and Golden Mosque attack with aftermath, 36

and political system vs. psychological citizens, 9

Irrationalist perspective, 4–5, 18, 48, 50–52

and democracy, 62–64

in equity and just-world theories, 111

Freud's psychology as, 50, 51, 52–58

and Marx, 50–51, 51, 62 (*see also* False consciousness)

and materialist approach, 61–62, 65

and subjective justice, 108

and terror management theory, 58–61

Islam (Shi'a), categorization of mullahs in, 35

Islamic fundamentalists, as intolerant, 64

Islamic societies

and incidents reflecting relations with West, 163

religious leaders' importance in, 97

Islamic terrorism, 10–11, 58

Islamic veil, 36

Japan

as ethnically homogeneous, 138

population decline vs. immigration for, xiii–xiv

Jury trials, similarity influential in, 136–137

Justice

distributive, 86, 113, 123, 163

evolutionary perspective on, 124

and minority cultures, 16, 24

procedural, 86, 113–115, 123, 163, 163–164

subjective or perceived, 4–5, 19, 48, 73, 108, 109, 119–120

universals, in, 121, 123–124

Justice motive, 109, 111

and instigators of rebellion and revolution, 118

and perception of injustice as justified, 123

Justice theories, 4–5, 19, 48, 108–109

and democracy, 122–124

and decision-making procedures, 115

equity theory, 111–113

just-world theory, 78, 79, 109–111

and procedural justice, 113–115

and relative deprivation, 115–119, 123

Just-world hypothesis or theory, 78, 79, 109–111

Kant, Immanel, 29

Kazakhstan, 7–8

Kerala (India), 21

Khomeini, Ayatollah, 163

King, Martin Luther, Jr., 54

Kwanzaa celebrations, 162

Kyrgyzstan, 7–8

Labor–management relations, as equity-theory example, 112–113

Laissez-faire multiculturalism, 148–149

Lambert, Wallace, 151

Lang, Sandra, 5

Language, national, 160

Language death, 14, 60

globalization as threat of, 13–14

Law

natural vs. positive, 119

obedience to, 114

Leadership, 56–58

democratic

and irrationalist models, 63–64

from Freudian perspective, 54, 55, 58

"Legitimizing myths," 77

Lemaine, Gerard, 99, 103
Lerner, M. J., 109, 110
Levin, Kurt, on theory, xiv
Libertarians, 68
Libidinal ties, 55, 56
Light, processing of, 30
London bombings (2005), 58
Lorenz, Konrad, 128
"Lottery" effect, in America, 42–43

Maastricht Treaty, 157
Madrid bombings (2004), 58
Manchester School of economic thought, 127
Mandela, Nelson, 54
Markets, economic, 28
Marriage, in Tiwi society, 34
Martin Chuzzlewit (Dickens), 29
Marx, Karl, and Marxist theory, 17, 18, 66
   on assimilation, 133
   on capitalism and religion, 97
   on class, 39, 67
   on consciousness, 87
   and false consciousness, 39, 62, 67, 68, 78, 79, 133
   on history, 66–69
   and ideology, 51, 115 (*see also* Ideology)
   and individual mobility, 81
   and instigators of rebellion, 118
   and irrationalist approach, 50–51, 51, 62
   on perceptions of fairness, 113
   on perceptions of mobility, 87
   and social dominance theory, 77
Mass media
   global conscience through, 128
   and identity, 91
Material conditions, and psychological experience (relative deprivation theory), 116
Materialist theories, 4–5, 18–19, 48, 51, 65–66
   and democracy, 86–88
   and genetics in competition for scarce resources, 84–85
   in historical views of Marx and Pareto, 66–70 (*see also* Marx, Karl, and Marxist theory; Pareto, Vilfredo)
   and irrationalist theories, 61–62, 65
   vs. justice-centered theories, 108
   and social identity theory, 98
   and theme of conflict (realistic conflict theory), 70–71, 82–84

and theme of monopoly of culture and resources, 70, 71
   resource mobilization theory, 18, 71–73, 87
   social dominance theory, 71, 73–78, 82–83, 117–118
   system justification theory, 71, 78–81
   and theme of social mobility, 70, 81–82
Mauritius, democracy in, 21
McGill University, Trudeau meeting at, 151
Melting Pot, The (Zangwill play), 132
Melting-pot assimilation, 132
Mendel, Gregor, 84
Meritocracy, 139, 142–143
   and assimilation policy, 139
   and democracy, 129
   perception of, 88
Mexico, and NAFTA, 8
Minimal group paradigm, 93–94, 94, 142, 162
   and Freud on minor differences, 50
Minority(ies)
   and accommodation, 60
   and authoritarian personality, 57
   and collective identity model, 99
   and common ingroup identity model, 102
   and conversion, 59
   and cultural diversity, 152–153
   and globalization, 24
   as identifying with communal identity, 77
   as identifying with sports and entertainment stars, 105
   identities of, 93, 105, 140
   and justice theories, 109
   equity theory, 112, 113
   languages of, 60
   maintaining of culture and language as right of, 145
   prejudice of against other minorities, 138
   and rights vs. duties, 16, 20, 77, 121, 122, 124
   under Roman Empire, 147
   and social identity theory, 96, 97, 98 (*see also* Social identity theory)
   stereotypes of, 80
   and system justification theory, 80
   as underclass, 144
   See also Assimilation; Immigrants; Multiculturalism

and democratic requirements, 62
and intergroup relations, 47
limiting psychological processes for, 11–12
Psychology, xi
social psychology of group dynamics, ix
Puerto Rican independence movement, 11
Putnam, Robert, 114–115, 144

Quebec, Canada
independence movement in, 11, 117
as monogroup, 96
similarity-attraction experiment in, 137
Racial prejudice, and fraternal deprivation, 117
Rand, Ayn, 38
Rationality, 4–5, 18
vs. rationalization, 53–54, 64
See also Irrationalist perspective
Rationalization, vs. rationality, 53–54, 64
Rawls, John, 28, 110
Reagan, Ronald, 88
Realistic conflict theory, 62, 83–84
as materialist theory, 18, 62, 65, 70–71, 83
and common ingroup identity model, 135
Rebellion, instigators of, 118
Regionalism, 10
Regression, 54
Relative deprivation, 115–119
health consequences of, 123
Relativism
in cultural free-market assumption, 153
limits to, 163
Religious carriers, 36
Religiosity
and just-world theory, 110
in U.S. and Islamic societies, 97
Repression, 59, 110
Republic, The (Plato), 70
Resource mobilization theory, 18, 71–73
and democracy, 87
Revolution, instigators of, 118
Right
and intergroup relations, 20
and minorities vs. majorities, 77, 121–122, 124
voting as, 104
Rule of law, 21
Runciman, W. G., 115, 116, 117, 118
Rushdie, Salman, 163

Russia (pre-Soviet), 1917 revolution in, 12
Russia (post-Soviet)
elections in, 11
population decline vs. immigration for, xiii–xiv
Rwanda
categorization in, 35
natural ethnic division in, 138

Satanic Verses (Rushdie), 163
Saudi Arabia, as monogroup society, 95–96
Scandinavian countries, income difference in, 123
Scottish nationalism, 4, 11
Selection compatibility, 136
Self, 89, 90. *See also* Identity
Self-categorization theory, 19, 101
and democracy, 104
Self-contained individual, 37–39
Self-esteem
as democratic right, 162
through "every child is a star" movement, 105–106
and hostility toward outgroup, 155
and terror management theory, 61
Self-help ideology, 40
Self-interest model, 114
"Selfish gene" view, 85
Separatist movements, 8, 11
in Iran, 7
in Quebec, 11, 117
Sherif, Muzafer, 83–84, 135
Shi'a Islam, categorization of mullahs in, 35
Shikibu, Murasaki, 33
Similarity, in intergroup relations, 55
Similarity attraction, 136–137, 140–141
Simpson, O.J., trial of, 136–137
Smith, Adam, 103, 115
Social capital, 114–115, 139
and diversity, 24
Social categorization. *See* Categorization
Social class, 39
and categorization, 39–40
and ideology, 39–40 (*see also* Ideology)
and language education, 161
and Marx, 39, 67
in United States, 41–43
Social comparisons, 96–97, 112
comparison targets in, 112–113
and relative deprivation, 116–117
Social construction, and collective identity, 99

Turkey, and European Union, 158
Turkmenistan, 7–8
Turner, F. J. (Frederick Jackson), 38
Turner, J. C. (John), 99, 101
Turn taking, as primitive social relations, 119–120

Ukraine, 7–8
Unconscious, in irrationalist perspective, 48, 50, 61–62
    and identification, 54
Unilingualism, vs. multilingualism, 160, 161
United Kingdom
    employee protection laws in, 159
    ethnic minorities in, 144
        South Asians, xiii, 11
    in European Union, 157
    London bombings (2005) in, 58
    resource inequalities in, 87
United States
    and American Dream, 41, 82, 88, 143
    and American exceptionalism, 40–43
    and assimilation policy, 132, 134, 150
    and "bowling alone," 143–144
    and China, 13
    elections in
        and fundraising, 86
        voting in, 22, 104
    employee protection laws in, 159
    ethnic minorities in, 144
    ethnic revival in, 151
    flags as carriers in, 36
    and founders' concern for irrational democracy, 63
    as free-market democracy, 22
    immigrants in, 59
        changing profile of, 149
        Latinos, xiii, 58, 159, 161
    independence movements in (Hawaiian and Puerto Rican), 11
    inequalities in, 41–43, 87
        educational, 106
        health consequences of, 123
    as meritocracy, 139
    minimum wage and poverty line in, 97
    and NAFTA, 8
    national language for, 160
    and problem of national identity, 159
    racial categorization in, 5
    Ayn Rand's novels in, 38
    religious leaders' importance in, 97

self-contained individualism in, 38–39
    social mobility infrequent in, 119
Universals
    and assimilation policy, 145
    in justice, 121, 123–124
University of Chicago School of Sociology, assimilation model of, 131–132
Utopianism
    of egalitarian societies (social dominance theory), 74
    of Marx and Pareto, 67
Uzbekistan, 7–8

van Gogh, Theo, 163
Veblen, Thorstein, 35
Veil of ignorance, Rawls on, 28, 110
Voting, as right vs. duty, 22, 104

Warfare
    prevalence of, 49
    World War II, 53–54
    World War II, 57
War and Peace (Tolstoy), 49
Wealth, relative vs. absolute, 119
Weber, Eugen J., 3
Weblogs, 17
Western Europe, immigrants and ethnic minorities in, 59, 144, 154
Western world
    fragmentation in, 10–11
    integration in, 8–10
What's the Matter With Kansas (Frank), 78
Whitman, Walt, 131
Wilson, E. O., 51
"Winner-takes-all society," America as, 42
Winner Takes All Society (Frank and Cook), 82
Women
    affirmative action for (and men's support), 118
    and social comparisons, 96
Women's movement (feminist movement), 72–73, 92
World War I, and Freud on rationalization, 53–54
World War II, and authoritarian leaders, 57
World Wide Web, 58

Yanomamo people, 85

Zangwill, Israel, 131

ABOUT THE AUTHOR

Fathali M. Moghaddam, PhD, is professor of psychology at Georgetown University in Washington, DC, and senior fellow of the Stanford Center on Policy, Education, and Research on Terrorism. He was born in Iran and from an early age received his formal schooling in England. He returned to Iran in the spring of revolution in 1979 and was researching there during the hostage-taking crisis and the early years of the Iran–Iraq war. During this period he also participated in United Nations (UN) World Food Program projects for Afghan refugees in Baluchestan and accompanied UN missions to the Iran–Iraq war front. Before moving to Georgetown University in 1990, he researched and taught at McGill University in Montreal, Quebec, Canada, for 6 years.

Dr. Moghaddam has conducted experimental and field studies of intergroup relations in numerous cultural contexts and has published extensively on conflict, justice, and culture. The American Psychological Association's (APA's) Society for the Study of Peace, Conflict, and Violence: Peace Psychology Division (Division 48) awarded Dr. Moghaddam the 2007 Lifetime Achievement Award. His first major book on intergroup relations was *Theories of Intergroup Relations: International Social Psychological Perspectives* (1994; coauthored with Donald Taylor), and his most recent books are *Global Conflict Resolution Through Positioning Analysis* (2008; with Rom Harré & Naomi Lee), *From the Terrorists' Point of View: What They Experience and Why They Come to Destroy* (2006), and *Great Ideas in Psychology: A Cultural and Historical Introduction* (2005). His book *Understanding Terrorism: Psychosocial Roots, Consequences, and Interventions* (APA, 2004; with Anthony J. Marsella) was recognized by *Choice* magazine (American Library Association) as a 2004 Outstanding Academic Title.